Blacks in a White Place

The original cabinet card photograph of Aunt Hattie, from the collection of the Oxford County Library. *Courtesy of the Oxford County Library.*

Blacks in a White Place
Ingersoll, Canada West and Ontario, 1850–1921

George Emery

Rock's Mills Press
Rock's Mills, Ontario • Oakville, Ontario
2024

Published by
Rock's Mills Press
www.rocksmillspress.com

Copyright © 2024 by George Emery.

All rights reserved. No part of this publication may be reproduced, distributed, or transmitted in any form or by any means, including photocopying, recording, or other electronic or mechanical methods, without the prior written permission of the publisher, except in the case of brief quotations embodied in critical reviews and certain other noncommercial uses permitted by copyright law. For permission requests, contact the publisher at: customer.service@rocksmillspress.com

For adoption, trade, and bulk orders, contact the publisher at:
customer.service@rocksmillspress.com

Library and Archives Canada Cataloguing in Publication data has been applied for.

This book is a work of history, and in the interest of historical accuracy and understanding it reproduces quotations and images from the time period it describes. Some of the terms and expressions are no longer used, and some are now considered offensive and derogatory.

CONTENTS

Preface | vii
The Plan of the Book | ix
The Ingersoll Study Area | xiii
Evidence for the Ingersoll Study | xiv

1. Coloureds and Whites in Ingersoll and the Townships | 1
Canadian Census Racial Designations and Issues of Interpretation | 1
Black and White Population Trends in the Ingersoll Study Area | 5
A Central Thesis of This Book | 6
Characteristics of Ingersoll Blacks, 1861 | 7
Jobs for Blacks during Ingersoll's Boom Years, 1850–1880 | 13
Ingersoll's Growth Stalled and the Rise of Great Cities, 1881–1921 | 15
Frame Houses, Log Houses, and Board Shanties | 16
Mixed Marriages, Blacks and Mulattos | 17
Black and Mixed-Race Households, 1861 | 17
Religious Affiliation | 18
Black Religious Affiliations in the 1871 Census: A Faulty Enumeration | 20
Blacks Listed in the 1881 Ingersoll Directory | 21
Alexander Fant, Ingersoll, Lone Black in a White Workplace, ca. 1902 | 23
Lone Black in School Class Picture, Ingersoll, 1900 | 24
Lone Black in School Class Picture, Ingersoll, 1931 | 25
Lone Black in School Class Picture, Ingersoll, 1933 | 25

2. James Sinclair (1844–1929), Ingersoll's First Local Historian: His Interpretation | 27
Biography | 27
The Sinclair Histories | 28
Document 1. James Sinclair, "The Coloured Church" | 30
Document 2. James Sinclair, Emancipation Day | 34
Document 3. James Sinclair, White Vigilantes and Ike Williams | 37
Document 4. James Sinclair, "Ike" Williams (1830–?) and His Boarding House | 40
Postscript 1: Fact Checking Sinclair's Story | 47
Postscript 2: Blacks as Remembered by Frank Wallace | 47

3. White Abolitionists and Runaway Slaves: Conventional Wisdom from the 1950s | 51
Summary of Conventional Wisdom of the 1950s | 51
Salient Features of the 1950s Narrative | 52
Local Historians and the White Abolitionist/Black Slave Interpretation | 53
Document 1. Stanley J. Smith, "Wesleyan Church" | 59
Document 2. Stanley J. Smith, "The Old Wesleyan Methodist Church" | 58

Document 3. Stanley J. Smith, "Old John Brown" | 60
Document 4. Stanley J. Smith's Quest for Evidence of John Brown's Army | 66
Document 5. "Town Role in Slave Abolition Forgotten" | 67
Document 6. Richard Houghton, "Town Was Full of Civil War Spies" | 68
Document 7. Tom Duralia, "Underground Slave Railway Stopped Here" | 72
Document 8. Joyce A. Pettigrew, *A Safe Haven* | 74

4. Conventional Wisdom of the 1950s about the 1850s Debunked | 77

5. Coloured Culture | 82
British Methodist Episcopal Church (Coloured) in Ingersoll, 1860–1899 | 87
The Ingersoll Congregation, 1881–1900 | 84
The Congregation's Cake-Walk Fundraisers: 1887, 1888, 1891, 1894, 1895, and 1899 | 90
The Rev. Lewis C. Chambers (Coloured), B.M.E.C. Ingersoll, 1860–62 | 93
A Selection of Letters from the Rev. Lewis Chambers, 1860–62 | 88
The Rev. Solomon P. Hale (Coloured), Ingersoll, 1876–1903 | 103
Stanley J. Smith, "Solomon Peter Hale, Fame without a Press Agent" | 106
Stanley J. Smith, "Hale's 'Discombobberation,' Delight to many Audiences" | 110
Charles Scoffin (1868–1954), White, Remembers Rev. Solomon Peter Hale (1948) | 114
Death Notice, Solomon Peter Hale (1816–1903) | 115
Ingersoll Newspapers Mock "Black Speak" (Negro Dialect) | 116
Emancipation Day Observances in Ingersoll | 117

6. Black-White Collisions in Ingersoll, 1860–80 | 119
Magistrate's Court before Reeve John Galliford, Esq. | 119
The White Magistrate, John Galliford (1811–75), Reeve of Ingersoll Village | 120
1858. White Merchant Cheats Black Customer, then Assaults Him | 121
1858. Black Fined for Assaulting White Bigot | 121
1858. A Spat between Coloured Gamblers | 122
1864. Magistrate Galliford Fines a White Bully | 123
1864. A Black Man's Gunshot Answers White Stone Throwers | 124
1864. Coloured Barber Battles White Bartender | 125
1865. White Man Sexually Assaults a Black Woman | 127
1878. Dominion Day. A Tavern Brawl, a White Mob, and the K.K.K. | 128

7. "Aunt Hattie," A Hard Life in Ingersoll, 1862–1913 | 133
1886. "Aunt Hattie's" Son Benjamin, Age 13, Arsonist | 135
1905. "Aunt Hattie's" Son, Isaiah, Death by Drunken Misadventure | 137

8. Black-race Entertainment for Ingersoll Whites | 141
Minstrelsy | 141
Street Minstrelsy: The *Darktown Fire Brigade* | 166
Racist Advertising | 169
Late Nineteenth and Early Twentieth Century Appearances of the *Darktown Fire Brigade* | 170
1910. "Aunt Hattie" and the *Darktown Fire Brigade*, Ingersoll, Victoria Day | 172

Conclusion | 175

Appendix A. Counting Blacks in Censuses, 1852–1921 | 177
Documentary Sources of Information in Census Enumerations | 177
Census by Census Appraisal of the Data for Blacks, 1852–1921 | 159

Appendix B. Michael Wayne's Interpretation | 187

Appendix C. Ingersoll and Township Blacks Enumerated in Censuses, 1861–1921 | 191

Acknowledgements | 211

The Author | 213

Index | 215

List of Maps

Map 1. Oxford County Townships, 1852–1974 | xiv
Map 2. Oxford Toll Roads, Mid-1850s | 14
Map 3. Tremaine, 1857 | 36
Map 4. Oxford County Atlas, 1876 | 36
Map 5. Town Lot Map, 1895 | 37
Map 6. Tremaine Map, 1857 | 43

PREFACE

This book examines Blacks in Ingersoll, Oxford County, during the years 1850 to 1921. Ingersoll was an incorporated Village until 1865 and thereafter a Town. The *Ingersoll area* refers to Ingersoll and its contiguous townships, West Oxford and North Oxford.

During the years of study Ingersoll was mostly a *White-race* place with a small *Black-race* minority. As measured by census statistics, its Black population peaked on the eve of the American Civil War (April 1861–April 1865). The 1861 Census enumerated 150 Blacks in Ingersoll and 48 in the village's contiguous townships—3% of the Ingersoll-area population. The Black census population remained substantial during the 1860s and 1870s, but then plummeted to 28 in Ingersoll and none in the townships by 1921.

There are several mysteries to solve. Why did a newly incorporated Village have a large and growing Coloured population on the eve of the American Civil War? Why did its Black population largely vanish during the decades following? How did Blacks and Whites get along in Ingersoll before, during, and after the American Civil War—cordially or with friction?

This book is about Blacks but also about how Ingersoll's White local historians have interpreted them. Here one must consider two sets of writings. One is that of James Sinclair (1844–1929), a life-long resident of Ingersoll (1854–1929) who published in 1907. The other is that of a second generation of local historians—Stanley J. Smith (1895–1979), Byron Jenvey (1881–1980), J.C. Herbert (1888–1999), and Harry Whitwell (1911–1979)—who published after the Second World War. For mid-20th-century Ingersoll readers, their work established what may now be called *conventional wisdom* about Ingersoll Blacks of the century before.

Conventional wisdom regards Ingersoll's Black history as a by-product of American slavery before the Civil War and its abolition in 1863. Blacks came to Ingersoll, so the story goes, to escape oppression in Southern Slave States; they then returned to the "sunny South" once slavery was over (because of the severity of the Canadian winter climate, suggests one local historian).[1] Thus, most pre-Civil-War Blacks were runaway slaves. Ingersoll was a terminus of a White-assisted Underground Railway that spirited runaways from Southern Slave States to Northern Free States or to the sanctuary of Canada. Ingersoll Whites actively welcomed these refugees, giving them "a safe haven."[2] In 1854 grateful Blacks contributed free labour to help erect a White-abolitionist Wesleyan Methodist Church.[3]

Upon investigation, however, this conventional narrative becomes problematic. Firstly, James Sinclair, Ingersoll's first local historian, who lived in Ingersoll during its village years, never referred to his Black neighbours as slaves; nor did he ever mention White abolitionists giving them refuge. Secondly, the second-generation local historians merely asserted their narrative, without supporting documentary evidence. Thirdly, a scholarly article published in 1995—Michael Wayne's "The Black Population of Canada West on the Eve of the American Civil War"—upended the assumptions and speculations of the Ingersoll conventional narrative.[4]

---

1. Stanley J. Smith, "Old John Brown," *Ingersoll Times*, centennial edition, 1967, p. 22.
2. Joyce A. Pettigrew, *A Safe Haven: The Story of the Black Settlers of Oxford County* (South Norwich Historical Society, 2006).
3. Stanley J. Smith (?), "Wesleyan Church, Once Haven for Slaves, is being torn Down in Ingersoll Now." *Ingersoll Tribune*, 1956 (Jenvey Scrapbook #3, p. 105); Richard Houghton, "Town was Full of Civil War Spies," *Ingersoll Times*, 31 March 1976.
4. Michael Wayne, "The Black Population of Canada West on the Eve of the American Civil War," *Histoire Sociale/Social History*, Vol. 28, no. 56 (1995, November).

The Plan of the Book

Chapter 1. Black and White in Ingersoll and the Townships: Profiles from Manuscript Censuses

This chapter summarizes information about race in Canadian censuses, 1852–1921.

Secondly, it presents statistical profiles as calculated from the census data. It tallies the Black and White census populations and calculates Black population turnover between censuses. It compares Blacks and Whites for place of birth, age and sex distributions, rates of adult illiteracy, and school attendance for children ages 5–11. For Blacks it examines professions, types of family dwellings (frame houses, log houses, board shanties), racially mixed marriages, and religious affiliation. The census profiles also show statistical differences between the census-defined races: Blacks have higher rates of adult illiteracy, proportionately more males, and larger proportions for the USA as place of birth.

Thirdly, the chapter reports Blacks listed in the 1881 Ingersoll Directory, which uniquely reports individuals by their place of residence. The chapter closes with images of Black children in Ingersoll school-class photographs.

Chapter 2. James Sinclair, Sr. (1844–1929), Ingersoll's First Local Historian: His Interpretation of 1907

This chapter opens with a sketch of the Sinclair family and a list of James Sinclair's publications. It appraises Sinclair's stories as *history* (what actually happened) and as a resource for *historiography* (a study of historians and cultural influences on what they think happened). It contrasts Sinclair's interpretation of Blacks with the abolitionist-hero interpretation of the 1950s (discussed in Chapter 3). The chapter closes with excerpts from Sinclair's publications on Blacks; these illustrate his assumption of White-race supremacy, but in a rather different manner than second-generation historians.

Chapter 3. White Abolitionists and Refugee Slaves: Conventional Wisdom from the 1950s

This chapter summarizes conventional wisdom about pre-Civil-War Ingersoll Blacks as written by local historians of the mid-20th century.

The body of the chapter then documents the conventional wisdom, as articulated in the summary. In the 1950s narrative, a great majority of Ingersoll Blacks were runaway slaves from Southern Slave States; Ingersoll was a terminus on the Underground Railway; White Abolitionists ran the Underground Railway; a White Wesleyan Methodist Church acted as a clearing house for refugee slaves; grateful runaways contributed free labour to help build the church; and the famous White-American abolitionist, John Brown, visited Ingersoll in April, 1858, a year before his capture of Harper's Ferry, West Virginia.

Chapter 4. Conventional Wisdom of the 1950s Debunked

This chapter debunks folkloric myths about Ingersoll Blacks before the American Civil War. As it shows, a majority of Ingersoll's USA-born Coloureds were Free Blacks *when they entered Canada,* not refugee slaves. Blacks came to Ingersoll for jobs, not refuge from slave catchers. Ingersoll Village was not a terminus on the Underground Railway. Ingersoll did not have White abolitionist heroes and grateful Blacks. The Wesleyan Methodist Church (White) was not a clearing house for refugees; nor did Blacks provide free labour to build that edifice in 1854. Local Blacks did not return en masse to the American Southern States after the Civil War and the end of slavery; rather they were leaving small towns for jobs in rapidly-growing cities. Ingersoll Whites regarded Blacks as an inferior race and gave them a rude welcome—truly the phrase "a safe haven" glosses over the harsh edges of the Black experience in the Village of Ingersoll.

Chapter 5. Coloured Culture: the Church and its Preachers, Black-Speak English, and Emancipation Day

This chapter documents the history of the British Methodist Episcopal (Coloured) congregation in Ingersoll, 1860–1899; sketches biographies of two Coloured pastors, Lewis Chambers (1860–62); and Solomon P. Hale (1876–1901); documents Black-Speak English (a.k.a. *Negro idiom*) as heard in White ears; and documents Black celebrations of Emancipation Day.

Chapter 6. Black-White Collisions in Ingersoll, 1858–1877

This chapter documents racial clashes, a number of which ended up in Magistrate's Court and one which featured a full-scale White race riot. The evidence gives the lie to the notion of "a safe haven" as a sufficient generalization about Black-White relations.

Chapter 7. "Aunt Hattie," a Black Life in Ingersoll, 1862–1913

This chapter sketches the life and family of a Black woman, Harriet Wright, who lived 50 years in Ingersoll. While most Ingersoll Blacks left Ingersoll a few years after arriving there, Aunt Hattie was a stayer. This biographical sketch sets the stage for mention of "Aunt Hattie" in Chapter 8.

Chapter 8. Black Entertainments for a White Audience

This chapter explores the portrayal of Blacks in Ingersoll's public entertainments. These included indoor minstrel shows (with white actors in *blackface*), and street minstrel performances of the *Darktown Fire Brigade* (1890–1910), a racist minstrelsy show that depicted Coloured firemen as comically inept buffoons in responding to a shack set alight. The chapter also treats *Jubilee Singers* (touring Black troupes depicting Blacks in a "plantation culture"); and theatrical performances such as *Uncle Tom's Cabin*.

Conclusions

This chapter summarizes the book's principal findings, as listed below.

- Local histories of Ingersoll Blacks have come exclusively from White local historians whose narratives assumed White racial supremacy and drew inspiration from small-town boosterism.
- James Sinclair's publications are unreliable for factual evidence but are useful sources of information if read with caution.
- The 1950s folkloric narrative is historical fiction, devoid of persuasive supporting evidence.
- The flawed local-history narratives, however, are essential evidence of Ingersoll's historical memory of Blacks in the town's past and how the historical memory of previous generations differs from that of the time of writing.
- A quest for jobs explains the influx of Blacks to Ingersoll before and during the American Civil War years and the exodus of Blacks from small places such as Ingersoll to cities after the Civil War.
- Conversely, the influx was not primarily about runaway slaves, White-abolitionist heroes, and the Underground Railway.
- Pre-Civil-War Blacks in Ingersoll differed from local Whites. Blacks were more heavily male; proportionately more of them were illiterate; and proportionately more of them had been born in the United States.
- Blacks differed culturally from Whites, as evidenced in their preference for Coloured institutions, religious practices, and their English-language dialect.
- Ingersoll Whites found local Blacks to be peculiar, amusing, primitive, and in some cases unhygienic and bad smelling. They patronized entertainments that featured unflattering Black stereotypes.
- Relations between Blacks and Whites in Ingersoll were sometimes abrasive, with street fights and in one instance, a White race riot. The conventional wisdom of "a safe haven" is misleading.

Appendix A. Counting Blacks in Censuses, 1852–1921

This appendix shows that Canada's census statistics were loaded with cultural values, notably White supremacy. They are not a neutral source of information. Census officials chose the questions for the enumerator's census forms and provided guidelines for acceptable answers. They also selected which variables and combinations of variables were included in published summary statistics.

Appendix B. Michael Wayne's Interpretation

This appendix elaborates Michael Wayne's methodology for overturning key assumptions of the conventional narrative.

Appendix C. Lists of Ingersoll and Township Blacks Enumerated in Censuses, 1861–1921

This appendix lists Ingersoll-area Blacks by name and census year.

The Ingersoll Study Area: Ingersoll and its Contiguous Townships, West Oxford and North Oxford

Ingersoll Village lay in the valley of the Thames River, south branch—midway between the future great cities of Toronto and Detroit; 32 kilometres east of London, a future regional metropolis; and 16 kilometres west of Woodstock, the Oxford County seat.

Ingersoll originated as a settlement in Oxford Township in 1819. The Village site was "laid out in 1831" and in 1846 contained "nearly 400 inhabitants."[5] In 1852 Ingersoll incorporated as a Village, with a population of 1,190 and a territory of 1,722 acres, taken from West Oxford and North Oxford townships. In 1865 Ingersoll incorporated as a Town, with a population of 3,151.

The original Oxford Twnship included three future townships: East Oxford, separated from the original township in 1820, and

---

5. *Smith's Canadian Gazetteer, Canada West*, 1846.

North Oxford and West Oxford Townships, created from the original in 1842.

In 1975 these townships disappeared in a restructuring of Oxford County.[6] West Oxford Township, Beachville Village, and part of Dereham Township merged to form the new township of South-West Oxford. North Oxford Township merged with the townships of East Zorra and West Zorra to form the new township of Zorra. The Town of Ingersoll continued as a separate municipality, situated on the border of Zorra and South-West Oxford townships.

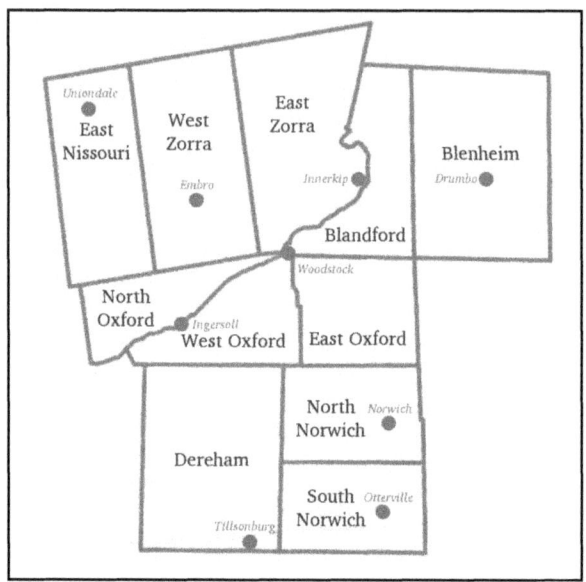

Map 1. Oxford County Townships, 1852–1974

Evidence for the Ingersoll Study

Documentary evidence is the basis for this book's local history. Citation of evidence is commonly missing in publications of local historians. Even so, all documentary evidence, statistical and literary, is biased and incomplete, to be used with caution. Nineteenth-century census enumerations, for example, express White-racist values and miss some types of people more than others.

---

6. Ontario, County of Oxford Act, 1974.

The documentary sources include census enumerations, 1852–1921; newspapers—*Ingersoll Chronicle* (1854–1919), *Woodstock-Ingersoll Sentinel-Review* (1920–40), *Oxford Herald* (1860–62), *Oxford Tribune* (1876–79), and Toronto *Globe* (1844–1921); materials in local archives (Ingersoll Public Library, Ingersoll Cheese and Agricultural Museum, and Oxford County Archives, Woodstock); publications of local historians (James Sinclair, Stanley J. Smith, Byron Jenvey, Joyce A. Pettigrew, and others); and scholarly literature (Michael Wayne, Hilary Bates Neary, Jack Blocker, Jr., and Cheryl Thompson).

CHAPTER ONE
Coloureds and Whites in Ingersoll and the Townships: Profiles from Manuscript Censuses

Canadian Census Racial Designations and Issues of Interpretation

Nineteenth-century Census officials assumed a humanity of four major *races* differentiated by *skin colour*, with the *White* race superior to the *Black*, *Red*, and *Yellow races*. The boundaries between race categories were arbitrary: *White* applied to persons of "Pure White blood." *Black* applied to persons with any Black blood, including full bloods (Negro), Mulattos, Quadroons, and Octoroons. This classification gave priority to *between-race* differences (*Black* versus *White*) over *within-race* differences (shades of *Black*, shades of *White*).

- **Definition.** Enumerator's Instructions, 1861 Census: "In this column mark a figure (1) [for] every Coloured person's name, i.e. Negro or Negress. If Mulatto, mark M after his or her name." 1901 Census, "only pure whites will be classed as whites; the Children begotten of marriages between whites and any one of the other races will be classed as red, Black or yellow, as the case may be, irrespective of the degree of colour."
- **The 1852 Manuscript Census**
  - The enumeration asked if "**Coloured persons—Negro,**" but the question "was much neglected, and the number of Coloured persons was not ascertained" (judgment of the 1861 Census commissioners).

- Microfilm copy of the enumerator's returns, one census page, does not display the column for **Coloured persons—Negro** (column 10 for the *rural personal Census*, column 11 for the *urban personal Census*). The relevant columns were on a second census page, which is not displayed.
- However, the *Oxford Gazetteer, 1852*, reports the numbers of Negroes in Oxford County and their distribution across the townships. Thomas S. Shenston, the editor of the *Gazetteer*, was also the census commissioner for Oxford County; as such he had access all manuscript pages for the County, including pages with Column 10–11).[7] As shown below, the census data show zero Blacks for Ingersoll and the townships of West Oxford and North Oxford.

1852	BLACKS
Blandford	0
Blenheim	0
Dereham	0
Ingersoll	**0**
Nissouri East	18
Norwich	101
Oxford North	**0**
Oxford East	1
Oxford West	**0**
Woodstock	6
Zorra East	0
Zorra West	0
Oxford County	126

- **The 1861 Census.** The enumerators' completed forms have good information for Coloureds (Column 5).[8] The published statistics

---

7. *Oxford Gazetteer, 1852*, p. 44; David G. Burley, "Shenston, Thomas Strachan," *Dictionary of Canadian Biography*, vol. 12 (1891–1900).

8. The 1861 Census published statistics for *Coloureds* are incomplete and unreliable. Wayne, "Black Population of Canada West," pp. 467–9; Bruce Curtis, *The Politics of Population: State Formation, Statistics, and the Census of Canada, 1840–1875* (University of Toronto Press, 2001).

THE OXFORD GAZETTEER;

CONTAINING A COMPLETE

HISTORY OF THE COUNTY OF OXFORD,

FROM ITS FIRST SETTLEMENT; TOGETHER, WITH A FULL ABSTRACT OF EACH CENSUS, CAREFULLY COPIED FROM THE ORIGINAL ABSTRACTS.

TO WHICH IS ADDED

A MAP OF THE COUNTY,

COMPILED EXPRESSLY FOR THE WORK,

FROM ROUGH DRAFTS, TAKEN BY THE ENUMERATORS ON THE SPOT.

BY THOMAS S. SHENSTON,

(COMPILER OF THE "COUNTY WARDEN,")

COUNTY CLERK & CENSUS COMMISSIONER, COUNTY OF OXFORD,

"This country cannot remain in its present state,—some great change *must* soon take place." *Annexation Manifesto. Montreal.*......."Quite true, Mr. Annexationist, it cannot remain in its present state, any more than our children and calves can; we expect to see the former 'change' into men and women, and the latter into cows and oxen. We, also, expect to see a continuation of the 'changes,' which has been going on for the last thirty years—well-poles giving place to wind-lasses, and wind-lasses to pumps; log houses to framed, and framed to brick and stone; oxen and sledges to horses and waggons, and waggons to carriages."—*Correspondent T. S. S. to the Hamilton Provincialist.*

HAMILTON, C. W.

PRINTED AND PUBLISHED FOR THE AUTHOR, BY CHATTERTON & HELLIWELL, OVER THE TELEGRAPH OFFICE, KING STREET.

1852.

PRICE, FIVE SHILLINGS.

are worthless; the Census clerks did not do their job.
- **The 1871 Census** replaced the precise question, *Coloured*, with an ambiguous question, *Origin*. The Enumerator's Instruction: "Origin is to be scrupulously entered, as given by the person questioned ... by the words English, Irish, Scotch, *African*, Indian, German, French, and so forth." The enumerator's reporting of Blacks as *African* is fairly good, despite the ambiguity of the race question.
- **The 1881 and later Census schedules** retained *Origin* (*Racial Origin* beginning in 1901). However, the 1881 Census enumerated some Blacks as *American* or *Canadian* rather than the intended *African*.
  - Including 25 *Americans* and one *Canadian* in Ingersoll and five *Americans* in North Oxford Township.
  - In North Oxford Township Henry Harris, USA-born, was of *Indian* "origin" in the 1871 Census but his "origin" was American in the 1881 Census; his wife Hannah Harris and their two children, born in Ontario, were of African "origin" in the 1871 Census but given the father's "origin," American, in the 1881 Census.
- **The 1891 Census** did not have a question about race.
- **The 1901 Census** asked two questions, *Racial Origin* and *Colour*, but Census officials used only *Racial Origin* for their published statistics. The data for race are good.
- **The 1911 enumerator's instruction** directed that *Racial Origin* be traced through the father (as in *English, Scotch, Irish*, etc.) but that "*the children be-gotten of marriages between white and Black or yellow races will be classed as Negro or Mongolian, (Chinese or Japanese) as the case may be.*" The data for race are acceptable.
- **1921 Census.** Enumerator's Instruction for Column 21. "The racial or tribal origin is usually traced through the father, as in English, Scotch, Irish, Welsh, French, German, Italian, Danish, Swedish,

Norwegian, Bohemian, Ruthenian, Bukovinian, Galician, Bulgarian, Chinese, Japanese, Polish, Jewish, etc. A person whose father is English but whose mother is Scotch, Irish, French or other race will be ranked as English, and so with any of the others. In the case of Indians the origin is traced through the mother, and names of their tribes should be given, as 'Chippewa', 'Cree', etc. The children begotten of marriages between white and Black or yellow races will be classed as Negro or Mongolian (Chinese or Japanese), as the case may be. *The words 'Canadian' or 'American' must not be used for this purpose, as they express 'Nationality' or 'Citizenship' but not a 'Race' or 'people'.*" [First mention of this caution, which had been sorely needed for the 1881 Census].

Black and White Population Trends in the Ingersoll Study Area

Nineteenth-century Ingersoll was a White-race village with a small Black-race minority, as tallied from Census statistics. The Black population in the Ingersoll study area peaked on the eve of the American Civil War (13 January 1861) at 198, held up well during the 1860s and 1870s, and then dropped to 28 in 1921. Meanwhile, Ingersoll's White census population increased sharply during the 1850s and 1860s, from 1,190 in 1852 to 4,022 in 1871, slightly declined during the 1880s, and then followed a flat trend, settling at 5,150 in 1921. Overall, the White population grew, while the Black population fell. Perforce, Blacks dropped from 6% of the Ingersoll population in the 1861 Census to 0.6% in the Census of 1921. In the townships the percentage drop was from 1.8 to zero.

POPULATION	1852	1861	1871	1881	1891	1901	1911	1921
Ingersoll	1,190	2,577	4,022	4,313	4,191	4,573	4,763	5,150
Oxford West	1,894	2,735	2,804	2,694	2,193	2,230	2,027	1,948
Oxford North	1,378	1,773	1,855	1,645	1,498	1,402	1,261	1,287
Ingersoll Area	4,462	7,085	8,681	8,652	7,882	8,205	8,051	8,385
N. BLACKS	1852	1861	1871	1881	1891	1901	1911	1921
Ingersoll	0	150	107	97	-	52	29	28
Oxford North	0	20	4	5	-	0	0	0
Oxford West	0	28	48	9	-	7	7	0
Ingersoll Area	0	198	159	111	-	59	36	28
POP. % BLACKS	1852	1861	1871	1881	1891	1901	1911	1921
Ingersoll	-	5.8%	2.7%	1.9%	-	1.1%	0.6%	0.5%
Oxford North	-	1.1%	0.2%	0.3%	-	0.0%	0.0%	0.0%
Oxford West	-	1.0%	1.7%	0.3%	-	0.3%	0.3%	0.0%
Ingersoll Area		2.8%	1.8%	1.1%		0.7%	0.4%	0.3%

A central thesis of this book: Jobs for Blacks were the driver for Black population trends in the Ingersoll area during the years 1850–1921.

The Black population was substantial during the 1850s, 1860s, and 1870s, when the Ingersoll area offered a booming economy and brisk population growth. This growth stalled during the 1880s,[9] a decade during which the town and both townships lost population. This was followed by slow growth for the local population into the 1910s alongside shrinkage in the local job market for Blacks. A powerful underlying cause was the growth of the job market for Blacks markets in rising great cities such as Detroit, Chicago, and Toronto. Significantly, similar Black population trends—a rise followed by a decline in small towns; and an increase of the Black populations of emerging great cities—obtained in the American Midwest during the years 1860–1930.[10]

9. The 1891 Census enumeration did not ask about race. Moreover, efforts to identify Ingersoll Blacks by linking family names from the 1881 and 1901 Censuses are futile, the reason being that microfilm copies of the enumerators' returns for 1891 are incomplete. The published Census for 1891 reports Ingersoll's population at 4,573, but the tally from microfilm copy is 1,553 (33% complete). Simply put, most of the enumerators' records are missing.
10. Jack Blocker, Jr., *A Little More Freedom, African Americans Enter the Urban Midwest, 1860–*

Aside: Blacks In Woodstock And Ingersoll

CENSUS YEAR	1852	1861	1871	1881	1891	1901	1911	1921
MUNICIPAL POPULATION								
Ingersoll	1,190	2,577	4,022	4,313	4,191	4,573	4,763	5,150
Woodstock	2,112	3,353	3,982	5,373	8,612	8,833	9,320	9,935
BLACK POPULATION								
Ingersoll	0	150	107	97	-	52	29	28
Woodstock	6	57	14	44	-	117	56	33
BLACKS AS PERCENTAGE OF MUNICIPAL POPULATION								
Ingersoll	0%	6%	3%	2%		1%	1%	1%
Woodstock	0%	2%	0%	1%		1%	1%	0%

During the 1890s the municipal populations dropped in Ingersoll and boomed in Woodstock—on 1 July, 1901, Woodstock became a city (styled "the Industrial City").[11] In this context, between 1881 and 1901, the Black population of Ingersoll fell by 54% (to 52), and that of Woodstock rose by 38% (to 117). The availability of jobs for Blacks influenced the trends in both communities. During the 1860s and 1870s, Ingersoll was an industrial village, while Woodstock, the County seat, was more of an administrative centre. When Woodstock industrialized during the 1880s, that is when its peak Black population showed.

Characteristics of Ingersoll Blacks, 1861
Place of Birth
INGERSOLL VILLAGE
- 53% of 150 Blacks had been born in the United States, compared with 10% of 2,427 Whites.
- 47% of 150 Blacks were born in Canada West, compared with 52% of 2,427 Whites.

1930 (Columbus, OH: Ohio State University Press, 2008).
11. *Woodstock Sentinel-Review*, 8 March to 3 July 1901

THE TOWNSHIPS

- Of 48 Blacks, 71% were US-born, compared with 6% of 2,427 Whites.[12]
- 29% of Blacks were born in Canada West, compared with 62% of 4,460 Whites.

Population Turnover

Populations are dynamic, the individuals in them changing. Between censuses, individuals enter the population through birth and in-migration; and individuals exit through death and out-migration.

- Of 150 Blacks in Ingersoll in 1861, just 21 (9%) were still there in 1871.
- Conversely, of 106 Blacks in 1871, just 18 (17%) had been in Ingersoll in 1861. (Thirty-five individuals in 1871 were not yet born in 1861.)
- Of 106 Blacks in Ingersoll in 1871, 21 (20%) were still there in 1881.
- Conversely, of 84 Blacks in 1881, 25 (30%) had been in Ingersoll in 1871. (Sixteen individuals in 1881 were not yet born in 1871.)

Ingersoll's Black population declined after 1861 because losses from out-migration and deaths exceeded replacements from in-migration and births.

Black Population Turnover: The Fant Family

Alexander Fant (1853–1937) was a long-term employee of the Ingersoll Packing Company (the former J.L. Grant Packing Company) on the north side of the river in Ingersoll. His trade was that of butcher. The family residence was on Skye Street nearby.

Between censuses, in-migration, births, and deaths changed the in-

---

12. Of 14 Township Blacks for whom the state of birth was entered, eight were natives of northern Free States and six of Slave States. For all Canada West Blacks for whom state of birth was recorded, 521 (70%) were born in Slave States and 223 (30%) in Free States. Wayne, "Black Population of Canada West," p. 473.

dividuals in Fant's Ingersoll family, and in the process individuals in the town population.

- **Additions through in-migration**. Alexander Fant, his widowed father, and other family members came to Ingersoll in the late 1870s, after spells in Middlesex and Kent Counties.
- **Additions through births**. In Ingersoll he married and parented many children—the 1891 Census enumerated seven of them.
- **Exits through deaths**. His extended family endured several deaths in Ingersoll, those of his father, Willis Fant, Sr. (1805–97); grandmother, Milley Fant (1775–1879), age 104; wife, Maggie Jane (1874–1925); daughter, Pliney Fant (1887–94), age 7; brother, Willis Fant, Jr. (1842–1917); and sister, Hannah Fant (1853–77).

Alexander Fant, Ingersoll, ca. 1902.

Biographical Details from Censuses

Alexander Fant (1853–1937) was born in the USA. In 1861, at age ten, he moved to Mosa Township, Middlesex County with his father, Willis Fant, Sr. (1805–97), a labourer and a widower; his grandmother, Mrs. Milly Fant (1777–1879), a widow who had been born a slave in Virginia; and five siblings ages five to 22. The 1871 Census found Alexander Fant, now age 18, in Bothwell, Kent County, in the household of his older sister, Selina, now married to Edward Walker and the mother of two children. The four Fants in the Walker household (excluding Selina) were Alexander, his older brother Willis Jr., age 20; grandmother Millie Fant, now 104 years old; and two sisters ages 16 and 19.

During the late 1870s some of the family removed to Ingersoll. There Alexander's sister, Hanna, died in 1877; sister-in-law Charlotte, wife of Willis Fant, Jr., died in 1879; and grandmother Milly Fant, now 112, died in 1879. The 1881 Census for Ingersoll listed Alexander and his father Willis, Sr., age 74, now a widower, and two children, possibly nieces by his late sister Selina. The 1881 Directory listed Alexander, his father, Willis Fant, Sr., and brother, Willis Fant, Jr., as labourers residing on the Thamesford Road. The 1891 Census enumerated seven Fants: Alexander, age 36, now married to Margaret Jane Miner, 22, and three daughters, ages 1–7; in a separate household were Alexander's father, Willis, Sr., age 86; his brother Willis, Jr., age 36, and his sister Elizabeth, age 36. The 1901 Census listed Alexander Fant, age 47, his wife, Margaret Jane Miner, age 31, and five children, ages 14–23; their oldest daughter's reported age, 17, dates Alexander's marriage at about 1883, when Margaret ("Maggie") would have been age 14. The 1911 Census enumerated Alexander and Maggie with nine children, ages 5–23; Maggie and two daughters were employed as domestics. The 1921 Census reduced their number of children to four.

Alexander's father, Willis ("Willie") Fant, Sr. died in 1897 "at the advanced age of 92 years … at the residence of his son, Skye Street." Alexander's brother, Willis Fant, Jr., died in 1917 at age 74 "after a comparatively brief illness … in his 75th year … at the home of his brother, Alex Fant [on], Skye Street … The late Mr. Fant had been a resident of Ingersoll for many years." His wife Charlotte had predeceased him in 1879.

Sex Distribution, 1861

INGERSOLL VILLAGE
- 58% of 150 Blacks were male; of 2,427 Whites, 48% were male.
- Blacks had 1.4 males for each female; for Whites, 0.9.

THE TOWNSHIPS
- 63% of 48 Blacks were male.
- Blacks had 1.7 males for each female; for Whites, 1.1.

Age Structure, 1861

In 2016, 25% of Ingersoll's 2016 population were under 20 years of age and 38% were aged 50+. In 1861 Blacks and Whites had much younger populations.

INGERSOLL VILLAGE

- 47% of 150 Blacks were under age 20 and just 5% were ages 50+.
- Of 2,427 Whites, 51% were under age 20 and 8% were aged 50+.

THE TOWNSHIPS

- 44% of 48 Blacks were under age 20 and just 8% were ages 50+.
- Of 4,460 Whites, 54% were under age 20 and 10% were aged 50+.

Illiteracy for Adult Blacks and Whites, 1861 and 1871

The 1861 and 1871 Censuses asked about literacy for persons over age 20. The 1861 questions were "cannot read or write, male" and "cannot read or write, female." The 1871 questions were, "cannot read" and "cannot write." Below are the illiteracy rates calculated for Ingersoll and the townships.

1861

- 23% of Ingersoll's 79 Black adults "could not read or write"; the rate was higher for women (30%) than for men (16%).
- The rate for 1,086 Ingersoll Whites was 2%.
- The Township rates were 41% of 24 Blacks and 3% of 1,850 Whites.

1871

- 40% of 45 Ingersoll Blacks could not read and could not write; another 16% could do one but not the other.
- Of 939 Ingersoll Whites, 4% could not read and could not write; and 2% more could do one but not the other.
- 50% of 18 Township Blacks could not read and could not write; and 6% (1 person) could not write.

- Of 1,057 Township Whites, 4% could not read and could not write; and 5% could do one but not the other.

Ingersoll and Townships, 1861: School-Age Children: Blacks, Whites and, School Attenders

Although Blacks had substantially higher rates of illiteracy than Whites, the difference was smaller for school attendance. The schooling rate for school age children in Ingersoll was 59% for Blacks and 64% for Whites. The schooling rate in the townships was 38% for Blacks and 62% for Whites, but the percentage for Blacks is meaningless due to the tiny number of cases. Schooling evidently was closing the racial divide for literacy.

The Census reported "attending school within the year," separately by sex. The writer collected data for all individuals within the census ages of 6–12; this arbitrary definition of "school age" meant actual ages of 5–11, the census data being for "age next birthday."

INGERSOLL

- Blacks = 21. Attenders = 12. School age (21) as % Population (150) = 14%
- Schooling Rate: (12/21) 57%
- School Age Male = 12. Attenders = 8. Schooling Rate = 66%
- School Age Female = 9. Attenders = 4. Schooling Rate = 44%
- Whites = 384. Attenders = 246. School age (384) as % Population (2,427) = 16%
- Schooling Rate: (246/384) 64%
- School Age Male = 180. Attenders = 115. Schooling Rate = 64%
- School Age Female = 204. Attenders = 131. Schooling Rate = 64%

TOWNSHIPS
- School Age Blacks = 8. Attenders = 3. School age (8) as % Population (48) = 17%
- Schooling Rate: (3/8) 38%
- School Age Male = 5. Attenders = 1
- School Age Female = 3. Attenders = 2
- School Age Whites = 755. Attenders = 470. School Age as % Population = 17%
- Schooling Rate = (470/755) 62%
- School Age Male = 378. Attenders = 250. Schooling Rate = 66%
- School Age Female = 377. Attenders = 224. Schooling Rate = 59%

Jobs for Blacks during Ingersoll's Boom Years, 1850–1880

Ingersoll boomed during the pre-Civil-War years. The hamlet became an incorporated Village in 1852 and a Town in 1865. Its population soared, by 117% during the 1850s and by 56% during the 1860s. New infrastructure triggered economic growth in Ingersoll during the 1850s. For east-west communications, the Great Western Railway between Hamilton and London was completed in 1853.[13] New toll roads extended Ingersoll's economic reach. To the south, the *Ingersoll and Port Burwell Plank and Gravel Road* (1849–52) and the Dereham, Ingersoll, and Dorchester Gravel Road; and to the north the North Oxford and West Zorra Gravel Road and the Thamesford and Nissouri Gravel Road (see the map on the next page).[14]

Black men worked on township road crews during the early 1850s, and some of them found jobs in Ingersoll beginning in 1857, building warehouses, stationhouses, factory buildings, sawmills, church buildings, and residences; cutting and clearing land for farms; and sawing and teaming timber from log-heaps—left over from land clearing,

---

13. David R.P. Guay, *Great Western Railway of Canada* (Hamilton: Dundurn Press, 2015).
14. From Brian Dawe, *Old Oxford is Wide Awake, Pioneer Settlers & Politicians 1793–1853* (1980), p. 88.

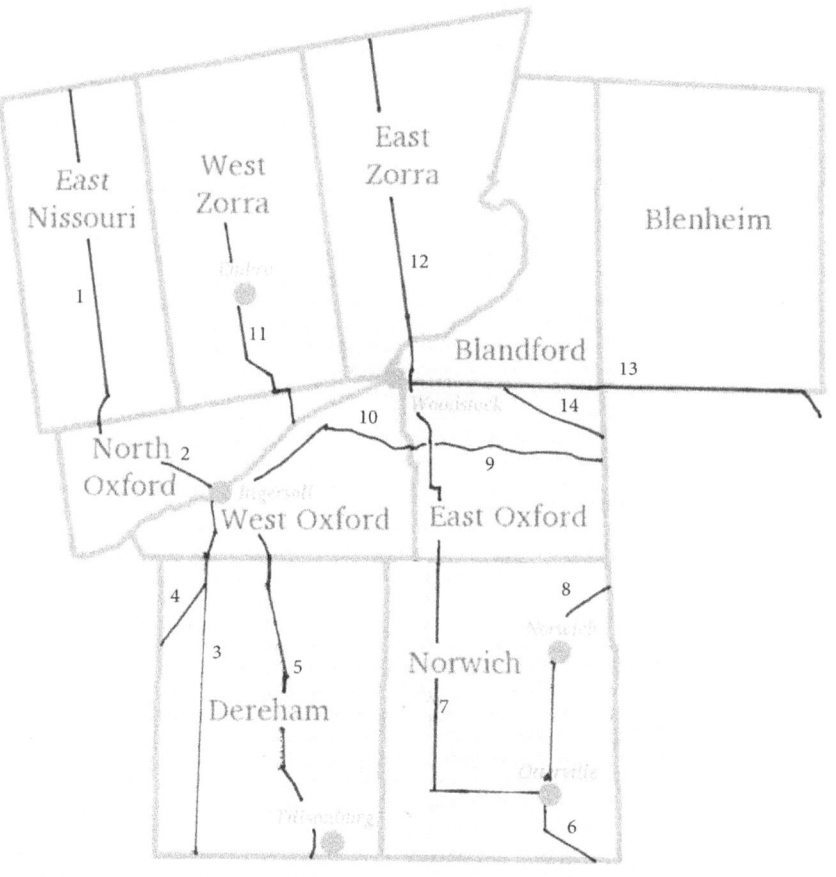

1. Thamesford and Nissouri Gravel Road
2. Ingersoll and Thamesford Gravel Road
3. Dereham, Ingersoll and Dorchester Gravel Road
4. Branch to Aylmer
5. Ingersoll and Port Burwell Plank and Gravel Road
6. Otterville and Port Dover Plank and Gravel Road
7. Woodstock and Otterville Plank and Gravel Road
8. Burford and Norwich Plank Road
9. Old Stage Road
10. Woodstock and Dereham Gravel Road
11. North Oxford and West Zorra Gravel Road
12. Woodstock and Huron Gravel Road
13. Dundas Plank Road
14. London and Brantford Road

Map 2. Oxford Toll Roads, Mid-1850s
(Based on information in Brian Dawe, *Old Oxford is Wide Awake*)

and formerly burned as a means of disposal—to meet the voracious wood-fuel appetites of railway locomotives.

Coloured men held low-skilled, low-paying jobs in Ingersoll. Their professions, as enumerated in the 1861 Census, were *labourers*, 26; *barbers*, 4; *waiters*, 2; and one each for *porter, plasterer, and gunsmith*. The sole woman listed was a *servant*. Township Blacks included 12 *labourers*, 1 *brickmaker*, and 1 *potter*. Black male professions in Ingersoll and townships in 1871 were *labourers*, 22; *barbers*, 4; *plasterers*, 2; and one each for, *carpenter, lumberman*, and *whitewasher*.

Black families in Ingersoll and London were poor, noted the Rev. Lewis Chambers (Coloured): "In the city of London they cannot get much to do. Wages is 62 cents per day for carrying the load, and for [common] work 50 cents per day. Women get 25 cents per day for washing, sometimes 37 [cents]. House rent is cheap and living cheap… Our people came here to Ingersoll about three years ago … they are poor. Wages is about the same as at London but cutting cordwood is better."[15]

Ingersoll's Growth Stalled and the Rise of Great Cities, 1881–1921

Ingersoll's growth stalled during the 1880s,[16] a decade during which the Town and both Townships lost population. This was followed by slow growth for the local population into the 1910s alongside shrinkage in the local job market for Blacks. Another factor was the growth of the job markets for Blacks in rising great cities such as Detroit, Chicago, and Toronto. This lured some Blacks out of Ingersoll and discouraged other Blacks from coming there. Significantly, similar Black

---

15. Chambers letters, 20 September 1860.
16. The 1891 Census enumeration did not ask about race. Moreover, efforts to identify Ingersoll Blacks by linking family names from the 1881 and 1901 Censuses are futile, the reason being that microfilm copies of the enumerators' returns for 1891 are incomplete. The published Census for 1891 reports Ingersoll's population at 4,573, but the tally from microfilm copy is 1,553 (33% complete). Simply put, most of the enumerators' records are missing.

population trends—a rise followed by a decline in small towns; and an increase of the Black populations of emerging great cities—obtained in the American Midwest during the years 1860–1930.[17]

CENSUS POPULATIONS: FROM AN "AGE OF VILLAGES" TO AN "AGE OF CITIES"									
	1852	1861	1871	1881	1891	1901	1911	1921
Chicago	29,953	112,172	298,977	503,185	1,099,850	1,698,575	2,185,283	2,701,705
Detroit	21,019	45,619	79,577	116,340	205,876	285,704	465,766	993,578
Montreal	58,000	90,323	130,833	177,377	256,723	328,172	490,504	618,506
Toronto	30,775	41,821	59,000	96,196	181,215	209,892	381,833	521,893
Buffalo	42,261	81,129	117,714	155,134	255,664	352,387	423,715	506,775
Hamilton	14,112	19,096	26,880	36,661	48,959	52,634	81,969	114,151
London	7,035	11,555	18,000	27,867	31,977	37,976	46,300	60,959
Brantford	3,877	6,251	8,107	9,616	12,753	16,619	23,132	29,440
Stratford	no data	2,809	4,313	8,239	9,500	9,929	12,946	16,094
St. Thomas	1,274	1,631	2,197	8,367	10,366	11,485	14,054	16,026
Chatham	2,070	4,466	5,873	7,873	9,052	9,068	10,770	13,256
Woodstock	2,112	3,353	3,982	5,373	8,612	8,833	9,320	9,935
Ingersoll	1,190	2,577	4,922	4,318	4,191	4,573	4,763	5,150

Frame Houses, Log Houses, and Board Shanties

In Ingersoll all Blacks and 87% of Whites lived in frame dwellings, not brick or stone. In the townships, 59% of dwellings were of frame construction, 10% were of brick or stone, and 31% were log houses and board shanties.[18] For Township Blacks, by contrast, seven of 11 heads of families lived in log houses, three in board shanties, and one in frame.

Some Black households were crowded. In Ingersoll, for example, Thomas Piper, a 52-year-old labourer, shared a one-story frame building with his wife Eliza Ann, seven children, and William H. Moore, age 25. In West Oxford Township Charles Galloway, a 64-year-old brickmaker, shared a one-story log house with his wife Barbara, age

---
17. Jack Blocker, Jr., *A Little More Freedom, African Americans Enter the Urban Midwest, 1860–1930* (Columbus, OH: Ohio State University Press, 2008).
18. Canada, 1861 Census, Published Statistics, vol. 2, table 15.

38, seven children under the age of 12, and a 26-year-old labourer, Jeremiah Johnston.

Mixed Marriages, Blacks and Mulattos

Ingersoll had married couples in which one or both partners were Black. A husband was not enumerated for four married Black ladies. Four Black men had White wives—that is, one in every eight Black married men had a White wife; the provincial average was one in seven.[19] None of the seven Black married men in the townships had a White wife.

- Isaac Williams, 32, a Coloured labourer, Black gang boss, and owner of a boarding house for Coloureds, was married to Asenath Williams, 30, a White born in Canada West.
- Noah Sommers, 38, a Coloured labourer born in the United States, was married to Emma Sommers, age 18, a White born in the United States.
- Sarah Piper, 31, a White born in Ireland, was the mother of five Mulatto children under age 6, living apart from her Black husband (name unknown) in Isaac Williams' Boarding House for Coloureds.
- John Miner, 46, a Coloured barber, was married to Eliza Ann Miner, 18, a White born in Canada West.[20]

Black and Mixed-Race Households, 1861

Forty-three of Ingersoll's 150 Coloureds (29%) were Mulatto. A few Blacks lived in White-headed households. Joshua Bryce, a 22-year-old, USA-born porter, was the sole Black resident of 15 inmates in Brady's Mansion House Hotel (southwest corner of Thames and King Streets).

---

19. For Canada West, 385 Black men listed in the Census had White wives—one out of every seven Black married men. Wayne, "Black Population of Canada West," p. 479.

20. This matches Michael Wayne's finding for Canada West: "385 Black men listed in the Census had White wives, mainly immigrant women from Europe or the British Isles. This represented one out of every seven Black married men." Wayne, "Black Population of Canada West," p. 479.

Washington Thomas (USA-born) and Washington Bryce, hotel waiters aged 19 and 20, resided with 15 other inmates in Daly House (northwest corner of Oxford and King Streets). John Beuford, a USA-born gunsmith, age 40, lodged in the household of a White shoemaker, Francis Mealy, age 35, and his wife, Catherine, age 19 (King Street East). Alexander Bedford, age 11, resided with Henry Taylor, Town Clerk, age 31[21]; his wife Harriett, age 26; and their ten-year-old daughter. Eliza Washington, age 16, was a live-in servant in the household of David Robertson, a White commission merchant, age 49; his wife Catherine, age 39; three sons ages 18 to 20; and Angelina Butler, age 11 (Victoria Street, near the G.W.R. depot).

In West Oxford Township a Black labourer, John H. Clark, age 19, lived in the household of a White miller, James Gustin, age 32; his wife, age 28; and five children under the age of ten. Elizabeth Galloway, age 17, roomed in a board shanty with John Peterson, a White labourer, age 33; his wife Fanny, age 34; and three children under age 4. In North Oxford Township, Sanford Nelson, a USA-born Black labourer, age 29, inhabited a frame house with William E. Dundas, a White farmer, age 49; his wife Ann, age 44; and three children under the age of ten.

Religious Affiliation

The British Methodist Episcopal Church (Coloured) was the principal denomination among Blacks of the Ingersoll area. In 1870 it erected the first (and last) Coloured church building in the town. Other Protestant denominations had followings, however—notably Baptist, but also Presbyterian and Anglican.

---

21. Henry Taylor (1830–83), born West Oxford, graduated from Albany, N.Y., Law School, practised in Ingersoll, married Miss Austin of Norwich, served as Town Clerk, emigrated to the southern U.S. States (Kentucky) to practise law and engage in mercantile pursuits just before the Civil War (1860), retired a wealthy man in New York. Death notice, *Ingersoll Chronicle*, 9 and 23 August 1883.

Postscript: Decoding Census Statistics for Religion

1861	Ingersoll	Ingersoll	Townships	Townships
Population	150	% Pop.	48	% Pop.
Br. E.M. (Col.)	0	0	0	0%
E. Meth	93	62%	20	42%
W. Meth	1	1%	3	6%
Baptist	22	15%	11	23%
C of E	18	12%	2	4%
Pres.	9	6%	1	2%
Advent	0	0%	8	17%
1871	Ingersoll	Ingersoll	Townships	Townships
Population	106	% Pop.	48	% Pop.
Br. E.M. (Col.)	0	0%	0	0%
E. Meth	6	6%	14	29%
W. Meth	51	48%	14	29%
Baptist	20	19%	20	42%
C of E	9	8%	0	0%
Pres.	4	4%	0	0%
1881	Ingersoll	Ingersoll	Townships	Townships
Population	97	% Pop.	14	% Pop.
Br. E.M. (Col.)	75	77%	0	0%
E. Meth	11	11%	0	0%
Meth	3	3%	0	0%
Baptist	7	7%	2	14%
C of E	0	0%	0	0%
Pres.	0	0%	7	50%
Meth C. C.	2	2%	5	36%

Census Returns for Religion for the Ingersoll Area, 1861, 1871, and 1881

Black religious affiliations must be teased out of the actual census statistics. The British Methodist Episcopal Church (Coloured) established a congregation in Ingersoll in 1860. Yet in the 1861 Census enumeration, Black Methodist Episcopalians were reported as "E.M." ("Episcopal Methodist")—the same as White Episcopal Methodists in the Village. Black Episcopal Methodists were not reported as such ("B.E.M.") until the Census of 1881.

The explanation lay in *Instructions to the Enumerators* "to give the religion, carefully distinguishing the class of Presbyterian or Methodist where such there are—thus, if Presbyterians in connection with the old Kirk, or Church of Scotland, mark them C of S; if with the Free Church or Presbyterian Church of Canada, mark them F.C.; and if United Presbyterians, mark them U.P. *The Methodists you will mark with W. for Wesleyans; E. for Episcopal; and N.C. for New Connection, and if none of these, mark them "Other" Methodists. There are no sects other than these two requiring special distinguishing marks.*" Effectively, Census officials did not recognize British Methodist Episcopal (Coloured) as a reportable denomination.

Thus, the "E.M." entered for 93 Blacks was a proxy for "B. Meth. E.C." This number approximates the "75 members and congregation" which the B.M.E. pastor reported for 1860. And the Enumerator's instructions proscribed a "special distinguishing mark" for the B.M.E. denomination; only "other Meth." was possible. If so, then 93 of the 422 Episcopal Methodists in Ingersoll were Black and 329 were White. Whites worshiped in Ingersoll's Episcopal Methodist Church on Charles Street; Blacks worshiped in a rented schoolhouse near Thames and King Streets.

Black Religious Affiliations in the 1871 Census: A Faulty Enumeration

Ingersoll statistics for Black religions in 1871 are bizarre and unreliable. These show 51 Wesleyan Methodists ("W.Meth."), not the expected Episcopal Methodists ("E.M.") as the principal religion of Ingersoll Blacks (51 of 104, thus 48%). The enumerators reported six Independent Episcopal Methodists ("I.Meth.E.") and zero Episcopal Methodists. These outcomes clash with other evidence. Firstly, Ingersoll's

British Episcopal Methodists had just erected Ingersoll's first and only Coloured church building in 1870, and B.M.E.C. statistics for Ingersoll in 1872 reported 40 members and probationers. Secondly, the Wesleyan Methodist totals were demonstrably higher than for the previous census (6% in 1861) and the census following (0% in 1881). At the level of individuals, the enumerators reported John Diggens's family as Episcopal Methodist in 1861, Wesleyan Methodist in 1871, and British Methodist Episcopal in 1881.

Enumerator confusion may explain the misleading 1871 statistics. The enumerator's instructions were, firstly, to enter the information given by the person questioned, with precision; but to enter it in abbreviated form (with initials) to fit within the boundaries of the column on the enumerator's sheets (e.g., "W. Meth." for Wesleyan Methodist). In 1871, Census guidelines did not recognize the British Methodist Episcopal Church (Coloured) as a distinct denomination (as would be the case in 1881). Thus, the enumerator's task was, it would appear, to represent Coloured Methodists with one of three truncated options on offer for Episcopal Methodist: "E.M.C.," "M.E.C." and "I. Meth. E." Somehow a false statistical surge in Coloured Wesleyan support was the outcome.

Blacks Listed in the 1881 Ingersoll Directory

The 1881 Ingersoll Directory flagged 33 of 1,115 persons as "(Coloured)." Of these three were not enumerated in the census for Ingersoll—the enumerator missed them, or they were not residents on Census Day (4 April 1881), or the writer missed them due to tricky spellings of family names.

The 33 "Coloured" persons included 21 labourers, 3 whitewashers, 1 horse trainer, 1 fish dealer, 1 pastor, and 1 lecturer. All five persons with no listed profession were married women or widows.

Unlike the 1881 Census the 1881 Directory reports the individual's street of residence: 9 Thamesford Road/Bell Street; 4 Victoria Street;

4 Wellington Street; 4 King Street E. (one at Zulu Terrance); 3 Hall Street; 3 Tunis Street; and one each for Alma, Inkerman, Carnegie, Skye, Margaret, and William Streets; and one Thames Street, the fish dealer's business address.

"COLOUREDS" IN 1881 INGERSOLL DIRECTORY			
FAMILY NAME	1ST NAME	RESIDENCE	PROFESSION
Moore	Robert L.	corner Inkerman	labourer
Sanders	Reuben	Bell	labourer
Hale	Rev. Solomon P.	Carnegie	lecturer
Holmes	Henry D.	Hall	plasterer
Van Patter	Henry	Hall	labourer
Van Patter	John	Hall	horse trainer
Henderson	Joshua	King St. N.	labourer
Henry	Peter	King St. N.	labourer
Graham	John	Alma	labourer
Fowler	William	Margaret	labourer
Johnston	Rev. Robert	Skye	B.M.E.C. Pastor
Sullivan	Mrs. George W.	Thamesford rd.	
Thomas	William	Thamesford rd.	whitewasher
Wright	Mrs. Benjamin	Thamesford rd.	
Hall	David	Tunis E.	labourer
Hall	Walter	Tunis E.	labourer
Piper	William	Tunis E.	labourer
Anderson	Joseph	Victoria	labourer
Diggings	Benjamin	Victoria	labourer
Diggings	Carey	Victoria	labourer
Mickey	Mrs.	Victoria	
Bevins	Washington	Wellington	whitewasher
Bird	Charles	Wellington	whitewasher
Bird	James	Wellington	labourer
Wilson	Andrew	Wellington	labourer
Mann	Mrs.	William	
Dier	Mrs. Jane	Zulu Terrance, King St. E.	
Green	Moses	Thames	fish dealer
Fant	Willis Sr.	Thamesford Rd	labourer
Fant	Willis Jr.	Thamesford Rd	labourer
Fant	Alexander	Thamesford Rd	labourer
Hughes	Benjamin	Thamesford Rd & Haines	labourer
Hughes	George	Thamesford Rd & Haines	labourer

Alexander Fant, Ingersoll, Lone Black in a White Workplace, ca. 1902

"Employees of the Ingersoll Packing Company, proudly displaying the tools of the butchering trade, circa 1902." Alexander Fant, 2nd Row, 4th from left.

From left to right:
First Row: Mr. Huntley, Jeff Lewis, James Huntley, Mr. C. C. L. Wilson, Mr. John Podmore, W. D. Hook, George Hambige, William Crookston, C. H. Sumner
Second Row: Neil McPhee, Doc Chambers, Tom Garlick, **Alex Fant**, Jack O'Brien, Bob McMillan, Harry Smith, Alex Lewis, Bill Stevens, Peter Sherry, Eddie McPhee [insert Bill Podmore behind Peter Sherry]
Third Row: Fred Lockery, Dan McGinnis, Jim Cane, Bob Tweedy, George Bowers, Jimmie Watson, John Noe, Dave Ely, Charlie Morley, Bob Gemmell, Nig Kyle, Tom Dutton
Back Row: Billy Murray, Jim Lockery, Cuff Thompson, Dick White, John Lockery, Ike Smith, Puss Chambers, John [Pointer] McMillan, Benny McMillan, William McCrea, John Thompson

George Emery

Lone Black in School Class Picture, Ingersoll, 1900

John Street Public School, Class Photo, ca. 1900:
Lone Black pupil, third row, fourth from left. (Detail below)

That the school class picture showed just one Black was unsurprising. Ingersoll then had two public elementary schools (Central, John Street), each with several classes.[22] And the 1901 Census for Ingersoll enumerated just four Black school attenders: Gormon Van Pater, age 14, Charles Van Pater, age 9, Fred Kelley, age 13, and Charles Kelley, age 8.

1900 detail   1931 detail   1933 detail

22. The public elementary schools were Central School, Thames and Ann Streets, site of future Victory Memorial School (1921); and John Street School, a.k.a. Ward 1 School (1882–1909), on John Street in the former New Connexion Methodist Church building (1868–74). In 1909 the John Street building was replaced by the new Ward School, between Alma and William streets, west side of George Street; in 1938 this school was to be renamed the Princess Elizabeth School.

Lone Black in School Class Picture, Ingersoll, 1931

Lone Black lad, sitting in first row, centre.
1931 Ward Street Public School, Ingersoll, Class Picture.
(Detail on facing page)

Lone Black in School Class Picture, Ingersoll, 1933

Lone Black lad, back row, third from left, 1933 Ward Street Public School Class Picture, Ingersoll. (Detail on facing page)

CHAPTER TWO
James Sinclair (1844–1929), Ingersoll's First Local Historian: His Interpretation

Biography

James Sinclair's family hailed from Dunbarton, Scotland, on the River Clyde, some 20 miles west of Glasgow. The Sinclairs were English-speaking Lowlanders, not Gaelic-speaking Highlanders. In Scotland they were Church of Scotland (Kirk) Presbyterians; however, following the "great disruption" in the Scottish Kirk in 1843, they became Free Church (Succession Church) Presbyterians. In Ingersoll they worshiped in Knox Presbyterian Church on St. Andrew's Street, a substantial brick building with a fifty-foot spire, erected in 1847.

James Sinclair (1844–1929) and his parents emigrated from Scotland to Ingersoll in 1854. His parents—John Sinclair (1803–84) and Nicholas McLaughlin Sinclair (mother, 1800–84)—settled on Catherine Street, north of the Thames River,[23] where John Sinclair was a teamster. However, John's four younger sisters had preceded him in the family's migration to Ingersoll. The eldest sister, Marion Sinclair (1805–87), had married George Rawson in Ingersoll in 1849. The second eldest sister, Catherine Sinclair (1809–?), had married Robert Haining (1810–71) in Scotland before coming to Ingersoll; the 1852 Census listed Robert as a tinsmith in Ingersoll, and his third child, Robert Jr., age 8, had been born in Ingersoll about 1844. The third sister, Janet Sinclair (1811–85), had married John Melville, a shoemaker,

---

23. The 1857 Tremaine Map and the 1887 *Bird's Eye* Map of Ingersoll show two Catherine Streets, one north of the River and one in the south part of town. The north-end Catherine Street (1857), on which Sinclair lived, was shown as Cathcart Street on the 1876 County Map and as Catherine Street on the 1895 Lot Map.

in Ingersoll in 1851. The youngest sister, Jean Sinclair (1813–82), had married John Buchanan (1811–1902) in Scotland in 1835; about 1841 the couple had come to Ingersoll, where John was tinsmith.[24] The 1861 Census listed three of the Sinclair sisters—Marion Rawson (no children), Catherine Haining (two children), and Janet Melville (one child)—as widows in the household of Donald Wallace, hardware merchant and Catherine Haining's son-in-law since 1858.

In 1862, at age 18, James Sinclair became a tinsmith, working at the King-Street shop of John Buchanan, his uncle.[25] In 1870 British Episcopal Methodists erected a Coloured church on Catherine Street, directly across the street from the Sinclair family home.[26] In October, 1876, James married Caroline Tune, who had come from England to Canada in 1867; children followed: three by 1881, five by 1891. At some point James became head of the family household. In 1881 his parents and his younger sister, Isabella, boarded with him. In 1911, at age 67, his household included three workers in the family shop: son George, a tinsmith, age 32; daughter Edith, a bookkeeper, age 22; and son James, Jr., 18, an errand boy.[27] By his year of death, 1929, he had resided in Ingersoll for 75 years. His wife Caroline survived him for four years more.

The Sinclair Histories

James Sinclair published five "Reminiscences of Ingersoll's Early Days" in the *Ingersoll Chronicle* in 1907 and a 43-page *History of the*

---

24. Sources: J. Miller, "Sinclair Family, Scotland 1744 to Canada," (2017); 1852 and 1861 Censuses; Oxford County Genealogical Index, 1793–1858. A brother James (1807) settled in St. Marys.
25. Or at the Thames-Street Shop of James Buchanan, John's son. Sinclair's entry states "at J. Buchanan."
26. The Church, on lot 9, was on the north side of Catherine, 3 lots east of George Street; Sinclair's house was the south side of Catherine St., 2 lots east of George St., on lot 7, directly across from the church. See 1911 Ingersoll Directory; 1895 lot map of Ingersoll.
27. Caroline, age 25, was a milliner in 1911; she was to marry Alfred B. Wilson in 1918. Edith Victoria, age 16, was to marry Walter Thurtell in 1917. Another daughter, Sarah Pet Sinclair, age 30, not in the 1911 household, had married S.T.H. Knight of Ingersoll in 1907.

Town of Ingersoll in 1924, on the occasion of the 1924 Ingersoll Old Boys' and Old Girls' Reunion. The first three of his *Reminiscences*, about Village Blacks, were "The Coloured Church," 15 and 22 August 1907; "Emancipation Day," 22 August 1907; and "White Vigilantes and Ike Williams," 29 August 1907. Two subsequent *Reminiscences*, although not about Blacks, held clues to the way James wrote his *History*. These were: "What's in the Pond? The Great Partlo Pond Hoax of 1857," 5 September 1907; and "The Old School House and Berry-Picking Party," 13, 20 September, 1907. Sinclair's *History of the Town of Ingersoll* (1924) made no mention of village Blacks—whose population of 150 when he was young had dwindled to 28 by the 1920s.[28]

Sinclair's work should be read with caution. Although he had lived in Ingersoll during its village years (1852–65), he wrote about those times decades later—in 1907, when he was 63 and in 1924, when he was 80. His published work amounted to an "old man's memories" of his distant past. His recall, understandably, was flawed: his Pond-Hoax article got the wrong pond and the wrong year. Moreover, the Pond article made stuff up: an imaginary crowd of 10,000 and dignitaries from away; this embellishment was moonshine—it never was. Simply put, old-man Sinclair's penchant for colourful storytelling overwhelmed his histories.[29]

28. The Pond-Hoax article was re-issued in the *London Free Press* in 1922 in a special section about Ingersoll; and in the *Ingersoll Tribune*, Centennial Edition, 1967. It had been copied by Byron Jenvey "from an old newspaper account written by James Sinclair, who watched closely the events of the Village Pond Hoax. My father-in-law, James Mayberry (born 1848) was also one of the spectators and I have heard him mention many of the foregoing details." The Ingersoll Library's Photographic Gallery featured it until 2017. Sinclair's *History of Ingersoll* was reproduced in the *Ingersoll Tribune*, Centennial Edition, 28 August 1952; and again in the Ingersoll and District Historical Society's reprint of 2009. In her foreword to the 2009 reprint, Diana Sinclair, James Sinclair's granddaughter, wrote with understandable pride: "My grandfather was a dreamer who felt that all information about the founding of Ingersoll should be preserved. This book provides some little-known information and flavour about our town in the 19th century."
29. *Ingersoll Chronicle*, 5 September 1907, "What's in the Pond? The Great Partlo Pond Hoax of 1857"; re-published in the *London Free Press*, as part of a special section on Ingersoll (7 September 1922, p. 17); "Local Historians Tell Tall Tales: the Great Ingersoll Pond Hoax of

That said, his *Reminiscences* hold valuable information for historians. Firstly, one can mine them for hard facts, which are scarce to come by. Secondly, they exemplify how Whites of Sinclair's times viewed other "races" through the lens of White supremacy. Blacks were inferior to Whites. Their culture was peculiar and amusing. They had low standards of hygiene and disagreeable body odour. A White woman married to a Black man was degraded and disgusting. Thirdly, the *Reminiscences* are noteworthy for what their interpretation of Ingersoll's early years did not do: Sinclair did not posit a narrative of an Underground Railway, White-abolitionist heroes, and grateful refugee slaves—an interpretation that was to emerge in the 1950s and receives discussion in Chapter 3.

To document the above arguments, excerpts from Sinclair's *Reminiscences* follow below. They appear in the following order: the Coloured Church, Emancipation Day, and Ike Williams.

Document 1. James Sinclair, "The Coloured Church," *Ingersoll Chronicle,* 15, 22 August 1907

[August 15]

… At this period the native Indians were numerous in this section, and their lessened numbers today confirm the rule that the aborigines of any country must eventually fade before the civilization of the white races. However, it can be said that so far as it was possible, the natives of Canada were seldom or ever harshly treated, and a kindly feeling was always shown towards them. In my boyhood days I asked no greater pleasure than to hear one, whom few recall, relating to past events. This was an old chief, Tim Maskelonge, then a man about 75 years of age, tall and straight as an arrow and intelligence beyond the average of his race. …

While dealing with the subject of race, it occurs to me that at this

---

1857," Ingersoll Historical Photo Gallery; George Emery, *Millponds, Millstreams, and People in Ingersoll, Ontario, 1819–2015* (264 Oxford Street Press, 2019), pp. 225–31.

time our Coloured citizens were a prominent factor in our population, but as remote in characteristics, habits, and sentiments from the native Indian as they are in complexion and physique. About this time the Coloured church was an institution that possessed features peculiarly its own, and if religion was ever allied to the ridiculous, this was the climax. The white man has tried to imitate him in burlesque, but one night at a protracted meeting in the old school house, which stood on the present Salvation Army barracks,[30] would take the conceit out of the best burnt cork artists in existence. The room was lit with candles set in tin sconces and hung on the walls. In winter it was heated by a large stove near the entrance, while the stove pipe zigzagged its way to the opposite end of the room. On a low platform the then leader, Mose Thompson[31] would, in language which would paralyze the author of the most comprehensive unabridged dictionary, announce the opening exercises, and should he discover in his audience any of our leading or prominent citizens, the initial remarks were of a still more elaborate character, which would at once banish every vestige of gravity and bring them at once into line for the ensuing performance, which being purely oral, for obvious reasons, generally resulted in an exhibition of the genuine humor and undisguised characteristics of this peculiar race. In my next communication, I will give an idea of some of their hymns.[32]

[August 22]

As promised in our last contribution to the above subject, our present chapter will relate to the method of conducting the services of the Coloured church as it was then known. In doing so I wish it under-

---

30. Thames St. S., west side, five buildings south of King St.
31. 1861 Census: Moses Thompson, age 20, labourer, born in Canada West, Episcopalian. Living with Lydia Thompson, age 48, born in the US, [British] Episcopal Methodist, probably Mose's mother.
32. For comparison, see Stanley J. Smith's article on the Coloured preacher Solomon P. Hale, Chapter 5. For a scholarly explanation of African American spirituals, see Sandra Jean Graham, *Spirituals and the Birth of a Black Entertainment Industry* (Urbana, IL: University of Illinois Press, 2018).

stood that we will not be guided by race prejudice or disrespect to this class of our population, as at the time of which we speak there were many families of this race who deserved and were treated with respect by all classes, and indeed many useful and industrious citizens were to be found amongst them, and as law-abiding people filled a place in our community. It is only with their peculiarities as compared with other members of our community we wish to deal. We have already introduced the reader to the leading figure in this connection. While it would be manifestly impossible to repeat his introductory remarks, and as singing formed a large part of the "performance" (a term we use advisedly), it will only be necessary to give the reader an idea, and he can let his imagination have free scope in supplying the detail. Take, for instance, one of their hymns, or songs, as the term best suits—

>Take your father by the hand,
>All suited in a band,
>March straight forward to the promised land
>And don't you leave me behind

>Chorus—

>Swing a-low dat chariot
>Swing a-low dat chariot
>Swing a-low dat chariot
>And don't you leave me behind

The chorus was repeatedly with hands joined, the only variation being in the first line, when all the relatives would be named. Nor must it be forgotten that some excellent voices were heard, and the genuine Negro melody maintained. It did not seem to matter what the import of the words were so long as a suitable chorus was attached, and time was also kept by stamping the feet, clapping the hands, etc. The frequent interludes of the more excitable members, when such exclamations would be heard as "B'res de Lod," "Come down fro de ruf, we'll pay for de shingles," "Goodbye children, I've gone to glory," "Hallelujah" etc. Many others such as the following—

> Zacariah clum a tree
> The Lod a massa for t see
> The limb it broke and he did fall
> He neber see the Lod at all

> Down by the river
> And he neber see the Lod at all
> Down by the river
> And he neber see the Lod at all

At intervals experiences would be related by both male and female, and often several at a time. Also impromptu words would be sung to some well known chorus, for instance—

> Good beefsteak and spare rib too,
> Fire bright, onions steeped in glue
> Glory, Glory, Hallelujah
> Glory, Glory, Hallelujah
> Swing a-low dat chariot, etc.

Also the following:—

> Chicken brof and possum pie,
> Song all day long, and neber die
> We'll sing an shout with the Israelites

An you'll see your fader dere
An you'll see your fader dere
And if you git dere afore I do
Tell them I'm a-comin too,
And see your fader dere,
And see your fader dere
And sing an shout with the Israelites
And see your fader dere

Document 2. James Sinclair, Emancipation Day, *Ingersoll Chronicle*, 22 August 1907

As the first of August was always observed by those people as Emancipation Day to celebrate the liberation of the slaves of the West Indies by the British government [on 1 August 1834], unusual services were held, and the name of Wilberforce and his influence on behalf of their race was made the theme of their oration. On one occasion a large gathering of these people held a monster picnic in a grove behind Dufferin Street [see Maps 3, 4, and 5 below],[33] then a suitable woods. A feature of the occasion was an elaborate barbeque, when an ox was roasted whole, together with other animals. In the evening a grand ball was held in the old Jarvis Hall (which stood where the Campbell Block now stands), for which elaborate preparations were made. At this time a hooped skirt for ladies was the prevailing fashion, and the larger the expansion of the dress, the more fashionable it was considered. This fashion antedated the crinoline, which with many modifications, was fashionable for some years afterwards. The hooped skirt was literally such, and the cane used for the purpose was exposed for sale at the leading dry goods

---

33. As shown below in Map 5, the 1895 Ingersoll lot map was the first to show a Dufferin Street. Maps 3 and 4 (1857 and 1876) show earlier names for the street that evolved into Dufferin. Interestingly, the 1857 Tremaine Map and the 1887 *Bird's Eye* Map of Ingersoll show two Catherine Streets, one north of the river and one in the south part of town; the north-end Catherine Street (1857) is shown as Cathcart Street on the 1876 Map and as Catherine Street on the 1895 Lot Map.

stores, in bundles resembling fishing rods, which mysteriously introduced into the underwear of our fashionably dressed ladies. It would not be supposed that our dusky beauties on such an occasion as this would be out-shone in fashion by their White friends. Consequently the prevailing fashion was not only adhered to by them, but was represented in an exaggerated form.

Assembling at the scene of pleasure, a most interesting spectacle presented itself. The male section of the party was arrayed in faultless evening dress, with white vest and full-dress coat, peg-top trousers, and white neck-tie, with elaborate stand-up collars which shone with added lustre against the sable background. The dignified bearing and the courtly manners of all the parties showed an association with the most refined of the age, as indeed many visitors were employed in situations where such experience could be gained.

However, when the exercises of the evening had fairly commenced, some unforeseen difficulty began to be experienced, and the frequent retirement of the ladies to the dressing chamber began to awaken suspicion that some insidious enemy had conspired to wreck the pleasure of their party, which upon investigation proved, alas, too true. Some miscreant had (perhaps as a practical joke) strewn the floor with some ingredient that, when wafted with the evolutions of the dance, and favoured by the expanded costumes of the ladies and fanned by the perspiring limbs and bodies of the dancers to their intense discomfort, for whatever the nature of the ingredient, it caused an intolerable itching, which necessitated instant retirement to the privacy of the dressing room.

However, the cause was discovered, and it was well that the perpetrators remained unknown, and after a brief recess and sundry repairs all around, the dancing was resumed and a most interesting program successfully carried out.

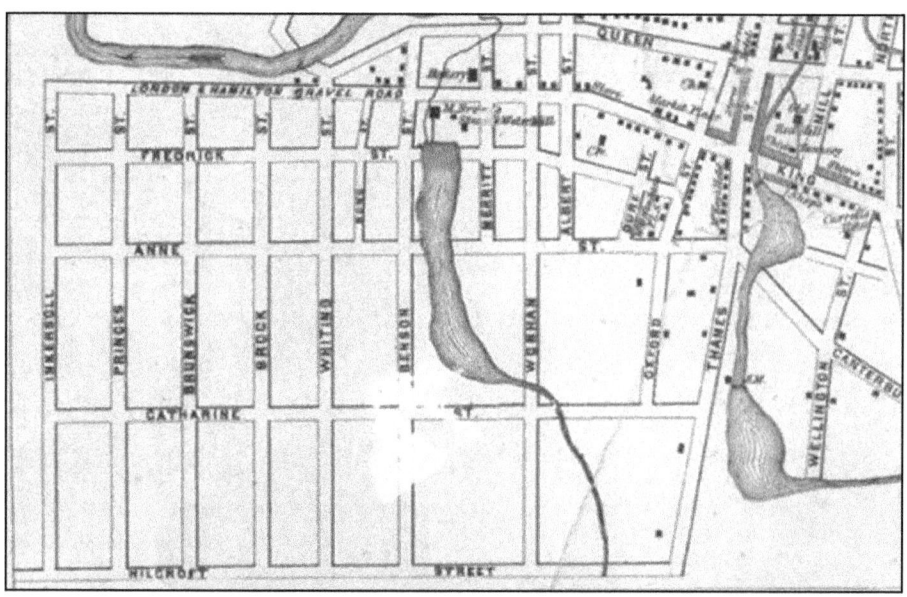

Map 3. Tremaine, 1857.

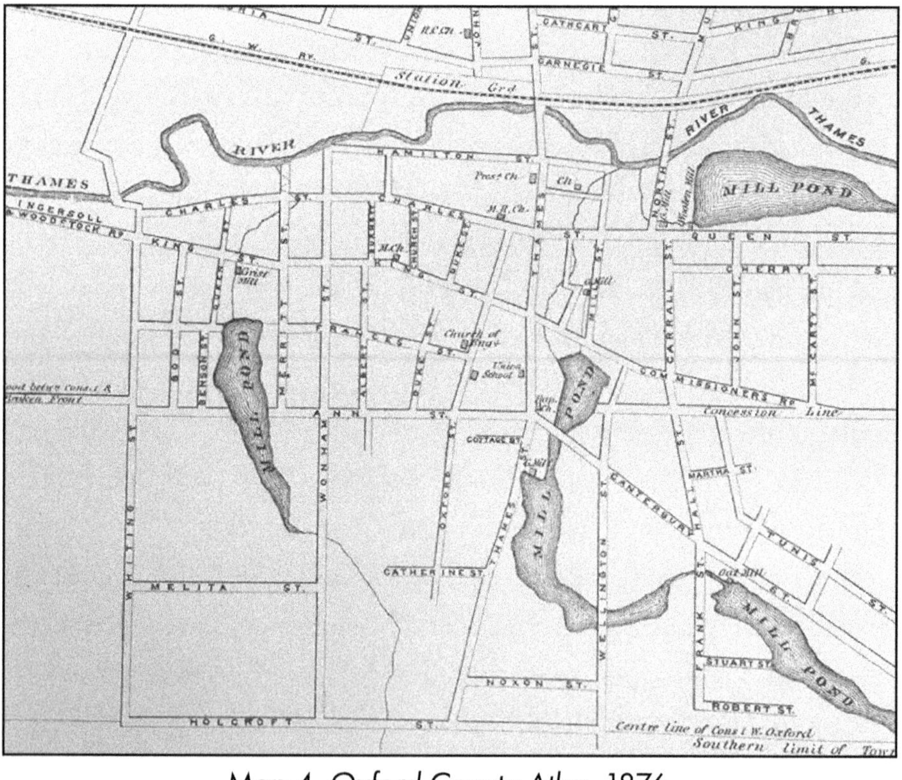

Map 4. Oxford County Atlas, 1876.

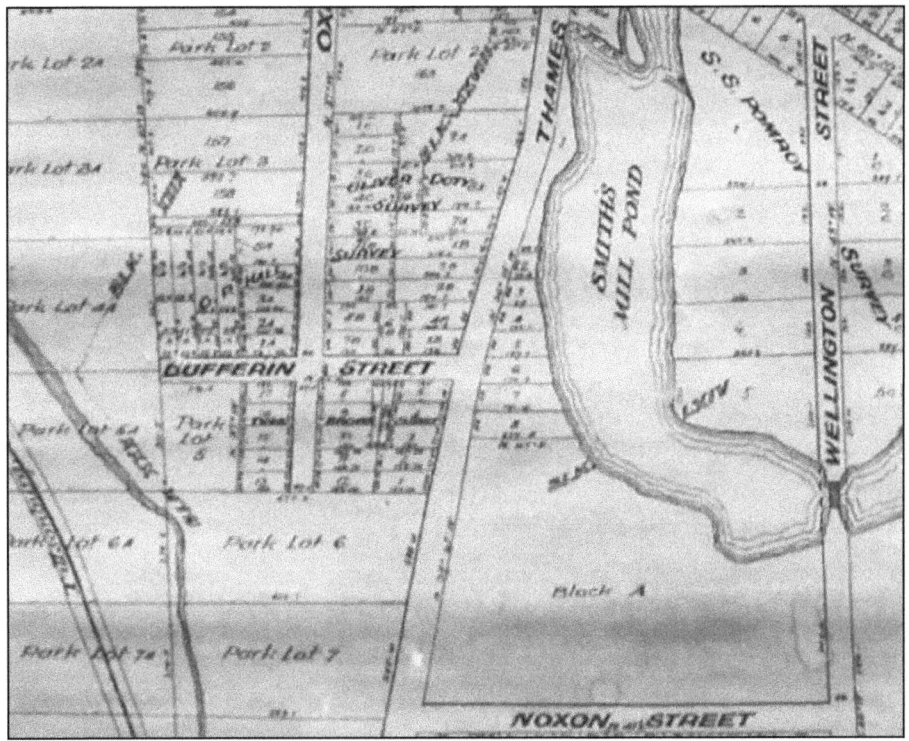

Map 5. Town Lot Map, 1895.

Document 3. James Sinclair, White Vigilantes and Ike Williams, *Ingersoll Chronicle*, 22 August 1907

Background: Wood, Root & Judd[34]

The cutting and clearing of farmland boomed during Ingersoll's village years, and a by-product was log piles, to be burned as a means of disposal. However, the arrival of the Great Western Railway in December, 1853, created a huge demand for log-pile wood to fuel the locomotives: "A car behind the engine carried the wood that was burned to fuel the train. Every 30 miles, *trains* needed to stop at *wood* sheds along the tracks to *wood up*." The railway contracted with an Ingersoll firm of Wood, Root, & Judd—American immigrants from Saginaw, Michigan

---

34. William G. Wood (1826–1885), Erastus T. Judd (1822–1899), and William T. Root (1823–1880) were American immigrants from Saginaw, Michigan, and residents of Ingersoll (two on Oxford Street, one on Duke). James Sinclair, "Reminiscences of Ingersoll's Early Days," *Ingersoll Chronicle*, 29 August 1907; *History of the Town of Ingersoll*, pp. 7, 16–17; *Oxford Gazetteer*, 1862–63.

—to fill the wood sheds. Wood, Root, & Judd, in turn, hired Blacks to do the work, housing them in a special car, which, states Sinclair, was "always given an isolated location in the station for obvious and odoriferous reasons." Isaac (Ike) Williams (1830– ?) hired on as boss of the Coloured work gang.

At some point Ike had enough savings to purchase (or rent) a building, situated on the east side of Thames Street and on the north side of the Thames River Bridge. In August, 1862, Ike petitioned the village council for a saloon license for what had become his "Boarding House for Coloureds":

> Councillors of Ingersoll this is the Second time I have made Applications to you for license or A permit to sell ardent Liquors Being I keep a Boarding hous the only house Kept for the Coloureds of Ingersoll true they can get other places But it is not very Common for them to Sit and Enjoy themselves with the White people for more than all some of my Boarders go any buy Whiskey and take it in their Bed rooms more than that they [order] Liquor other places come to my house and then I bear the blame of to them.
> I am
> With respecks
> Yours truly,
> ISAAC WILLIAMS[35]

The 1861 Census enumeration of Ike's Boarding House lists seven Coloureds and three Whites. The enumeration may be incomplete: it reports four families in the Household, but just three are evident from family names. As shown below, Ike's wife was a White woman, Asenath Williams; Catherine Martin, an unmarried lodger age 19, was White; and Sarah Piper, a third White, living apart from her husband, boarded with her five Mulatto children.

35. *Ingersoll Chronicle*, 8 August 1862.

		Age	Place of Birth	Religion	Race	Mar./ Single	Profession	House	N.	N. Families
Williams	Isaac	32	U. States	Episcopal	Black	M	labourer	frame	2	4
Williams	Asenath	30	U. Canada	W. Meth.	White	M				
Williams	Emma	2	U. Canada	W. Meth.	Mulatto					
Martin	Catherine	19	U. Canada	Baptist	White					
Piper	Sarah	31	Ireland	Episcopal	White	M				
Piper	Ann E.	7	U. Canada	Episcopal	Mulatto					
Piper	William	6	U. Canada	Episcopal	Mulatto					
Piper	Thomas	5	U. Canada	Episcopal	Mulatto					
Piper	John	3	U. Canada	Episcopal	Mulatto					
Piper	Jacob	1	U. Canada	Episcopal	Mulatto					

Sarah Piper, living apart from her Black husband, was desperately poor. In 1860 she "appeared before the Council and stated the reasons on which she applied for relief. She had five young children to support, and she was sick and unable to get work even if she could get it, or could leave her children to do it"; she received $6. She again sought municipal assistance in December 1862 (granted $4) and April 1864.[36]

By August 1865, Ike was gone from Ingersoll, but not his Boarding House for Coloureds. "DISORDERLY CONDUCT," thundered the *Chronicle*!

> On Monday evening last a crowd of Coloured people, male and female, collected on Thames Street bridge in front of a disreputable saloon kept by a Mrs. Williams, who is a White woman but had at one time a Coloured man for a husband [who, however, some time ago took refuge under the "stars and stripes," having been engaged in *crimping*].[37] On the evening above mentioned, one Lucretia Wilson, a "Coloured" person of considerable mus-

---

36. Ingersoll Census, 1861; *Ingersoll Chronicle*, Village Council minutes, 1860–64.
37. *Crimping*: illegally enticing Canadians to serve in the Northern Army of the US during the American Civil War. For Mrs. Williams, see Sinclair's saga of Ike Williams in Document 4. For crimping, see William F. Raney, "Recruiting and Crimping in Canada for the Northern Forces, 1861–1865," *Mississippi Valley Historical Review*, vol. 10, no. 1 (1923, June): 21–33.

cular appearance, was shouting and swearing at the top of her voice, using the grossest kind of language, towards the keeper of the saloon—the screaming and yelling baffling all description, which continued for some time when the Mayor happened to pass and ordered Lucretia to be locked up for the night, which put an end to the row for the time being. Lucretia was discharged next morning on payment of one dollar for her lodgings and making a promise that she would behave better in future. We might add that such news at that particular place [is] almost of nightly occurrence. Our Town Council should take the matter in hand, as it is hardly possible for ladies to pass that way without being subjected to insult of some kind. We hope that we will not have to refer to the matter again.[38]

Document 4. James Sinclair, "Ike" Williams (1830–?) and His Boarding House for Coloureds, or, "How the young men of the times removed a nuisance which defied removal by persuasion," *Ingersoll Chronicle*, 22 August 1907

I would ask the reader [begins Sinclair] to place himself at the northeast end of the Thames St. Bridge and imagine that he is looking at a one and a half story building, standing on the site of the present brick structure, but *extending some distance over the channel of the river* [my italics]. Its southern supports being of timber, and formed independently of the building proper, the lower ends of the uprights being framed into what is known in building as a "mud sill" [scaffold poles set on firm foundations to support the overhead structure] and tenanted[39] into a corresponding timber, running parallel with it, on which the building proper rested. This place at one time was quite respectable, but with the steady growth and popularity, together with

---

38. *Ingersoll Chronicle*, 4 August 1865.
39. *The mortise and tenon joint* functions by inserting one end of a piece of wood (the *tenon*) into a hole in another piece of wood (the *mortise*).

the excellent accommodation provided by the Adair House, which stood on the present site of Mr. Scott's warehouse, the place to which our remarks apply gradually fell away, until it became the home of transient Coloured people, to whose use it was now entirely devoted. The proprietor of this place was a huge Negro, who will be a leading character in the present narrative. His wife was a White woman, to whom we will refer to later on.

Allow me [continues Sinclair] to introduce our leading personage in the person of Isaac Williams, or as he was commonly known, "Ike." Now Ike was a full-blooded Negro and could qualify on the fourteen points that differentiate the Caucasian from the race to which he belonged.... Ike stood six foot two inches in height, his chest measurement was fifty-four inches, and as he often proudly stated, with a characteristic lacking in measurement at the hips. His body was disproportionately long, and his legs were ill-shaped, with a decided inclination to interfere at the knees, and then his feet, Oh My! It was customary for boys at the time on meeting "Ike" and knowing his vanity, to ask him such questions as his height, chest measurement, etc.; also the size of his shoes, when a genuine smile of self-admiration would overspread his sable countenance, and looking down at his feet, would reply, "Dat Mr. Kelly (the shoemaker) said dat dey is 17s, sah." Now this was the time when small feet were fashionable, and shoes were made to fit tight, that it led a celebrated American humorist to exclaim that "the man who invented tight shoes must have been a narrow contracted cuss." That no one could appreciate them until he had walked almost five miles with a pair of No. 8 feet in a pair of No. 7 shoes. Returning to "Ike" we could not overlook the great length of his arms, reaching as they did nearly to his knees. Good-natured as a rule, and although absolutely illiterate, [he] was most polite in manner. He took pride in being a champion of his race, and was always so regarded by them.

His word was law to them, and with physical force sufficient to compel respect, was never disputed. Ike was employed as manager of this element, exclusively employed by the then firm of *Wood, Root & Judd*, who were contractors for cutting the wood, then the fuel of the locomotives of the G.W.R. [A car behind the engine carried the wood that was burned to fuel the train. Every 30 miles, trains needed to stop at *wood* sheds along the tracks to "wood up."] The Coloured men were housed in a special car, always given an isolated location in the station for obvious and odoriferous reasons, while the building with which we have to deal, for the same reasons, had become a standing object of disgust, from a combination we will now attempt to describe.

Looking north from the Thames-Street Bridge, Ingersoll, late 1850s. North side of the Thames River, on left: Great Western Railway freight house and station. Right side: Ike's Boarding House for Coloureds (the white building, half over water).

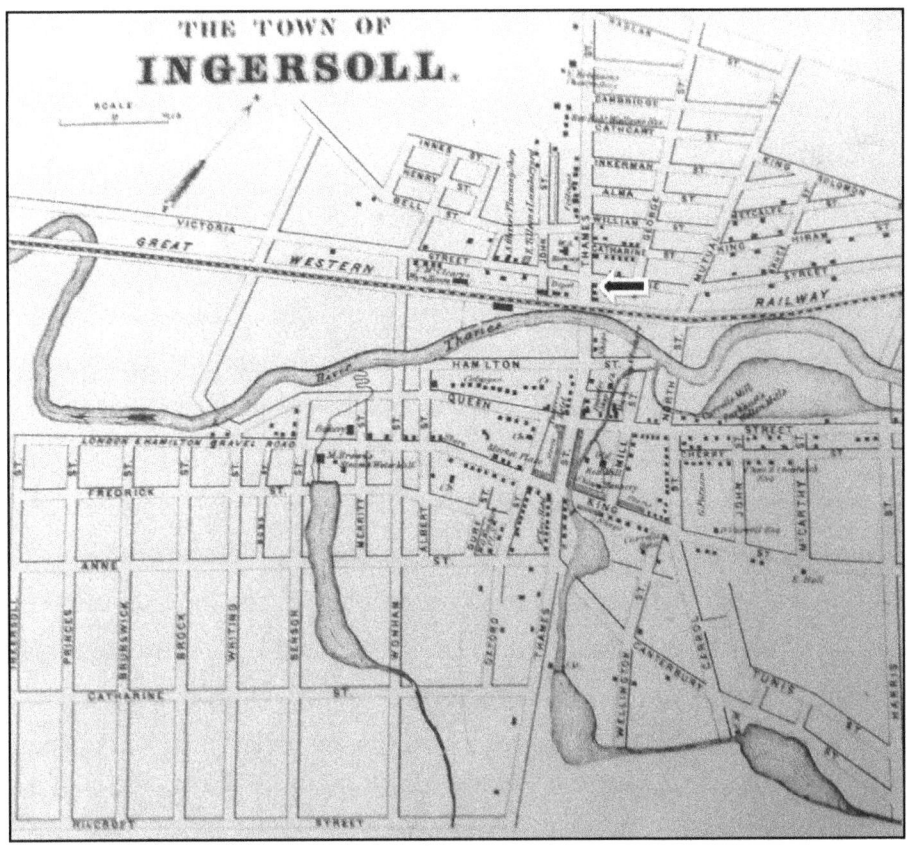

Map 6. Tremaine Map, 1857.
Arrow marks location of Ike's Boarding House.

Asenath Williams: "White Denizen of a Darky Dive"
Here, indeed, we may well pause [continues Sinclair] before making the descent. The sights, smells, and sounds witnessed and experienced daily and nightly for a period of years is more fitting to be told in a camera, which would make the existence of such a place a vastly greater crime than its destruction. With the principal figure in the paragraph a White woman ... the reputed wife of him we have just described. Of this woman it can be said that she, in her earlier womanhood, possessed personal attractions sufficient to make her the object of admiration, endowed with a splendidly developed physique, above the aver-

age in height and well proportioned, erect and graceful in movement, with that dignity of manner that commands respect. Her eyes were dark, though not Black, which seemed to possess a hypnotic influence when interested, her hair luxuriant, and of a raven Black inclined to waviness. Her face was bold and striking, every feature indicative of force, which lent an impression of austerity to the casual beholder, yet beneath doubtless burned with intensity the fire of an ungovernable passion which, once centred on an object of its affection, knew no retreat. It has been said, "Man's love is of his life a thing apart, a woman's whole existence," and in charity may we not believe what was currently reported at the time, that unrequited affection had produced the condition we are about to portray. So far as the woman in this case is concerned, such natures as hers do not as a rule make confidants of her sorrow, while it remains indelibly inscribed on the innermost recesses of their being, and controls their destiny. Thwarted in this, the supreme object of her life, disappointment usurped the throne of reason, and dissipation floats her to certain destruction, in the present case to a condition worse than death itself—the degree superlative of human degradation, for a White man or woman, the *denizen of a darky dive* [my italics].

Now that we have endeavoured to show this woman as she once was, it becomes our painful task to describe her as she was of the time of which we speak. The building we have described was a low-ceiling structure, with the bar-room opening into the street. In and around there were always a number of Coloured people, and when the sewing machine was at work here the whole gang would frequent "Ike's place," until it had assumed the condition already mentioned. There were three children born her by Ike's wife, the two oldest being able to run about when the third was born. These children were a most repulsive sight, never half-dressed, and dirty to the last degree, wholly uncared for, and the faces of both of them were blotched with open sores of a character that shall be nameless. The youngest, even in early infancy, showing the same taint, while the mother would often sit in front of her home in full view of all passers-by, and performing the offices of maternity with her person barely covered, and with her feet encased in worn-out slippers, with her stockingless limbs exposed beyond the limits of decency, singing songs and vulgar Negro melodies, with unkempt hair and a besotted expression, seeming to take delight in her depravity. Nor was this by any means an exceptional case, and often varied by more disgusting exhibitions. Ike did not seem to mind the condition so long as his wife did not get too intoxicated. His frequent absence from home gave her this opportunity, and the orgies of the inmates were better left to the imagination.

The Vigilantes Move In

Conditions such as these [Sinclair continues] could not be allowed to continue, as the first view the stranger got on leaving the train was the unsavory spectacle of a White woman nursing a half-caste child, surrounded by a lounging group of Negroes who were sure to be in evidence when "de train com'in."

After deliberation matters began to take form. Directly across the river from the doomed house, where Ackert's pump shop now stands, was a dense growth of willows of the same kind now growing on the opposite banks. Into this thicket, under cover of the night, the ropes and tackling were concealed for days previous to the event. However, one important obstacle had to be removed before the proceedings could go farther. This was Ike. How was he to be disposed of? As with Ike at home and the crowd he could command, the scheme could not be carried out. However, this was got over by taking into their confidence a party in Chatham, who arranged to have him detained for a few days. Another obstacle presented itself. How could the tenents [tenons] be sawn off, as was necessary before the uprights could be pulled from their place, without the suspicion of the inmates being aroused? This was arranged by a crowd of our young men, masked in Calithumpian attire, who arranged for a dance at Ike's in his absence. To this Ike's wife readily consented, and with her helplessly intoxicated, and her children laid away in safety, it was not too difficult to arrange the balance. Here they were, jumping, dancing, and making every conceivable noise, while a man on a ladder at each post vigorously sawed the tenents [tenons] of the uprights, and with ropes attached to each post in such a manner that, when the posts were pulled clear, the ropes came home and were speedily concealed. When everything was in readiness the dancers seized the women of the party and hustled out of the house, and on a given signal the uprights yielded to the vigorous force simultaneously applied, and with little warning the house turned a complete somersault, and was viewed in the morning a complete wreck. However the day of reckoning with Ike had to come. He was in a measure prepared for this by the tale that a locomotive had left the track and wrecked his house. However, on coming home and viewing the wreck, there was not the slightest evidence to support the idea that it had been pulled over. As the wreck effectively concealed all the evidence, no one knew how it happened, and the parties in the house could assuredly have had no hand in it. Supposing it was, as he had been told, of course, the officers of the law were invoked to discover the parties, but nothing came of it, and it was soon hushed up, and a standing object of disgrace effectively removed.

We regret that in the recital of the foregoing we were obliged, in order to be faithful in the portrayal of the circumstances connected with our subject, to touch upon the prurient and unchaste. The conditions I have endeavoured to present were witnessed by hundreds of our citizens, and as we stated at the outset, were such as could not obtain in the present, which shows great advance made by us as a people in social order and public morality, and if ever an occasion presented itself where the end justified the means, this was the one.

Postscript 1: Fact Checking Sinclair's Story

One may be sceptical that Sinclair's vigilante action ever happened. "With little warning," he claimed, "the house turned a complete somersault, and was viewed in the morning a complete wreck." Yet the *Ingersoll Chronicle* made no mention of that event. Moreover, the boarding house was still in business in August 1865, by which time Ike Williams had fled to the United States to escape a charge of crimping, leaving his White wife, Asenath, in charge.

Postscript 2: Blacks as Remembered by Frank Wallace, a Sheltered White Boy, 1849–1862[40]

Frank Wallace (1851–1930) was raised in Ingersoll until 1862, when his family moved away. His memoir, written in 1921 when he was 70 years of age, reflected on his childhood in Ingersoll, during his first decade of life.

His father, the Rev. Robert Wallace, was the inaugural pastor of Knox Presbyterian Church on St. Andrews Street (1849–1860). In 1850 Robert married Mary Anne Barker, daughter of Joseph Barker, a shoemaker, at whose house he boarded, and Frank and his siblings were born in Ingersoll. Their home was "a good-looking, comfortable brick cottage, set nearly in the middle of the eight acre lot" on the north side of the Thames River. Although not rich, the family were upper-crust Whites.

- "We always kept a maid."
- "My school life began at six years of age. I was never sent, nor my sister, to the 'common school,' public school, as we now call it. The distinction of classes kept us from that. My first private school was that of Mrs. Atkins, far from our own house, not far from grand-

---

40. Francis Huston Wallace, "A Boy's Life in Ingersoll in the 1850s," taken from *Memories: A Family Record* (1921). Courtesy of Ingersoll Cheese and Agricultural Museum; Ingersoll Library.

father's. So I had a good long walk each day, down the hill, across the river, and east in the southern part of the town. The school was small and the pupils were mostly girls older than myself. What I learned from Mrs. Atkins or her daughter I have not the remotest recollection. But this I well remember, that I suffered tortures of the mind from the teasing of the girls who called me 'little preacher.'"

- "I was kept very carefully away from association with 'common' children. Other boys were supposed to be mostly 'bad boys,' with whom I must not mingle. Indeed I was badly 'molly-coddled.' It was positively forbidden that I should go into the water to swim or on the water to row."

- "*How well I remember the Coloured man, Warren by name, who used to do our garden and cut down our trees.* One of the keenest pleasures of my childhood was to watch the cutting down of those big maple, ash and beech trees; to see them sway and fall, and to hear them crash to the ground. Another great pleasure was to listen to Warren tell of his escape from Southern slavery, for those were the days 'before the War.' As soon as I was old enough, Father gave me 'Uncle Tom's Cabin' to read, and I recall very vividly the picture in his copy of Eliza escaping, babe in arms, on floating blocks of ice across the Ohio River on her way to Canada."

- "Another pleasure which came to me from Warren were bows and arrows which he made for me and in the use of which I spent many happy hours in our bit of woodland sloping down to the creek which ran near the western boundary of our place. There were plenty of squirrels and chipmunks to shoot at. …"

- "One of the most interesting visits of my childhood was, with Father and Mother, to Rev. William King, of Buxton in the Elgin Settlement near Chatham. Mr. King, the 'Clayton' of Mrs. Stowe's story 'Dred,' had married a Southern wife who inherited a large number of slaves. They set the slaves free, paid their passage to Canada and accompanied them 1500 miles to that land of freedom. With the help of many friends, Mr. King formed the Elgin Association in 1850, purchased 9000 acres of land, gave each Coloured settler a farm of 50 acres, and devoted his life to superintending the settlement. Over two hundred families of former slaves prospered under his care. Schools were built, a church was erected. After the war many young Coloured men and women went back from Buxton, as the centre of the settlement was called, and became teachers among the emancipated slaves of the South...."

- *"Mother took home with her one of the young Coloured girls as maid, but she did not keep her long. I remember that one of the counts in Mother's indictment against her was that she was quite too fond of the sugar bowl."*

After his Ingersoll childhood days, Frank Wallace attended Upper Canada College and the University of Toronto, was ordained a Methodist minister in 1878, and retired as Dean of Theology, Victoria College, in 1920.

CHAPTER THREE
White Abolitionists and Runaway Slaves: Conventional Wisdom from the 1950s

This chapter summarizes the predominant White interpretation of the years 1950–2022 and documents it with excerpts from published local histories.

Summary of Conventional Wisdom of the 1950s

- A majority of Ingersoll Blacks were refugee slaves (runaways from Southern Slave States).
- The notion that most Blacks were runaways dated from the nineteenth century.[41] What was new in the 1950s was the notion that White abolitionists, not slaves, were the centrepiece of the story.

---

41. For pre–Second World War references to Blacks as Slaves, see: (1) Death Notice, 1887. Washington Bevins, a resident of Ingersoll for over forty years, died at his home on Friday at the advanced age of 111 years. The old man was a slave on the plantation of Gen. Ross in 1812. He, together with his wife, now dead, ran away to Canada along with many other slaves, and coming to Ingersoll, has lived here ever since. ... At one time there were nearly 400 runaway slaves here, most of whom returned to the South at the close of the Civil War. *Ingersoll Chronicle*, 19 May 1887. (2) Death Notice, Solomon P. Hale, 1903: Mr. Hale "was born a slave and after having attained to manhood became desirous of freedom and made a bold attempt in obtaining the same, and about fifty years ago arrived at the Fifty-Ninth Creek, County of Wentworth (near Winona), and was fortunate in getting employment with Hugh B. Wilson, Esq., brother of the Hon. John Wilson, for over eleven years, meantime buying his first wife out of slavery." (3) Pre-1867: John Grieve Oliver (1846–1920), son of Adam Oliver, recalled driving teams with some Scotchmen and two men who were "late from slavery just after the USA rebellion." To John the two men were "Black as ebony but ... innocent and good. ... They took their master's name and language." The Scots forced the former slaves to speak Gaelic. "We enjoyed the sport," remembered John, and the Blacks "appeared not to mind it." George Emery and Glenna Oliver Jamieson, *Adam Oliver of Ingersoll, 1823–1882: Lumberman, Mill Owner, Contractor, and Politician* (Ingersoll & District Historical Society, 2002), p. 43.

- Ingersoll was a terminus ["the most northerly"] on the Underground Railway.
- American slave catchers—bounty hunters—were active in Ingersoll.
- Whites ran the Underground Railway in Ingersoll, billeting refugees in safe houses and fixing them up with jobs.
- Grateful Blacks provided free labour to build the White Wesleyan Methodist Church.
- A White Wesleyan Methodist Church in Ingersoll (1854–64) on Oxford Street acted as a clearing house for refugee slaves in Ingersoll, hiding them from slave catchers and giving them a place to worship until they could acquire a Black church of their own.
- The White American abolitionist John Brown visited Ingersoll in April 1858, a year before his capture of Harper's Ferry, West Virginia. He stayed in the Daly House and spoke either in the Wesleyan Church or the Town Hall, his purpose being to raise troops for an abolitionist army to overthrow slavery in the American South.

Salient Features of the 1950s Narrative
- A paucity of evidence. There exists scanty documentary evidence to support the folkloric wisdom of the 1950s and an abundance of documentary evidence to refute it (see Chapters, 4, 6, and 8).
- The folkloric narrative expresses a widely-shared belief in White supremacy over other "races"—the view that Ingersoll Blacks were passive recipients of a history made by their White-abolitionist minders.
- The folkloric narrative exaggerates the cordiality between Whites and Blacks and the deference shown by Blacks to Whites. Conversely, it ignores racial conflict.
- This interpretation expresses local boosterism by presenting the old home town as part of larger events on the world stage—the evil of American slavery and its abolition in 1863.

Local Historians and the White Abolitionist/Black Slave Interpretation

By contrast with James Sinclair, writing in 1907, the 1950s local historians, Stanley J. Smith and Byron Jenvey, made the *White abolitionist/Black slave thesis* the centrepiece of their interpretation. Smith was the principal generator of the interpretation. Jenvey was the archivist, the keeper of Smith's clippings—the clippings, commonly without dates and the names of newspapers in which they appeared, were the documentary authority for Smith's colourful, fabulist stories.

The White abolitionist/Black slave narrative continued into the 21st century. In 1967 the *Ingersoll Tribune, Centennial Edition*, showcased an article, "The Blacks: Travelling the Underground Railroad to 'Freedom' in Canada." In March 1976 the *Ingersoll Times* featured an article by Richard Houghton, "Town was Full of Civil War Spies" ("based on research by Harry Whitwell and Stanley J. Smith"). On 19 July 1980, Michael Barris of the *Woodstock-Ingersoll Sentinel-Review* published "Helped to End Slavery's Tide: the Railway Stopped Here." In the *Sentinel-Review's* issue for 5 December 1981, Tom Duralia published "Underground Railway Stopped Here." In 2006 Joyce Pettigrew of South Norwich Township published *A Safe Haven: The Story of the Black Settlers of Oxford* County,[42] a pioneering work in local history that, unusually for the genre, reports documentary evidence for her findings. That said, her work shares the White abolitionist/Black slave narrative and, where her primary evidence is thin, she draws on the undocumented publications of local historians for coverage of Blacks in Ingersoll.

Stanley J. Smith (1895–1979) was born in England and came to Ontario with his parents in 1901, at age six. After a stint as a trainman in Sarnia, 1913–14, he served in France as a private and was wounded during the Great War. He returned to Sarnia in 1919 and lost a leg in a

---

42. Joyce A. Pettigrew, *A Safe Haven: The Story of the Black Settlers of Oxford County* (Otterville, ON: South Norwich Historical Society, 2006).

train accident in 1925. He moved to Ingersoll 1931 and there lived out his life. In 1933 he became a proud member of the Wisconsin Liar's Club. As an historian, "by his own admission he was an authority on, among other things, Abraham Lincoln, Wyatt Earp, Billy the Kid, Wild Bill Hickock, John Brown, Aimee Semple Macpherson, Cattle Kate, Kitty Leroy, the original First Canadian Division that left Canada in 1814, and the complete histories of Chatham, Sarnia, and Ingersoll." "When Stanley Smith Speaks," remarked Adrian Ewins of the *Woodstock-Ingersoll Sentinel-Review*, "it's a Tall Tale or Spicy History."[43]

Byron G. Jenvey (1881–1980) was best known for his nine scrapbooks of newspaper clippings on current and historical events.[44] By the 1970s Jenvey was widely respected as the town historian. Mr. Jenvey modestly denied this title, saying, "I merely like to keep the facts straight."[45]

The balance of the chapter presents excerpts of publications that set out the White abolitionist/Black slave thesis. Chapter 4 follows with evidence that overturns the thesis.

---

43. Adrien Ewins, "When Stanley Smith Speaks it's a Tall Tale or Spicy History," *Woodstock Sentinel-Review*, 28 January 1976; Yvonne Mott, "Colourful 'Character' disdains 'Cut, Dried,'" *Woodstock Sentinel-Review*, 6 December 1976.
44. See Ingersoll Public Library website.
45. *Ingersoll Times*, 13 February 1980. Byron Jenvey was born in Hawtrey, South Norwich Township. With the exception of five years as an economics professor at the Ontario Agricultural College (1918–23), he spent his life in the Ingersoll area. He farmed in West Oxford Township, 1904–18, 1923–26, and; was Clerk and Treasurer of West Oxford Township, 1908–18. In 1926 he retired from farming and relocated to 23 Ann Street, Ingersoll. During the 1960s, Mr. Jenvey was gracious and helpful when introducing the writer to Ingersoll's local history. He was a positive influence for the Town.

Left: Byron Jenvey, Local Historian, Ingersoll (Ingersoll Cheese & Agricultural Museum).
Right: Stanley J. Smith, Local Historian, Ingersoll (Ingersoll Public Library).

Document 1. Stanley J. Smith, "Wesleyan Church, Once Haven for Slaves, is being torn Down in Ingersoll now," *Woodstock Sentinel-Review,* **5 June 1956 (Jenvey Scrapbook #3, p. 105)**

In this article, Stanley Smith discussed "[t]he old Wesleyan church on Oxford street," whose construction he dated to August 1854. Smith described the church as "one of the old landmarks of Ingersoll," going on to claim that "through its portals have passed some of the most famous speakers, ministers, and lyceum lecturers of the past century."[46]

According to Smith, the church became famous in the mid-1850s as a "clearing house" for slaves fleeing the United States. At the beginning

---

46. Pure folklore. This building was a Wesleyan Methodist Church for only ten years; in 1865 the congregation moved to a new church building on King Street (the present Trinity United). By 1874 the old building had become a Bible Christian Methodist Church. *Ingersoll Chronicle,* 1 July 1864; *Oxford Gazetteer,* 1874–1875, p. 61. In the Methodist Church union of 1884, the Bible Christian denomination was absorbed into the Methodist Church of Canada, which apparently ended the use of the original Wesleyan Church building for denominational purposes.

of the twentieth century, the town's older residents could still recall "the ladies of the church giving succor to the poor wretches who had been smuggled through the slave states [from] even as far away as New Orleans."

Smith cited as a source Joseph T. Fitzgerald, who managed the *Woodstock Sentinel-Review*'s Ingersoll office and who (according to Smith) "made an extensive study of this old landmark." Fitzgerald is credited with uncovering "many interesting facts" about the church and its congregation. The Wesleyan congregation had previously gathered in "the old Episcopal Methodist church which was situated nearby on Charles street west and in later years became known as the Charles Street Methodist church," Smith noted. "In the rear of the church was the common burial ground for adherents to Methodism, but in 1861 their bodies were transferred to the Ingersoll Rural Cemetery."

The building contractor for the new church was Adam Oliver, who would later serve as the member of the Ontario Legislative Assembly for the riding of Oxford South from 1867 to 1878. Although the original cost estimate for erecting the church was $2,800—more than $100,000 in today's dollars—"by purchasing material at cost, and donation of much volunteer labour, the brick building cost less than $2,500! And," asked Smith, "from where came the volunteer labor? *Naturally, the ex-slaves, to reciprocate their thanks to the Wesleyans for their kindness and tolerance, shown to them upon their arrival in Ingersoll* [my italics]." Indeed, Smith asserted, "[e]very historian of Ingersoll has mentioned that the Coloured people became very skilled in the building trade—especially brick-layers, plasterers, and roofers."

Two other notable buildings—the first town hall and the Daly House—dated from the same year as the Wesleyan church (1854), but less than two years later, on the first day of February 1856, the town hall was destroyed by fire. Left without a venue for large meetings, Ingersoll turned to the new Wesleyan church as a stopgap. Since it "could seat 500, *it became almost the Town Hall until a new municipal building could be erected* [my italics]."⁴⁷

Under the heading "Famous Speakers," Smith wrote that the prominent abolitionist leader John Brown visited Ingersoll to raise money and recruit Blacks to his movement. Brown was executed in 1859 for trying to incite a slave rebellion by raiding the federal arsenal at Harper's Ferry, Virginia (later West Virginia).

In the years leading up to the American Civil War, Ingersoll's Black community used the Wesleyan church to hold "meetings pertaining to the obnoxious slave trade." The church choir included "many Coloured singers," wrote Smith; "one can imagine them banding together and singing Negro spirituals which they had probably learned 'back in plantation days' upon their mothers' knees."

Smith went on to note that while a "Coloured church" had been built on the north side of the Thames River in 1858, it was too small to hold a large crowd. For instance, in 1861 a troupe of Black singers from Oxford and Middlesex counties sang there, "and an old account states that a repeated performance occurred a week later because the church could not contain the crowd."

Smith concluded the 1956 article with a description of the physical structure of the Wesleyan church:

> On entering ... one would walk under a gallery (it held 100) and the pews were placed on each side of the church. At the rear, a stairway led to the third storey, and this was the resident minister's private home. Above this, was a half storey ... an attic where the church records were stored, and tradition has it, that in a pinch, it became a temporary haven for the slaves who arrived during the night.

47. Not true. The Council met in the Mansion House through February 1856, and then in the Town Clerk's office in a new temporary market building. Two ratepayers' meetings in May 1856 were held in the school house.

Document 2. Stanley J. Smith, "The Old Wesleyan Methodist Church" [newspaper unknown], June 1956, Jenvey Scrapbook #3, pp. 116–17

By Stanley J. Smith

Smith returned to the subject of the soon-to-be-demolished ("for the valuable timber it contains") Wesleyan Methodist Church in a second newspaper article from June 1956. The article is preserved in one of Byron Jenvey's scrapbooks, though the name of the newspaper in which the piece first appeared is not given.

With the demolition, wrote Smith, "vanishes one of the most historic buildings in this part of Ontario because it was the headquarters of Harriet Tubman's most northerly terminus of the Underground Railway for escaped slaves." Smith described the "unique organization to aid slave refugees" as extending from Plaquemine County, Louisiana, to Oxford County, Canada West:

> The "railroad" ran mostly on moonless nights across cotton fields, dense thickets, and upon certain occasions, openly in daylight. Some friend of the anti-slavery society would have five or six Negroes chained together, and if questioned, he would produce some false sale bill that the Negroes were his "property" and he was moving them "further up the river", to the site of a new plantation.
>
> Or he might produce a false "Runaway Slave" circular which offered a substantial reward for their safe return to their legitimate owner J. Invariably, the "owner" resided almost on the borders of Ohio (a free state) and somehow mysteriously crossed the Detroit River to Canada a few days later.

Smith went on to claim that in the 1850s, Ingersoll boasted a larger Black population that any other "inland community" in Canada West apart from Chatham: "Just previous to the outbreak of the Civil War, its Coloured inhabitants numbered 'upwards to four hundred' according to the obituary of the late Washington Bevins (1887)."

In this article, Smith repeated the claim that abolitionist John Brown visited Ingersoll, and provided a few additional details. Brown, he noted, was "advertised to speak in the Ingersoll Wesleyan Methodist Church, April 15, 1858 upon the outrages perpetrated on the 'Free Soilers' by the 'Border Ruffians' in the Missouri-Kansas border war…" He gave credit to a "Mr. Stutler," who

> closed a link when he kindly supplied us with a copy of John Brown's correspondence whilst in Ingersoll. He was to have met Mrs. Tubman at the Daly House, corner of Oxford and King Streets, Ingersoll, but she did not put in an appearance. Brown wrote to a friend in St. Kitts by the name of W. H. Day and asked her whereabouts. Mr. Day replied that he did not know, but "Jackson" put her on the same train which Brown traveled to Ingersoll and Mr. Day was under the impression she would look him up en route.

In this article, Smith placed the construction of the Wesleyan church in the context of "a great building boom [that] took place in the struggling Village of Ingersoll during the year of 1854. Absalom Daly constructed a new hotel; the village fathers met in the Royal Exchange Hotel and decided the village should have a new town hall and market building; the Board of Management of the Wesleyan Methodists decided to construct the latest design in church architecture. All of this proposed building activity was within a 300 yards radius."

The church itself was described as being three and a half stories high, with each floor "designed for a set purpose." On the first floor, which was slightly below street level, were "the kitchen, banquet hall, and sewing room." The second floor housed "the church proper, with a small gallery facing west." Above that were "the residential quarters of the presiding ministers; and the half floor, or attic, was used as a general utility and storage room. Tradition has it that the high attic was often called into use by the arrival of a new batch of 'contraband,' as the slaves were called."

To the rear of the lot was a drive shed, to provide shelter for church-goers' carriages and wagons as well as their horses.

Construction of the new church was funded by "public subscription," with "nearly every other denomination" also contributing to the cost. According to Smith, services in the new building were first held on "Sunday, September 15, 1854"—apparently an error, as September 15, 1854, was actually a Friday.

Document 3. Stanley J. Smith, "Old John Brown in Ingersoll," *Ingersoll Tribune*, Centennial Edition, 1967, p. 22

(A condensation from the book *Capt. John Brown In Canada*, copyright 1960 by Stanley J. Smith)

In this article, Smith went into even more detail about Brown's supposed visit to Ingersoll. He began with mention of "two remarkable characters in history who gained international fame," both (according to Smith) with ties to Oxford County: "One was the notorious Aimee Semple McPherson of Dereham township who was top news for seven years because of her exploits," and who was "dubbed the Barnum of Religion by many church critics." The second was "Old John 'Osawatomie' Brown, [the] American abolitionist who led a raid on the government arsenal at Harper's Ferry, W. Virginia, 1859, to establish a stronghold for escaped slaves and was hanged for treason, December 2, 1859, in Charlestown, W. Virginia." (Charles Town was in 1859 actually still part of Virginia, as West Virginia did not separate from the state of Virginia until 1861.) "The hanging," Smith wrote, "was the spark that lit the fuse to cause the American Civil War."

Referring to Brown's "mad scheme to free those who were in human bondage" and to recruit converts to the cause from the Ingersoll area, Smith noted that "[i]t is only within the last couple of years that further light has been shed on Brown's activities whilst in Ingersoll and his plan to meet Mrs. Harriet Tubman, conductor of the Underground Railway." That meeting, "which failed to materialize," had been set for April 15, 1858, at Ingersoll's Daly House. Smith pondered the question of why Brown had decided to visit Ingersoll to begin with:

> One of the enigmas to any student or keen historian delving into the activities of John Brown previous to his preparation of his famous but futile raid ... is why did he choose a small Canadian village as the site to conspire to flaunt the laws of our friendly neighbour to the south in an attempt to overthrow the government's authority to impose slavery on the Negro population dwelling in the southern states. The small Canadian village of course was Ingersoll, Canada West, and it was in the year 1858 that the conspiracy transpired, doomed to failure from its outset.
>
> This writer has been an active researcher into the life of John Brown since 1902 when we first heard the story of Brown from the lips of the daughter of an escaped slave by the name of Martha Matthews of Chatham, Ontario. Chatham was the eventual place where a meeting was called of very prominent Negroes and a provisional constitution was adopted to govern the people of the southern states if, as, and when the overthrow was accomplished. We have received the greatest assistance from America's greatest authority on the life of John Brown in the person of Dr. Boyd B. Stutler of Charleston, West Virginia, whose collection of John Brown lore cannot be surpassed by any other gatherer of John Brown material. His photos and documents run into the thousands.

Smith cited an obituary of resident Washington Bevins, who died at age 112, in support of the claim that in the 1850s Ingersoll's Black population topped five hundred. (Many Blacks, Smith noted in an aside, "returned to the Sunny South upon the termination of the conflict [i.e., the Civil War] because of the severity of the Canadian winter climate.") Ingersoll's Black population was "blessed with an over abundance of worldly goods compared to their brethren of the southern states," Smith wrote, as they were "highly skilled men" who were "chiefly engaged in the building trade" and therefore commanded high wages. "Naturally this would be a magnet to Brown who relied on a meagre existence to garner in money to purchase needed arms and ammunition."

Another reason for Brown to come to Ingersoll was the fact "the village was the halfway station of the Underground Railway which existed between Detroit and Niagara Falls." What Smith termed "influential Ingersollians" backed the movement. They included Max and Leonard Bixel, who had come to Ingersoll in 1848 from Wurttemburg, Germany, "to escape militarism when Prussia was about to take over," and Thomas Brown, owner of one of the largest tanneries in the province. "Most of his labourers were Coloured and he paid excellent wages based on their ability to produce leather instead of the colour of their skin," Smith wrote, adding that the list of other organizations in Ingersoll supporting anti-slavery activity "is too lengthy to mention at this writing other than to write it was very comprehensive and composed of members of all other fraternal bodies."

Fugitive slaves arriving in Ingersoll found "a temporary haven" in the Wesleyan Methodist church's basement, with additional quarters in the stables of the New Daly House, "which were run by Peter Van Patter, another escaped slave and noted horse trainer."

Smith cited "a Simcoe lady who wishes to remain anonymous" as telling him that abolitionist John Brown had a "staunch friend" in Ingersoll "in the person of Harvey C. Jackson, a Mulatto and one-time sailor on a schooner, who injured his back and was compelled to give up sailing and seek a position on shore." Jackson worked as a driver on Edward Doty's stage line between Port Burwell and Ingersoll.

John Brown was a very reticent person [Smith continued] and his most intimate friends were unaware of his next move. Harriet Tubman was an exception and probably knew all his plans to invade the south and she wholeheartedly threw in her support to support John Brown. It could have been she who informed Brown of the existence of Jackson and his knowledge of ex-slaves who had settled in the district. In all of Brown's correspondence there are mentioned only three or four places where he visited whilst in Canada, namely St. Catharines and Chatham. However, his son, John Brown, Jr., was more communicative and mentioned other spots where Brown, senior had made contacts. Again, through the kindness of Dr. Boyd B. Stutler, America's greatest authority on Brown, this writer is advised that Brown posted a letter from Port Robinson, Canada West, while he was in Canada to gather men and money. One can obtain further information from letters which Brown received in Ingersoll which was sent by a printer, W. H. Day of St. Catharines. Brown wrote Mr. Day that he was to have met Mrs. Tubman at the Daly House and was under the impression that she was on the same train that he was but occupying a different car. Day replied by telegraph that "Jackson" had put her on the train and also informed Brown of five Ingersoll men who might join him in his southern venture.

Drawing on information provided by his anonymous Simcoe source, Smith deduced that the "Jackson who drove the stage for Doty was the Jackson who placed Mrs. Tubman on the cars. Moreover, after Brown was sentenced to be hanged it was F. C. Jackson [who] made an appeal for funds for Mrs. Brown and her family," requesting "that sums be allotted to the others who were also sentenced to die."

The telegram sent by the St. Catharines printer W. H. Day told John Brown "that he could pick up his recruits by going to 'Patterson's Hotel,'" and asking for "the location of Bachelor's Hall." John Patterson ran the Royal Exchange Hotel, but a few weeks prior to Brown's arrival in Ingersoll in February 1858, had assumed control of the New Daly House. He was also Town Clerk.

As for Bachelor's Hall, Smith described it as "an undesirable nest which sat on piles at the Thames Street Bridge. It was constructed half on land and the other half on mud sills situated on the river bed." Its actual name was the "River House," but it had been dubbed Bachelor's Hall because of its "unsavoury character," such that "no lady would venture through its doors." James Sinclair, Sr., "an accurate historian of Ingersoll," provided one of the best descriptions of Bachelor's Hall, and also described the building's "destruction … by irate citizens while the proprietors were absent in Chatham on a binge." The building was pulled off its foundations and tumbled into the Thames River.

After arriving at the Great Western Railway station, Brown was to go to Patterson's Hotel—the Royal Exchange—where he would receive further instructions to carry on to the the New Daly House, the site of his planned meeting with Harriet Tubman.

At this point in the article, Smith noted that in 1933 he had interviewed many of the town's older residents, asking them "for their earliest memories of the town":

> There were two nearing their one hundredth birthdays and they possessed all of their faculties. One was Clarence Brown of King Street East who maintained that he had seen [John] Brown on more than one occasion as he recognized him as a stranger to the town and was dressed similar to a deacon in a church. He

had noticed in particular his military bearing and his very long strides. Mr. Brown further claimed that John Brown often visited Thomas Brown's tannery on Mill Street and conversed with the Coloured employees of the firm. Mr. Brown was under the impression that the two Browns were related.

The other person interviewed was Mrs. Mary McCaskell on Victoria Street. She possessed a remarkable memory. Born in Ingersoll in the early 1830s she remembered her mother running a boarding house on Water Street and having as lodgers the top executives of the construction firms who had the contract to build the Canada Great Western Railway in 1853.

Smith credited Charles Scoffin[48] as the source of "a list of the Coloured boys who were reputedly members of the Brown Army of Liberation," which was known in Ingersoll as "John Brown's Army." When he showed the list to Mary McCaskell, "she claimed she knew most of them personally, especially the Hughes and Baileys mentioned in W. H. Day's telegram to John Brown," though she could not recall whether they had ties to Brown's Army or the American Civil War. "In retrospect," Smith concluded, "one can imagine that the story that Clarence Brown had seen John Brown more than once had a certain amount of truth. It is common knowledge that Brown was forced to remain in Canada from April to the end of May 1858, because he was so strapped for funds. It is also known that Brown made some addresses to the people interested in slavery." Smith had seen in the the *Oxford Herald* an advertisement for a meeting at the Wesleyan church, and Neil McFee[49] remembered John Brown speaking at the town hall, that speech being "one reason he had enlisted in the Union Army when he was just over

---

48. Charles Scoffin (1868–1954) was born and died in Ingersoll. See *Charles Scoffin, Memoir*, Ingersoll Cheese and Agricultural Museum.
49. Neil McFee (1847–1940), born Scotland, came to Ingersoll with his parents, ca. 1850. According to his death notice, he was a resident of Ingersoll "for over 90 years except for a short while spent in the USA at the time of the Civil War."

sixteen years old." Smith described McFee as "the most informative" of the early residents he had interviewed, with his detailed knowledge of Civil War battles furnishing proof of his factual reliability.

Another Ingersoll resident with a "remarkable memory" was John (Husky) Henderson, whose father credited John Brown for acquiring a farm in North Oxford Township. According to Smith, Boyd Stutler said John Brown, Jr., likely had visited this farm, "as he was in Canada while his father was organizing the Harper's Ferry raid, and he was forming societies in various places to help abolish slavery." Henderson, who had been was born in 1866 in North Oxford, told Smith that his father was given the land on the condition that "he took off the timber for the original owner" and transported it into Ingersoll to be sawn up as lumber.

Document 4. Stanley J. Smith's Quest for Evidence of John Brown's Army

Source: Excerpt, Stanley J. Smith, "It Happened One Hundred Years Ago. John Brown's Death Incensed Canadians," unidentified clipping, 2 December 1959, possibly *Sentinel-Review*.

For over half of a century this writer has been trying to trace down the so-called "John Brown's Army," but known more familiarly as the Army of Liberation. Some of the oldsters of 25 and 50 years ago insist that it was a reality, and three detachments originated in Chatham, Buxton, and Ingersoll. We have spent countless hours and travelled many miles to obtain the authenticity of this 'mythical' army but to no avail.

The late Mary McCaskill of Ingersoll, when shown a list given to us by the late Charles Scoffin, Ingersoll, maintained that the list was the enlistments of Coloured citizens who joined some army, but she was under the impression that it was for the Civil War. Mr. Scoffin declared that it was … found in his father's effects in answer to some newspaper enquiry during the 1870s. A Miss Martha Matthews, Chatham, gave us the first inkling when she claimed that her father was among some who went to Detroit from Chatham.

The Scoffin list gave us the names of Carey Diggins, Tizzard Diggins, Benjamin Diggins, Cornish Costin, Darcy Anderson, Charles Bird, Henry Van Patter, John Van Patter, Reuban Sanders, Benjamin Hughes, George Hughes, Henry D. Holmes, Peter Henry, Walter Hall, David Hall, S. Fisher, James Bird, and George Mickey. According to Mr. Scoffin the advertisement mentioned that a Coloured contingent was marshalled in Ingersoll and proceeded as far as Toledo, Ohio, or some Lake Erie port, and then returned home.

Document 5. "Town Role in Slave Abolition Forgotten," Interview with Byron Jenvey, *Woodstock Sentinel-Review*, 8 November 1971

This 1971 newspaper article opened by declaring that "Ingersoll's role in helping slaves to freedom in the mid-1800's is all but forgotten. Town residents now wash cars where once stood a clearing house for slaves." The claim made in Smith's earlier articles—that the town's Black population topped 400, with Ingersoll having the "the largest Coloured population in Canada, with the exception of Chatham"—is then repeated.

Noting that few Blacks lived in Ingersoll in 1971, the writer quotes "town historian Byron Jenvey" as saying that that most Blacks "returned home after they were freed." Adding that "he knew a few of them," Jenvey said that "[m]any died here of tuberculosis. Some moved to Dresden. I remember how ignorant they were, uneducated. They worked for 50 cents per day. It was pitiful."

Jenvey then recounts the story (again familiar from Smith's earlier articles) of the Wesleyan Methodist Church on Oxford Street, which became a refuge for slaves fleeing the United States: "Built in 1854 at a cost of $2,500, the [church] was demolished in 1956.... Slaves were smuggled into an attic over the church in the wee hours of the morning. They travelled on foot and many of them trekked from as far as New Orleans."

The story of how abolitionists "led the slaves to safety and [away] from their masters by telling soldiers they were transferring the slaves to work in other areas" is retold, and the church's role in rallying support against slavery is mentioned. "[E]ven noted abolitionist leader John Brown supposedly spoke at the church on one occasion," the article notes. "Probably, some of the money raised in Ingersoll helped John Brown capture the U.S. arsenal at Harper's Ferry."

The article concludes with a brief description of Brown's attack: "With only 18 men, John Brown made the attack on Oct. 16, 1859, taking about 60 leading citizens prisoner. John Brown was captured and hanged in Virginia in 1859. Married twice, he was the father of 20 children, two of whom were killed at Harper's Ferry."

Document 6. Richard Houghton, "Town Was Full of Civil War Spies," *Ingersoll Times*, 31 March 1976, second section (based on research by Harry Whitwell and Stanley J. Smith)
This 1976 newspaper story reiterates much of the material published by Stanley J. Smith in earlier pieces, beginning by noting that while the "old Wesleyan Church which stood on Oxford Street has been torn down for more than ten years now … doubtless … there are still many area people who remember the stately old edifice." The article continues:

> The church was built with much volunteer labour from ex-slaves who had been smuggled into Upper Canada from plantations in the Southern United States [my italics]. The church was built from huge pine trees, hewn in Oxford County. Many of the boards from these trees measured as large as 12 to 14 inches wide.

In the same year, 1854, two other buildings of note were constructed in Ingersoll. The town's first town hall was built and across from it a hotel called the Daly House. The town hall was to burn down shortly after being built, and the Daly House was to become the Ingersoll Inn.

After February 1, 1856 when the first Ingersoll town hall went up in flames, the Wesleyan Church was used often for town meetings until a new town hall could be built.

However, the church was "most noted for ... those times in the early morning hours when an abolitionist would smuggle into town a bunch of slaves who had left their bondage on plantations in Virginia, Georgia, and Louisiana to try and make a new life." At the church, the fugitives were "hidden in the loft safe from agents of the plantation owners who were anxious to take them back to the deep south for bounty." While the Blacks remained safe in the church attic, "abolitionists would find places for them on farms in rural areas around the town."

Writer Richard Houghton's piece went on to quote from Stanley Smith's earlier articles:

On entering the church one would walk under a gallery, and the pews were placed on each side of the church. At the rear, a stairway led to the third storey, and this was the resident minister's private home. Above this, was a half storey ... an attic where the church records were stored, and tradition has it, that in a pinch, it became a temporary haven for the slaves who arrived during the night.

Houghton's article claimed that "[a]ccording to historians" the town was "a hot-bed for the plotting of the [American] Civil War." The reasons for this included the large number of ex-slaves who came to Ingersoll "to escape bondage on plantations," as well as the town's position midway between Detroit and Niagara Falls, making it a "major overnight stop" for those travelling between the two cities.

Houghton went on to describe Ingersoll's involvement in the lead-up to the Civil War:

At the height of the plotting for the American Civil War, the traffic was so intense in Ingersoll that there were two weekly newspapers in town. One was controlled by the Southern Confederate faction, and the other by the abolitionist Northern faction. Also the hotels in town at the time were supported by either the north or the south, and much spying and espionage went on in all the hotels.

The famous abolitionist John Brown arrived in Ingersoll in April of 1858 to gain money and recruits for his army of liberation. He visited the Daly House expecting to find the famous conductor of the Underground Railway, Harriet Tubman of St. Catharines. The Underground Railway was a group dedicated to getting Negro slaves out of the United States and spirited away onto farms in Upper Canada.

The story of how Ingersoll resident Neil McFee, inspired by hearing John Brown speak at the town hall, later enlisted in the Union Army following his sixteenth birthday, is recounted in the article.

While visiting Ingersoll, Brown (the article noted) "frequented a hotel of ill-repute called Bachelor's Hall." Once one of the "finest hotels in Oxford," it had fallen into "a dilapidated state." Houghton quoted an unidentified "historian ... in a newspaper report that is many years old" on the decline of the hall: "[U]tter ruin ... came when a temporary saw-mill was situated less than 100 feet from the hotel. The employees were recruited from a low class laboring element with the result that they converted the hostel into a low-down groggery and a house of ill fame." Appalled at the eyesore, "[i]rate citizens" demolished the building by "sawing through the wooden piles which rested on mud-sills in the river bed. Strong ropes were attached to the piles and a mighty tug dumped this eyesore into the river."

Following the failure of the Harper's Ferry raid, Virginia governor Henry A. Wise became aware of Brown's recruiting efforts in Ingersoll. As a result, the governor "dispatched detectives … to make discreet enquiries as to any plots to free slaves."[50] The fact there were more than "five hundred Coloured residents" in the town made Ingersoll "a natural magnet to the southerners to keep them under surveillance." Indeed, both the Union and the Confederacy "set up recruiting stations under the pretext of them being purchasing agents for their respective governments." The North's representatives based their headquarters at the Daly House, with "recruiting rooms in the old Commercial Hotel," while agents of the Confederacy were headquartered at the Royal Hotel, with their recruitment centre based at the Anglo-American Hotel, located at the intersection of Charles and Carroll Streets. Since the Royal Hotel faced the Commercial Hotel across the street, the two sides could easily spy on one another.

The article concluded with more details about U.S.-controlled newspapers in the town:

> The two newspapers in Ingersoll at that time were the *Ingersoll Chronicle* and the *Oxford Herald*. The *Chronicle* was published by John S. Gurnett and the *Herald* was published by T. A. McNamara. The *Chronicle* published a weekly sheet for the United States government called the *Ingersoll Plain Dealer*. The *Herald's* pro-South paper was called the *Sickle*.

---

50. Improbable. See Craig Simpson, *A Good Southerner: The Life of Henry A. Wise of Virginia* (Chapel Hill, NC, 1985), Ch. 11, "Two Men at Harper's Ferry," pp. 202–18.

Document 7. Tom Duralia, "Underground Slave Railway Stopped Here," *Woodstock Sentinel-Review*, 5 December 1981

(Reprinted in *Ingersoll Times*, 25 July 1984, Ontario Bicentennial souvenir edition, section 2, p. 26)

This 1981 article evoked the atmosphere of bygone days: "The parking lot just south of Big V Pharmacy doesn't look overly exciting.... But were you to close your eyes and bring your thoughts back to the 1850s, you might feel somewhat different...." The article continued:

> Envision a bustling Ingersoll of 2,000 persons, an old church, a mysterious Underground Railroad, and a fiery-tongued orator plotting to overthrow the American government. And think of the period. The American Civil War was less than a decade away, there were growing tensions between the north and the south, and the Fugitive Slave Act, passed in 1850, meant that Blacks were not safe from extradition even in free states.

Duralia told of the building of the Wesleyan Methodist Church, constructed in 1854 for $2,500, and then turned to Ingersoll's Black population and the town's involvement in the Underground Railroad:

> [B]etween 1854 and the outbreak of the Civil War in 1861, fugitive slaves in the black of night were whisked into that church's attic, the most northerly terminus of the Underground Railroad. During the 1850s Ingersoll was host to between 400 and 500 Blacks, the second highest Black concentration in Canada behind Chatham. And many of the slaves that made it to Ingersoll via the Underground Railway were from as far away as New Orleans.
>
> According to an abolitionist newspaper, "The Voice of the Fugitive," in the early 1850s a large concentration of Blacks worked

on the railroad, and Ingersoll attracted a number once the line was open to Windsor, because wood for the locomotives was cut and stored here.

The Underground Railroad was "a source of considerable mystery to the slavers of the U.S.," even though "in some northern states the routes were actually published in anti-slavery newspapers." Of course, it was not a railroad at all, but rather a mutual agreement between the friends of the slaves, predominantly the Quakers, to aid the fugitives on the way to Canada."

The article concluded by retelling the story of John Brown's visit to Ingersoll:

Born in 1800 in Connecticut, opinions vary on this man from calling him a madman to a martyr, and his direct approach to freeing the slaves by force, if necessary, often lost him the respect of the other Abolitionists, who idealistically dreamed of a peaceful emancipation for Black slaves. Brown reportedly came to Canada in April of 1858, where he spent much of his time in travel, gathering support for a planned guerilla-style strike on the U.S. Federal arsenal in Virginia, Harper's Ferry.

Some of that time was spent in Ingersoll, where he met with others at the Daly House, now Marco's Landing, to discuss a plan of attack. He is also said to have spoken at the Wesleyan Church to rally support against slavers in the U.S. ...

Although the Wesleyan Methodist Church was replaced by a car wash in 1956 and later by a drugstore parking lot, "when you walk by that lot and close your eyes, the parking lot can be very exciting."

Document 8. Joyce A. Pettigrew, *A Safe Haven: The Story of the Black Settlers of Oxford County* (South Norwich Historical Society, 2006)

(Excerpts from Chapters 4–5, "The Effect of the 1850 Fugitive Slave Act," and "International Stories with an Oxford County Connection")

There was one Black in Ingersoll in 1852, but the figure changed dramatically as fugitives began to arrive in the mid-nineteenth century. It is not known where they were billeted originally. Perhaps the arrivals were taken immediately to places of employment. Soon the Wesleyan Methodist Church, built in Ingersoll in 1854, became the refuge on arrival from which they were taken to places of employment. The church had a second story where the minister lived and a basement which was used as a hiding place for fugitives when they arrived. The minister could keep a watchful eye out for slave catchers. The Daly House stables run by Peter Van Patter, himself an escaped slave, accommodated the overflow of fugitives as they arrived.

The hotels in the town played a key role in the fugitives' protection as well. The Daly House across from the Town Hall was the biggest hotel, owned by Absalom Daly. Daly not only built the hotel but in 1840 started the stage service from Port Burwell to Ingersoll. ... It is said that the Daly House was noted for accommodating those visiting Ingersoll to assist the fugitives. The front rooms of a hotel across the street were occupied by slave catchers who watched as the stage coach unloaded daily, in the hope that they would find a Black that they could return to slavery and thus collect a bounty. ...

One of Ingersoll's most interesting Black history episodes concerns John Brown of Harper's Ferry fame. The Black population was doing so well in South Oxford in the 1850s that when John Brown came to Canada to seek funding and recruits for his intended take-over in the Southern States, he came to Oxford County for assistance. Ingersoll was one of several places that he visited in April of 1858. He knew about the large population of Blacks because his son, John, Jr., had visited Ingersoll the previous year when he was forming societies in various places to help abolish slavery, and he met Henderson, Van Pipe, and Fant in North Oxford Township.

John Brown's itinerary in 1858 was a busy one, as seen from his diary and letters. On April 9, 1858 he was in Woodstock, Norwich, and Tillsonburg, and the following day in Ingersoll and London. He returned to St. Catharines and Toronto. He then returned to Ingersoll on the 12th of April and stayed until the 17th. While in Ingersoll he stayed at the Daly House hotel and is known to have preached in the Wesleyan Methodist Church.

CHAPTER FOUR
Conventional Wisdom of the 1950s about the 1850s Debunked

This chapter overturns White-folkloric myths of the 1950s (documented in Chapter 3). It draws on scholarly literature, the absence of documentary evidence for folkloric interpretations, and the documentary materials in Chapters 5–8.[51]

MYTH. A majority of Ingersoll Blacks were refugee slaves (runaways from Southern Slave States).

- Ingersoll and Canada West had zero refugee slaves. Slavery had been unlawful in Canada West since 1793.[52] When a runaway crossed into Canada, he or she ceased to be a slave and became an immigrant.
- Michael Wayne's analysis of sex distributions in the 1861 Census (see Appendix B) indicates that just 34% of 9,806 Blacks born in the United States had been fugitives when they entered Canada West. "Since American-born Blacks represented only 57.5% of all Blacks in Canada West, slightly under 20 per cent of all Blacks in Canada West had been fugitives from the United States"—not "a great majority."
  o The difference matters. In the eyes of local Whites, Black skin colour, illiteracy, and slave status were badges of racial and social

---
51. Useful literature for this chapter: Michael Wayne, "The Black Population of Canada West," pp. 469–70; Jack S. Blocker, Jr., *A Little More Freedom*; Hilary Bates Neary, *A Black American Missionary in Canada: The Life and Letters of Lewis Champion Chambers* (McGill-Queen's University Press, 2022).
52. *Upper Canada Statutes*, Chap. VII, 1793, Act to Limit Slavery.

inferiority. By overstating the proportion of Ingersoll Blacks who had been runaways, local Whites exaggerated what, in their eyes, was a measure of Black inferiority.

- o As Wayne elaborates, US historians have shown that 75–80% of fugitives from Slave States were men—ergo, 3.5 to 4.0 males per female. By contrast, sex parity (1.0 male per female) obtained in the family-based populations of northern US Free States and Canada West.[53]
- o Enumerators listed state of birth for 744 US-born Blacks in Canada West, 521 born in Slave States.[54] Of these 324 were males and 197 were females (i.e., 1.7 males per female, considerably less than the 3.5 to 4.0 expected if all were fugitives). Thus, through simple algebra (see Appendix B), 51% of 521 Canada-West Blacks born in Slave States were Free Blacks, not refugees, when they crossed into Canada. One such case was that of Lewis Chambers (discussed below), a Maryland slave who had purchased his freedom in 1844 before immigrating to Canada West in 1854.
- Michael Wayne's evidence for the province applies to Blacks in Ingersoll. Of Ingersoll's 80 US-born Blacks, 51 were male and 29 female—a ratio of 1.8 males per female—closer to family-based parity than the fugitive ratio of 3.75 to 4.0. For all 150 Ingersoll Blacks, the ratio was 1.4.
- The facts of the matter: no Blacks in Canada West were refugee slaves; less than 20% of all Blacks in Canada West had been fugitive slaves when they crossed into Canada, albeit some Free Blacks entering Canada had once been slaves.[55] Wayne's findings for Canada West apply to Blacks in Ingersoll and the townships.

53. For Canada West, 1.1 (calculated from 1861 published Census statistics).
54. The provincial totals for state of birth included 15 Blacks in North Oxford and West Oxford townships, none in Ingersoll. Of these nine had been born in northern Free States (New York, 8; New Jersey, 1) and six in Southern Slave states (Virginia, 4; Georgia, 1; Louisiana, 1).
55. For example, the Rev. Lewis G. Chambers (discussed in Chapter 5), had been born into slavery in Maryland in 1816, purchased his freedom in Maryland in 1844, and immigrated to Canada as a Free Black in 1854.

MYTH. On the eve of the American Civil War Ingersoll had some 400 Blacks and Canada West had 40,000.

- As enumerated in the 1861 Census, the Black population was smaller than has been thought. Ingersoll Blacks numbered 150, not the 400 indicated in the 1887 Washington Bevins death notice. Canada West had 17,000 Blacks, not the 40,000 estimated in the literature. Michael Wayne cautions that 19th-century censuses may undercount population by as much as 20%.[56] If an undercount of such magnitude applied in Canada West, then Blacks in Canada West numbered 20,500 and Blacks in Ingersoll, 180. The corresponding statistics for the Ingersoll study area are 198 and 238.
- As Michael Wayne explains, "abolitionists, because they were determined to bring the horrors of slavery to the forefront of public consciousness, had reason to exaggerate the number of fugitives; so did many White Canadians who were opposed to Black immigration."

MYTH. American slave catchers, bounty hunters emboldened by the *1850 Fugitive Slave Act* and lured by bounties, were active in Ingersoll.

- The American *Fugitive Slave Act of 1850* empowered Slave Catchers to pursue Slave State fugitives *in northern Free States* (my italics).[57] This American statute did not apply to Canada. No evidence exists to show that Ingersoll had slave catchers, lurking about to snatch local Blacks, in defiance of British law.

---

56. Wayne, "Black Population of Canada West," p. 470–1.
57. The Act made the U.S. federal government responsible for finding, returning, and trying escaped slaves, even if they were in a Free State. It required officials and individuals in Free States to assist in the return of slaves to their owners. It supported the efforts of slave catchers to return fugitives to their owners, in return for bounties.

MYTH. Ingersoll was a terminus of the Underground Railway.[58] **White abolitionists ran the Underground Railway in Ingersoll, billeting refugees in safe houses and fixing them up with jobs.**

- An inland community such as Ingersoll was never a "terminus on the Underground Railway." The *Underground Railroad* was a clandestine network of White abolitionists and safe houses *in Northern Free States* (my italics) that helped fugitives from Southern Slave States to reach northern Free States and Canada. Slavery had been illegal in Canada since 1793. Thus, a slave entering Canada ceased to be a slave and became an immigrant.[59] The Canadian border was the terminus of the Underground Railway, not inland communities in Canada.

MYTH. The White Wesleyan Methodist Church in Ingersoll (1854–65) was a clearing house for fugitives, hiding them from slave catchers and giving them a place to worship until they could acquire a Black church of their own. Grateful Blacks contributed free labour to build the church in 1854.

- The White Wesleyan Methodist Church in Ingersoll was not a clearing house for fugitives because *the village had no fugitives*. All Blacks in Canada were, by law, free. The American Fugitive Slave Act of 1850 did not apply to Canada. We find no evidence that American slave catchers were illegally at work in the province.
- The White Wesleyan Methodist Church in Ingersoll was not a clearing house for fugitives because *the village had no Blacks* before 1857.

---

58. Similarly in folklore St. Catharines was "one of the final stops in Canada on the Underground Railroad for refugee African-American slaves"; "by the 1830s, Brantford became a stop on the Underground Railroad, and a sizable number of runaway African-Americans settled in the town," and "Guelph was established as a village in 1827 and it became part of the Underground Railroad." Wikipedia posts for St. Catharines and Brantford; https://krassoc.wordpress.com/2012/10/20/british-methodist-episcopal-church-essex-street-guelph-wellington-county/
59. Upper Canada Statutes, Chap. VII, 1793, Act to Limit Slavery.

- Ingersoll Blacks in 1857 were described as impoverished. Had Blacks been in the village in 1854, they would not have been in a position to build a White Church with free labour.
- A majority of Ingersoll Blacks were Episcopal Methodists. Thus, it is unclear why the White Wesleyan Methodist Church would have been a clearing house for Black fugitives—rather than the White Episcopal Methodist Church nearby.
  - In 1860, when Ingersoll Blacks had no church building, they rented space in a schoolhouse for worship—they *did not use the White Wesleyan building*.[60]
- We have no evidence of Blacks in Ingersoll before 1857.
  - The *Ingersoll Chronicle* made no mention of Blacks in the village until 1857.
  - In 1860 the Rev. Lewis Chambers (Coloured) noted that "Our people came here to Ingersoll about three years ago" [1857].[61]
  - Elisha Hall was a contractor for building the Ingersoll & Port Burwell Plank and Gravel Road during the years 1849–1851 and recruited Blacks for his road crews.[62] (See advertisement to the right).

> LABORERS WANTED IN CANADA WEST.
>
> We learn from a private letter which was directed to a gentleman of this place, that labor is in great demand near Oxford, in the London district. Elisha Hall Esq., has a contract of making plank roads, and has expressed a wish to give employment to as many as 20 colored men who are needy. He will pay $10 in cash per month and have their washing done, or $10.50 with board and they do their own washing. Any person wishing employ here can address Mr. Hall, at Oxford, C. W. He lives 21 miles East of London, on the Hamilton road.
>
> We understand also that there is 200 laborers wanted to work on the railroad near London, at $10 per month.

60. Nor, as was alleged, was the Wesleyan Methodist Church used for public meetings after the Town Hall burned in 1856; the Village Council met in the Mansion House in February 1856; then it met in the Town Clerk's office in a new temporary market building. In May 1856 the Council held two large ratepayers meetings in the School house. Simply put, we have no evidence that the short-lived Wesleyan Church on Oxford Street was anything out of the ordinary. See Stanley J. Smith, "Wesleyan Church, Once Haven for Slaves, is being torn Down in Ingersoll Now." *Ingersoll Tribune*, 1956 (Jenvey Scrapbook #3, p. 105): "When Ingersoll's original town hall burned in 1856, the Wesleyan Church provided a gathering place for town meetings, as it could seat 500."

61. *Ingersoll Chronicle*, 29 May 1857; Rev. Lewis Chambers correspondence with George Whipple, Secretary of the American Missionary Association, courtesy of Hilary Bates Neary, 20 September 1860.

62. This newspaper was published in Sandwich, Canada West, from January 1851 to June 1852, in response to the enactment of the pro-slavery 1850 Fugitive Slave Act in the United States. Hall's advertisement is the sole item pertaining to Oxford County during this two year period.

However, while Coloured men in road crews passed through the Oxford countryside, they were unlikely to be job-holding residents of Ingersoll.

- Pettigrew reports that in 1851 Ingersoll had one solitary Black: Abraham Brock who was a servant to Elisha Hall, a gentleman farmer, President of the Agricultural Society in 1850.[63]

  o The January 1852 Census does indeed enumerate one Abraham Brock, a servant, in Hall's household, but it does not identify him as Coloured. Indeed, the 1852 Census for Oxford County enumerated 126 Blacks in Oxford County, but none in Ingersoll and the townships of North Oxford and West Oxford.[64]

- *Ingersoll Chronicle*, 2 September 1854. **Signor Costillo:** "Coloured," **but probably not Negro.**

  An Imposter. On Monday morning last *a coloured man* [my italics] bearing the rather important cognomen of *Signor Costillo* called at our office and ordered 100 bills, announcing an entertainment in ventriloquism, intermixed with other tom-foolery performances. Almost two hours after leaving the order, the sable son entered the office for the second time and said, "he guess'd he wouldn't have them bills now." The bills being partly "set up" we demanded remuneration for our trouble; but this the Signor refused and made for the door with the deep conviction, we presume, that he might

---

63. Pettigrew, *A Safe Haven*, p. 64. Elisha Hall became a miller, a mill-pond operator, and real estate developer. More importantly for the 1850s, Hall was the contractor and a shareholder of the Ingersoll and Port Burwell Plank and Gravel Road toll road company during the years 1849–1851. See Robert G. Moore, "Ingersoll & Port Burwell Road Company, 1849, History and Comments," 2002, https://elgin.ogs.on.ca/ancestor-indexes/online-publications/ingersoll-port-burwell-road-company/.
64. *Oxford Gazetteer*, 1852, p. 44.

endanger his person did he remain in longer. The country is flooded with humbugs of this sort…

MYTH. The White American abolitionist John Brown visited Ingersoll in April 1858, a year before his capture of Harper's Ferry, West Virginia. He stayed in the Daly House and spoke in the Wesleyan Church or the Town Hall, his purpose being to raise troops for an abolitionist army to overthrow slavery in the American South.

- A dubious claim. The *Ingersoll Chronicle* made no mention of John Brown visiting the village for the purpose of raising a private army, a sensational newsworthy action which would have been illegal under Britain's *Foreign Enlistment Act of 1819*.[65]

MYTH. Blacks came to Canada West and Ingersoll to escape oppression.

- Reality: they came for jobs building warehouses, stationhouses, factory buildings, sawmills, church buildings, and residences; and cutting timber to meet the voracious wood-fuel appetites of railway locomotives. In 1861, for example, Black Ike Williams bossed Black road crews to supply wood for Great Western Railway locomotives, while also operating a "boarding house for Coloureds."

MYTH. Refugee Blacks in Canada West returned to their Southern States of origin at the end of the US Civil War and slavery in the Southern States ended. This explains why the Black population in Ingersoll peaked before the Civil War, but had largely vanished by 1921.

- Ingersoll Blacks did not return *en masse* to their old homelands,

---

65. William F. Raney, "Recruiting and Crimping for the Northern Forces, 1861–1865," *Mississippi Valley Historical Review*, vol. 10, no. 1 (1923, June), pp. 21–33; https://api.parliament.uk/historic-hansard/lords/1819/jun/28/foreign-enlistment-bill.

the former Southern Slave States. Their lodestar was jobs, which increasingly by the 1880s were in rapidly-growing cities: Chicago, Detroit, Montreal, Toronto, Buffalo, Hamilton, and London. By the 1880s Ingersoll's economic boom was over; its population actually declined during the decade.

Census Populations: from an "Age of Villages" to an "Age of Cities"								
	1852	1861	1871	1881	1891	1901	1911	1921
Chicago	29,953	112,172	298,977	503,185	1,099,850	1,698,575	2,185,283	2,701,705
Detroit	21,019	45,619	79,577	116,340	205,876	285,704	465,766	993,578
Montreal	58,000	90,323	130,833	177,377	256,723	328,172	490,504	618,506
Toronto	30,775	41,821	59,000	96,196	181,215	209,892	381,833	521,893
Buffalo	42,261	81,129	117,714	155,134	255,664	352,387	423,715	506,775
Hamilton	14,112	19,096	26,880	36,661	48,959	52,634	81,969	114,151
London	7,035	11,555	18,000	27,867	31,977	37,976	46,300	60,959
Brantford	3,877	6,251	8,107	9,616	12,753	16,619	23,132	29,440
Stratford	no data	2,809	4,313	8,239	9,500	9,929	12,946	16,094
St. Thomas	1,274	1,631	2,197	8,367	10,366	11,485	14,054	16,026
Chatham	2,070	4,466	5,873	7,873	9,052	9,068	10,770	13,256
Woodstock	2,112	3,353	3,982	5,373	8,612	8,833	9,320	9,935
Population of Ingersoll over the Same Period								
Ingersoll	1,190	2,577	4,922	4,318	4,191	4,573	4,763	5,150

MYTH. Ingersoll Whites befriended local Blacks; Blacks were passive and grateful.

- Although Ingersoll Whites opposed slavery, they assumed and asserted White supremacy. They committed to a belief that Black subservience was a precondition for White equality.
- Blacks endured oppression from local Whites, but they also pushed back, as shown by evidence in Chapter 6. Blacks had *agency*—they were active agents, not passive recipients, in the history that happened to them.

Postscript

When Blacks left Ingersoll, where did they go? Three cases from death notices.

Enoch C. Brown (Coloured) an old resident of Ingersoll, and for a long time employee in the Tillson lumberyards, and for various other departments under George Ross, Adam Oliver, and others, passed away at his home in Lansing, Mich. At 8:10 a.m. March 24, at the age of 81 years, 3 months, and 25 days.
(*Ingersoll Chronicle*, 29 March 1900)

Word has been received in town announcing the death in Illinois of Charles Bird, an aged Negro who for many years claimed Ingersoll as his home. In years gone by he is said to have become a bus driver for different hotels here, and he was always a prominent figure about the streets.
(*Ingersoll Chronicle*, 25 December 1902)

Word has been received of the death in Evanston, Ill., of Mary Bird, beloved wife of Mr. Chas. Bird of this town. She leaves behind two daughters and two sons besides her husband.
(*Ingersoll Chronicle*, 1 April 1897)

CHAPTER FIVE
Coloured Culture: Emancipation Day, the B.M.E.C. Church and Its Preachers, Black-Speak English

The British Methodist Episcopal Church (Coloured) in Ingersoll, 1860–1899

In 1858 the Canadian Congregations of the American-based African Methodist Episcopal Church separated to form the British Methodist Episcopal Church (B.M.E.C.). In 1860 the Rev. Lewis Chambers (B.M.E.C.) organized the London Circuit, comprised of congregations in London and Ingersoll.

In the 1861 Census, taken in January, 93 of 150 Ingersoll Blacks (62%) reported *E. Methodist* as their religious affiliation—which meant *British Methodist Episcopal*, given that the Rev. Lewis Chambers reported "about seventy-five" members and congregants in Ingersoll in September 1860.[66]

Throughout its existence, the Ingersoll congregation was too small and its members too poor to support a resident minister. Accordingly, for pastoral supply, the Ingersoll congregation was always part of a circuit that bundled it with one or more nearby congregations (shown below, partial list). In each circuit, two or more congregations shared one minister. In 1860, for example, the Rev. Lewis Chambers (London Circuit) commuted between London and Ingersoll; in 1862 the Rev. Benjamin Whipper (Simcoe Circuit) commuted among five congregations: Woodstock, Ingersoll, Simcoe, Otterville, and Guelph.

---

66. Lewis Chambers letters, 20 September 1860. The 1861 Census reported 373 Episcopal Methodists; ergo 280 were White-Church Episcopal Methodists, assuming that the 93 Coloureds were with the British Methodist Episcopal congregation.

- 1860–61. London Circuit (London and Ingersoll).
- 1862. Simcoe Circuit (Ingersoll, Simcoe, Otterville, Woodstock, Guelph)
- 1863–64. Ingersoll Circuit (Ingersoll, Woodstock, Otterville, Princeton)
- 1865. London Circuit: (London, Ingersoll, Woodstock, St. Thomas)
- 1872. London Circuit: (London, Ingersoll, Woodstock, Lucan, Brantford)
- 1880. Ingersoll Circuit (Ingersoll, St. Thomas, Strathroy, Lucan)
- 1881. Ingersoll Circuit (Ingersoll, Otterville, St. Thomas)
- 1888. Brantford Circuit (Ingersoll, Woodstock, Otterville, Simcoe, Seneca)
- 1893–94. Ingersoll church closed.
- 1894–99. Woodstock Circuit (Woodstock, Ingersoll)

The pastors charged with the Ingersoll congregation changed every two years, in part because the B.M.E.C. Conference rearranged circuit territories to provide the best possible financial support for pastors, and partly because, in all Methodist denominations, the "iron rule of the itinerancy" limited a pastoral appointment in one place to three years.[67]

Ministers to Circuits that included Ingersoll (partial list)
- Lewis C. Chambers, 1860–61 (London Circuit)
- Benjamin Whipper, 1862–63 (Simcoe Circuit)
- C.H. Rollins, 1864 (Ingersoll Circuit)
- Peter R. Anderson 1870–72 (London Circuit). Suspended for six months in 1871 for practising fraud upon several persons in London and Ingersoll. 1872: charged with insubordination, tried,

---

67. W.T. Minter, *The Doctrine and Discipline of the British Methodist Episcopal Church* (1892). See p. 62 (Section III, Item 2): "no minister shall be allowed to remain in charge of any Circuit or Station longer than three years, except in particular cases; the General Superintendent shall have the power to allow him to remain longer."

condemned, and excommunicated from the B.M.E. Church
- Thomas Jefferson, 1875 (London Circuit)
- Solomon Peter Hale, 1876–77 (Ingersoll Circuit)
- Robert Johnson, 1878–80 (Ingersoll Circuit)
- James A.D. Podd, 1880–82 (Ingersoll Circuit). 1881 Census: Baptist clergyman, married, native of British West Indies, London resident
- T.H. Slater, 1887 (Ingersoll Circuit)
- Minister yet to be appointed, 1888 (Brantford Circuit)
- George Blount, 1892 (Woodstock Circuit)
- S.A. Lucas, 1894 (Woodstock Circuit)
- J.W. Brown, 1899 (Woodstock Circuit)

During the 1860s the Ingersoll congregation was without a church building. In Ingersoll, reported the Rev. Lewis Chambers in 1860, "we have no church, but rent a schoolhouse for to worship in at $2.00 per month." In 1863 the congregation worshipped in a carpenter's shop.[68] In 1864 the congregation acquired a $400 chapel for worship, but it promptly burned down.

In 1870 the congregation finally purchased lot N.9 on Catherine Street on which they erected a chapel. The B.M.E.C. valued the chapel at $900 in 1872; $1,000 in 1873; $600 in 1877; and $550 in 1887. Trustees managed the property, their appointments subject to approval by a majority of the congregation's male members.[69]

The Ingersoll Congregation, 1881–1900

In 1881 the British Methodist Episcopal Church was the principal Coloured religious denomination in Ingersoll, and the sole one with a church building (erected 1870). In the 1881 Census for Ingersoll, 89%

---

68. Chambers letters, 20 September 1860; B.M.E.C. Conference Minutes, 1864.
69. Land Records Abstract, Ingersoll Library. Interestingly, the BME church faced the residence of James Sinclair. The Church, on lot 9, was on the north side of Catherine, three lots east of George Street; Sinclair's house was the south side of Catherine, two lots east of George St., on lot 7 (1911 Ingersoll Directory; 1895 lot map of Ingersoll).

of the African population reported the B.M.E.C. or Episcopal Methodist as their denominational affiliation.[70] In 1881 the B.M.E.C. Annual Conference reported 19 church members in Ingersoll, about 20% of the denominational total by census affiliation.

By other measures, however, the numerical strength of the church was slipping. The number of church members, 19, was down from 45 (and 30 probationers) in 1860, the founding year of the congregation. The culprit was the shrinking of the town's Black census population, from 150 in 1861 to 97 in 1881 and 52 in 1901. The Ingersoll church was closed in 1893–94 and shuttered in 1900. The last mention of the congregation in the *Ingersoll Chronicle* (shown below) was 28 December 1899.[71]

The Congregation's Cake-Walk Fundraisers: 1887, 1888, 1891, 1894, 1895, and 1899

As Ingersoll's Black population shrank, the B.M.E.C. church turned to Cake-Walk fundraiser concerts in the Town Hall to pay church bills. A "Cake Walk" was a dance competition for which a cake was awarded as a prize. Whites commonly served as judges (e.g., M.T. Buchanan, Charles Kennedy, and Dorland Noxon in 1888).

"The Coloured Folks' Entertainment"
(*Ingersoll Chronicle,* 31 March 1887)

There was a fifty dollar audience composed of many of our leading and most trustworthy citizens, assembled in the Town Hall on Tuesday evening to witness the entertainment got up by our Coloured friends in aid of their church in this town. The programme consisted of songs, recitations, dialogues, music on the dulcimer by Misses Matilda and Elsie Pryor of London, who played the instrument in a remarkably fine

---

70. Of Ingersoll's 97 Blacks, 75 reported their affiliation as B.M.E.C. and 11 Episcopal Methodist.

71. By 1901 Woodstock had a larger Black population than Ingersoll (117 versus 52). Woodstock Blacks erected a church building in 1888, and during the years 1894–1899 the Ingersoll congregation was the junior partner in a two-point Woodstock circuit.

manner. Miss Brown presided at the organ, playing the accompaniments with good effect. A "cake walk" closed the entertainment, three prizes being given to the best walkers. The judges were selected from the audience and were Messrs. F.H. Brady, H. Goble, W.K. Sumner, T. Seldon, and Rev. Mr. Lawrence.[72] They gave the prizes as follows and their decisions were pronounced by the audience to be correct:— 1st prize, Mr. Will Smith and Miss E. Brown;[73] 2nd, Rev. S. P. Hale[74] and Mrs. A. Thomas;[75] 3rd, Mr. W. McLeod[76] and Miss H. Evans. The large audience was most enthusiastic in their applause, some of the well-known participants being greeted familiarly and vigorously as they appeared. Everything passed off in the utmost good humour, both participants and the audience enjoying the fun immensely. The Rev. Mr. Slater states that $48.65 was realized and wished to thank those who purchased tickets for their kindness.

"Cake Walk"
(*Ingersoll Chronicle*, 16 February 1888)

The members of the British Methodist Church will hold an old folks concert and cake walk in the Town Hall on Tues. evening 28th inst. Vocal and instrumental music will be rendered by the old folk. The Misses Pryor of London will be present and accompany them on the dulcimer and violin.

"Cake Walk"
(*Ingersoll Chronicle*, 1 March 1888)

The cake walk held in the Town Hall on Tuesday evening under the auspices of the B.M.E. Church was very successful in point of finances.

---

72. 1881 Directory: H. Goble, contractor; Rev. G. Lawrence, superannuated minister; Thomas Seldon, drover; W. Sumner, labourer.
73. Emma Brown, age 14, Coloured, 1881 Census.
74. Solomon Peter Hale, former Ingersoll B.M.E.C. Coloured pastor.
75. Alice Thomas, servant, Coloured, 1881 census, then age 21.
76. William McLeod, Town Assessor, 1881 Census, White, then age 50.

The audience was highly amused and kept pretty fair order. The cake winners were: 1st Miss Evans and Mr. Case; 2nd, Mrs. Thomas and Rev. S.P. Hale. Judges: M.T. Buchanan, Chas. Kennedy, and D. Noxon. On behalf of the society Rev. Mr. Slater desires us to thank the audience for their attendance and good order. $50 was realized above expenses.

"Entertainment"
(*Ingersoll Chronicle*, 22 January 1891)

There will be a free concert in the B.M.E. Church, Tuesday evening, January 28. Come one, come all.

"The B.ME. Church"
(*Ingersoll Chronicle*, 8 November 1894)

The Rev. S.A. Lucas of Woodstock has been appointed by the B.M.E. Conference to reopen the preaching appointment at Ingersoll of the Coloured people, which has been closed for the past two years. The churches in the two towns will in the future be in the charge of Mr. Lucas. The first service was held Sunday afternoon at 3 o'clock.

"Cake Walk"
(*Ingersoll Chronicle*, 12 December 1895)

The double cake walk in the Town Hall on Friday evening under the direction of Rev. Solomon Peter Hale was fairly well attended. Six couples competed, the judges being [3 Whites] Mr. C.N. Harris, John Richardson, and C.B. Ryan.[77] T. Chambers and G. Sage and partners were so nearly matched that the judges could not decide, and accordingly they cast lots as to which should take first prize, when Mr. Sage was declared the lucky one, Mr. Chambers taking second.

---

77. Charles H. Harris, butcher; Charles B. Ryan, cheese buyer; John Richardson, 30 Carroll St.

[Untitled]

(*Ingersoll Chronicle*, 28 December 1899)

The jubilee concert and cake walk given in the Town Hall Thursday night, under the auspices of the B.M.E. Church, was not as successful as it might have been. The audience was limited to almost thirty and the entertainment was of a strictly amateur character, some of the songs having been on the "voters' list" for some time. The cake walk was the funniest part of the programme. We will not give the names of the competitors.

The Rev. Lewis C. Chambers (Coloured), B.M.E.C. Ingersoll, 1860–62

The Rev. Lewis Champion Chambers (ca. 1816–1900) was a British Methodist Episcopal Church (B.M.E.) preacher in Canada West during the years 1858–67.[78] He had been born a slave in Maryland in 1816, but in 1844 he had purchased his freedom, moved to Philadelphia, and joined the African Methodist Episcopal Church (A.M.E.C.), a body formed after white Methodists had insisted on racial separation in congregational worship. He married Anna Marie Harris in 1845 and purchased a four-acre farm in New Jersey in 1850. Then in 1854 he led a party of 14 family members and friends to Dresden, Canada West.[79]

He was ordained a deacon in the A.M.E.C. in 1856, ordained an elder in the newly-constituted Coloured B.M.E.C. in 1858, assigned to two Kent County congregations, and granted a $200 annual stipend from the American Missionary Association (A.M.A.), an abolitionist, biracial (mostly White), Protestant organization founded in New York State in 1846. Chambers was the sole Black pastor to receive a

---

78. Hilary Bates Neary, *A Black American Missionary in Canada*.
79. The 1861 Census for Middlesex County, London Township reports Lewis Chambers, age 43, his wife Ann, age 41, five children, ages 2 to 13, his mother-in-law, Anna Jane Harris, age 62, George Chambers, 35, married to Rebecca, age 32, all born in the US. The agricultural Census located Lewis on Con. 2, Lot, 12, with one John Chambers, age 32, nearby in a log house on Con. 1, Lot 7. See Neary, *Black American Missionary*, for some of the hard-to-find details.

stipend during the brief history of the A.M.A.'s Canada Mission field (1848–62).

In the fall of 1860 the B.M.E. Annual Conference stationed Chambers on the London Circuit, comprised of London and Ingersoll. The London congregation was the stronger of his two charges, with 65 members and a paid-for church building. "At Ingersoll, we have no church, but rent a schoolhouse to worship in at $2.00 per month.... The number of members is forty-five. The members and congregation are about seventy-five. They attend very regular. This is a new place. Our people came here to Ingersoll about three years ago. There [were] four families but they are still increasing."[80]

His livelihood was to come from farming, on land purchased or rented for his family, the meagre financial offerings from his congregations, and the A.M.A. grant.

He planned to live on a farm near Ingersoll. "In our small society," he explained, "a White man and his wife joined our church and have been very vigilant attenders of church and Sabbath school.... When I made up my mind to move they were much pleased and wanted me to put up a house on their farm. He said that he would find the logs and haul them. So, he let me have a piece of ground and I found the lumber and we went to work and put up a house. The Coloured friends all turned out and put it up. I bought the lumber. It did cost much, but it was my money in this hard country. It cost $40."

1860. The New House Torched: Welcome to Ingersoll!

But Chamber's house was torched on the 24th of September, 1860, the very day that its construction was completed: "Some enemy done it. I have learned that they did not want a preacher to live in that place."[81] As he elaborated, "Different ones have told me that they had not anything against me but they did not want our slaves and wife to attend

---

80. Chambers letters, 20 September 1860.
81. The *Ingersoll Chronicle* made no mention of this fire.

our meeting. But they say under my preaching God blessed their souls and will attend. Their prayer is to God that I will continue. By the help of God I will." In the event, he located his residence near London, not Ingersoll, on five acres of rented farmland in London Township.

Chambers was to serve as pastor of the London Circuit for two church years (1860–62). Then in 1868, after spells in St. Thomas and St. Catharines, Chambers returned to the United States and the A.M.E.C. He died in Philadelphia in 1900.

A Selection of Letters
from the Rev. Lewis Chambers, 1860-62[82]

An Editorial Note—What to Look For: Black Preference for worship in a Coloured church rather than a White one—link to Black preference for a Coloured boarding house in Chapter 2; reference to some church members (like Chambers) having once been slaves; expulsion of church members for drunkenness, adultery, prostitution; sickness and the poverty of church members; the evangelical style of worship—link to James Sinclair's "the Coloured Church," Chapter 2, and to White description of Solomon Hale's lecturing, below in this chapter.

August 15, 1860

One of our members has died at Ingersoll, a female. She said that she was willing to die for she was going home. At Ingersoll, there was a man who has been for a long time a desperate drunk, and about a week ago he came forward to join the temperance society. We made it a matter of prayer for that was the request of his wife, for poor woman she was in trouble. So, he came forward and said will you let me join the Church under your watch care? From that day to this he has been a praying man and the town is astonished at him to think he is such a changed man. So, the work of God is going on. My heart's desire is to

---

82. Courtesy of Hilary Bates Neary, author of *A Black American Missionary in Canada*.

God for his cause that it may prosper. The man that I spoke about was slave and came to Canada about ten years ago. He married a free woman. She was a fine woman, but drink has ruined him. Sometime after I had been there she asked me to do her a favour, to talk to husband and pray for him. So we made it a matter of prayer and he came and joined the temperance pledge the next night. He asked if [he] might join the church under my watch care. So, he joined, and from that day until this he has been walking upright....

September 14, 1860
To Rev. Lewis Chambers. Annual Report, Rooms of the American Missionary Association, New York.

Months of labor herein reported, ten. Hopeful conversions, at London 2, Ingersoll 26. Additions to the Church on examination ... London 2, Ingersoll 26. One young man at Ingersoll wants to go in the ministry. Additions do. by letter: London, 3; Ingersoll, 12. Whole number of members in each of the Churches to which [I] minister, London members 65, Ingersoll members 4. Church members pledged to total abstinence, London 32, Ingersoll 26. *Former slaves 3 have come to London. 12 have come to Ingersoll.* They appear to be very industrious. I want to build a house to worship in at Ingersoll. Number of Sunday-school and Bible-class scholars, Ingersoll, 45 scholars 1 Bible class. Our schools are all one with the Whites.

February 13, 1861

The meetinghouse at Ingersoll has closed with the blessing of God upon it. I never was in a meeting where there was a deeper feeling of God's goodness than in that one meeting. These were eight who professed to obtain the blessing. They united with the Church, stating that they had obtained the pearl of great price, and more desired to flee the wrath to come. And two women and three men were before desperate [dancers] and intemperate, and one female was a prostitute, but she now prayeth. Her parents told her if she did stop going to meeting then she must leave. So she said that she would for before she would do as she had done that she would, for before she would do as she had done, that she would beg her way through the world. She asked the church to pray for her. She has left the town and is two miles in the county, and comes to church every Lord's Day. That is a blessed change.

June 8, 1861

We have lost us another one of our members. Her last remembrance was paid to her on last Sunday. She was a member at Ingersoll. When she was first taken with the fever she was in her perfect mind. She was well composed. Her death was a happy one. She died in the seventeenth year of her age.

July 29, 1861

Mr. Whipple Rev. Dear Sir: These lines will inform you that I am well and my wife was delivered of a fine daughter on the 20th. I am glad to say that she getting along tolerable well. She is not so well today, but I hope that by the blessing of God she may get well again. Well dear Brother, do not get wearied with me for writing to you so soon, for I have the confidence in you for my love for [you] shall never be forgotten. But I am now in a straight at this time. I had to have a doctor for my wife and daughter and that must be paid cash, but he says that he will wait a few days. Well, London pays me on average about one hundred and fifty cts. per week. And Ingersoll pays me five dollars per quarter. Well my rent is eighteen dollars per quarter. I pay my own passage from London to Ingersoll and they pay it back again. Well, if it was not for my brother with my team[83] I do not know what I should do. He as well as I have everything to buy and they may that promised to pay me after I

---

83. Lewis must now have owned a team of horses that his brother George used as a carter. Many Blacks earned a living in that occupation.

had received my quarterly pay. Now on the 10th of August I have money due, and who I can borrow I do not know. I do hope that if you can do something for me before August, by that time you will oblige me much. If I live to see next November times will better with me. Dear Brother, the good work of the Lord is still going on and my heart feels warm for the work of God. I will station myself in London. Please write to me in a few days. If I have said anything pardon me for I do not want to do wrong. May the God of all grace bless, preserve and keep you[84] so that [you] may live to do much good for the cause of the poor slave that makes his way to Canada. I do hope that you will pay us another visit in Canada. Yours truly, L.C. Chambers

August 14, 1861

The quarter just closed has been one of some trouble owing [to] some bad conduct of some of the members at London and Ingersoll. At London three of the members went a fishing and taken with them a pint of ardent spirits. So, they fell out and we had them up before the church. Two confessed their faults and [I] pardoned them. They would not [confess their faults] at Ingersoll. Two I turned out for immoral conduct. This quarter I have preached twenty-six times on the Lord's Day and attended Sabbath school ten times, prayer meeting six times, preached in the week four times. I have taken this quarter by letter three, and two on profession of faith; one at Ingersoll by letter and one on profession of faith; at London two by letter and one on profession of faith. The number added to the church the quarter is five, and two turned out by the rules of our church.[85]

November 14, 1861

The quarter just closed has been one of much joy. I do not think I have

---

84. Chambers is echoing the words of blessing in Numbers 6: 24–26.
85. See *The Doctrine and Discipline of the British Methodist Episcopal Church*, Chapter V, Trial of Lay Members, Section VII: Concerning Spirituous Liquors, p. 104–108.

ever felt more of the power of God and peace of mind. Although there is some disturbance in our connection in Canada about the Bishopric, two thirds of the members are at peace. More than two thirds of the members in my two stations at London and Ingersoll are quiet, except four members. I have delivered four discourses on love and peace, which has done much good. On the 13th of Oct., which was the Lord's Day, our meeting was one of deep interest. The Lord's spirit was felt powerful all day. On last Lord's Day was our sacrament. I administered the Lord's Supper at 6:00 in the evening to a large number of devoted followers of our Redeemer, whose hearts did seem to feel much of the burning love of God.

I have preached twenty-four times this quarter, twenty-two times on the Lord's Day, twice in the week; attended Sabbath school ten times, prayer meetings ten times. Our concert prayer meeting has been well attended excepting our last meeting owing to a wound that I got in the foot, which prevented me from uttering. Also two Sabbaths I have not been able to attend. I have added to the church at London by letter one this quarter. The church in London has a membership of good standing members seventy-eight, congregation two hundred and fifty, and a good Sabbath school. Our congregation is on the increase in London. The church in Ingersoll has a membership of good standing members 50. The congregation is from seventy to eighty. The Sabbath school is poor, but the meetings are well attended as a general thing. The two churches has paid me this [year] $62 dollars. This finishes my year's labour, with the exception of that the members in [my] station are at peace on the matter, except two. Therefore I am settled down in London to labour in the cause of missions for my poor & rejected people who may come to Canada. Now, Mr. Whipple, so here is my heart and hand in the cause of Christ and liberty. Give me a place visiting the sick and baptizing. Every week I am engaged three days in visiting [and] reading God's word to members that cannot read.

November 14, 1861

Mr. Whipple Rev. Dear Brother: These lines will inform you that I am prostrated under the care of the Doctor, I having cut my foot very bad on last Wednesday trying to get a little fire wood, but it is now a good deal better and I think by next Lord's Day week that I will be able to preach to my people. They have showed great kindness [to] me by coming to see me, then taking up small contribution on last Sunday night. The amount was $2, 19 cts. ... I hope that you will pay us a visit this winter. Will you come, Mr. Whipple? Let me know when you will come. Dear Brother, will you please send me a draft next week by the 8th of the month for I am in great need of it this time. I have not wasted my little means. One year ago I was burnt out, or my house was burnt. Now I lease a small farm[86] near London and built another log house on it and placed my family on it with brother so that my team may earn me something for my family. So, I thank God that I have all paid for except 150 dollars will pay all that I do owe. I have 50 dollars now, 50 on the first of December. Please send me 50 as soon as you get this. I did not beg one cent of money, but my brother with the team has done well or a stranger. You know that I have a large family, and my salary is very small. The [congregations] at London and Ingersoll pay me about 125 cts per week. The people are poor, very poor. All my family are well. I hope you and yours are the same. I am now in the bed and I notified today for the fifty for 8th. Please let me hear some kind word from you. I remain yours truly in the Gospel. L. C. Chambers in haste.

December 23, 1861

On the 8th our quarterly meeting was at Ingersoll, although it was a stormy day. Our meeting was one of deep interest. On last Lord's Day

---

86. The Chambers extended family had now moved to Lot 3 in Concession 2, London Township, with more acreage and thus more potential for earnings from their farms.

we had the Rev. Mr. Tearne[87] with [us] at eleven and at three o'clock. He has preached for me four times. My heart praises God, and by his help I will go on in his cause, for I know that my reward will be a glorious one. Well you say that you cannot give but one hundred dollars per year. Well I will not complain. By the help of God I will do the best I can. I am determined to spend and be spent in the missionary cause. My mind is made up. Money or no money I will be like good old Paul. With my own hands I will work and preach to my brethren. Dear Brother, pray for me. You will please send me the 50 dollars to me on the last year's salary. That 50 I promised to pay on the first of this month. Please write and let me know when you can send it. I will look for the 50 dollars by the first of January. I hope that I may get it by that time and then the 100 per year after or for this year. I will be satisfied. There is great deal of talk about war with States now in London. I hope not. I hope that the north will not go to war with the British nation.[88] Will you please write as soon as you get this and let me know what you think about the war. No more but remain yours truly, L.C. Chambers.

February 15, 1862

There is a good deal of sickness in Ingersoll. I have taken in one by letter this quarter, and turned out two for living together in a state of adultery. There was a little child died at Ingersoll week before last. She told mother that she might give her playthings to her other sister for she was going home to heaven. Her aunt asked her if she was afeared to die. Her reply was no, for she was going home to Jesus. She died in the Lord. She was about eight years of age.

---

87. In the words of the CCSS Annual Report for 1860 (p. 24), Mr. Tearne was a still a "Scripture reader", and not ordained until he moved to the United States

88. In the aftermath of the Trent Affair, November, 1861, there was fear that Britain would declare war on the United States. British troops were already being sent to Canada, and 2,000 were stationed in London.

April 2, 1862

Mr. Whipple Rev. dear Sir: I am happy to inform you that I and my family are well. We had have been the most of us sick, but thank God we are at this time well. It has been a very sick time both here and in Ingersoll among the children. The people have suffered much this winter [from] colds and the sore throat. Two men fell dead in their houses. One was a White man, the other was a Coloured man. The White man got up well in the morning, and while washing himself he fell dead. He was a very nice man. He leaves a wife and three children, but he was well to do.

The Coloured man was a hard-working sober man, labouring to pay for a home. He came into his house from work and fell dead. He leaves a wife and five children. The man at Ingersoll that I baptized last summer who has been in a decline for two years is now able to attend to his work. He praises God for his goodness. The good work is going on in Canada. The Lord is pouring out his spirit among us.

May 14, 1862

I have preached twice a day and attended Sabbath school every Lord's Day and preached every [Thursday] night. Our prayer meeting has been poorly attended this quarter. Our concert prayer meeting has been well attended. We have not had any revival this quarter, but everything is quiet and the peace of God is with us. On last Lord's Day I preached twice to a large congregation at eleven and at six. I felt of a truth that God was in our midst for his Holy Spirit was felt powerfully. Many gave great attention. Our congregation has increased at Ingersoll since last quarter.

July 21, 1862. Blacks Prefer Black Churches

I pen you a few lines which afford me much pleasure to let you know that the Lord is still carrying on his good work. On last Thursday the

17th, I was sent for to go to St. Thomas to preach to my brethren who had come to Canada so I sent an appointment and on the above date I went and at 15 minutes past eight o'clock we met in Mr Steward's house and preached from the first chapter of Matthew and the last part of the 21 verse and I do not know when I ever felt more of the power and goodness of God. For there was "good feeling" in the house. There [were] twelve that joined. Some said that they had been praying to God for some time to send some preacher. That way the condition of the Black man is not good in Canada as some would think.

If our people go to the White church they cannot enjoy themselves. You know the feeling is not good. So, this [is] the great cause that so few of our people go to White churches. We are poor unfortunate class of people, but I am thankful that God has opened a way for us so that our people have the Gospel preached by men of our own. [My italics]

The Rev. Solomon P. Hale (Coloured), Ingersoll, 1876–1903

Solomon Peter Hale (1816–1903) was born a slave in Maryland. He married Ellen (1816–?), a fellow slave, with whom he had at least two children, (Ellen, Jr., 1849–?) and Isaiah (1852–?). In 1860, leaving his wife and family behind, he fled to Canada West and freedom.[89]

He found employment as a labourer in the Hamilton area[90] and, according to his death notice, bought his first wife out of slavery (if so, then presumably before 1865 when emancipation of the slaves took effect).

In 1870 he was naturalized as a British subject. After eleven years in Canada, his wife and US-born grown-up children joined him in Hamilton.[91] His marriage ended with the death of his wife. In Ingersoll

---

89. *Ingersoll Chronicle*, 24 September 1903, death notice: "He was born a slave and after having attained to manhood became desirous of freedom and made a bold attempt in obtaining the same."
90. According to his death notice, he worked eleven years for Hugh B. Wilson, Esq., brother of the Hon. John Wilson. If so, then he was John's man after 1867 when City Directories listed him as a labourer in Hamilton. See *Hamilton City Directories*, 1867–68, 1868–69, 1870.
91. *Canada Census for Hamilton*, 1871.

(1876–1903) he was married to Julia Ann (born 5 February 1840 in Maryland); in 1880 their only son, Joshua, died at the age of 2 years, 10 months.

Meanwhile, he began an eight-year ministry in the Coloured British Methodist Episcopal Church. He was a "travelling preacher"[92] in 1871, ordained as a Deacon in 1873, and appointed to the Ingersoll Mission (Ingersoll and Otterville) in 1876. At the B.M.E.C. Annual Conference of 1877 "Sister M.J. Hughes, complained that Rev. S.P. Hale had expelled her from the Church without giving her a fair trial. Bro. Hale acknowledged that he had turned out not only Sister Hugh[e]s, but also Maria Moore, Harriet Gaines and George Selvin [Sullivan]—all turned out without trial. Whereupon the Conference restored Sisters M.J. Hughes, Maria Moore, Harriet Gaines, and George Selvin to membership in the Church in Ingersoll, and passed a resolution that Rev. S.P. Hale be reproved by the Bishop for mal-administration."[93]

In 1878 the Conference called out Hale "for travelling through the country and misrepresenting the Church and his own sacred calling by delivering lectures, which have been construed in the light of burlesques." As a condition of remaining in the ministry, Hale agreed "to deliver no more burlesque lectures." The Conference appointed him to Puce River (Essex County). In 1879 the Church expelled him from the ministry for "insubordination and contemptuous treatment of Conference." In addition the Conference resolved that "Bro. Hale be published as a refractory preacher in the London and Ingersoll press, and in any and every other place where Elder Hale may try to impose

---

92. "Travelling preacher" may explain his apparent double enumeration in the 1871 Census, once in Guelph and once in Hamilton. One Solomon P. Hale in Guelph was a lodger age 49, married but with his spouse not listed. One Solomon Hale in Hamilton was 59, married to Ellen, age 57 and father of two children ages 22, 19.
93. The expulsion of the four individuals potentially affected the several other individuals in their respective households. The 1871 Census reports Hattie Gaines, 35, her husband, a barber age 39, a son 8, and William Bass, 16 as Presbyterians. The 1881 Census reports Maria Moore, age 40, husband Robert, a labourer age 64, and three children ages 9 to 17; Mary Jane Hughes, age 35, married to Benjamin, a labourer age 50, and two teen-age sons; George Sullivan, a labourer, age 50 and five unmarried adults, aged 30 to 55.

himself on the public as a minister in good standing in connection with the B.M.E. Church."[94]

Ingersoll Chronicle Mentions of Solomon Hale

19 April 1877: We have received a letter from Embro complaining of the manner in which the Rev. S.P. Hail [sic], pastor of the Coloured church, was treated by prominent citizens of the above village. If the statements made are correct, it reflects great discredit on the man [sic] in question.

18 April 1878: We regret to learn that the eminent lecturer on "Hell," the Rev. Solomon Peter Hale, is about to leave this town.[95] He informs us that he is about to retire from the pulpit and intends raising chickens and lecturing for a living in future. Rev. Hale lectured in St. Mary's a few weeks since and was received with great favor.

23 May 1878: Bro. Hale delivered his lecture on the "British Empire" to a large and enthusiastic audience in the Town Hall Friday evening last. Considerable "backing up" was indulged in by the audience, which prevented much of the Rev. Solomon Peter Hale's discourse being heard.

7 August 1879: Rev. Solomon Peter Hale was stirring up the citizens of Strathroy on Tuesday. Rev. Sol. P. Hale has lately been lecturing at Embro. The *Express* in referring to it says, "the elucidations and annotations of Mr. Hale in his enlarged capacity as the rhetorician on "the originality of the British Empire," kept his audience in a continual roar of laughter. Although, as Mr. Hale says, is "sable complected" and was born in the Southern States, yet he claims to be a full-blooded Englishman; and judging from the plethora of knowledge he presumes

94. British Methodist Episcopal Church, Ontario Conference, Annual Conference Minutes.
95. He remained in Ingersoll through to his death in 1903.

to possess on every question that concerns England and the Queen in her "beautifully and gorgeous enlarged capacity," one would think he had seen and learnt all the momentousness of that highly dignified and monarchial institution. Yet he has never been within 3,000 miles of the place he prognosticates and expostulates upon with such unflagging volubility. Mr. Hale, for a self-educated slave, is certainly an intelligent man; but it would try the risibility of the gravest motels to hear him fling his misplaced jaw-breaking adjectives all over the house."

Stanley J. Smith, "Solomon Peter Hale, Fame without a Press Agent," *Ingersoll Tribune* (March 1956)

After the Civil War, wrote Smith, "Ingersoll's Coloured population returned to the sunny Southern States, but this fact had no effect on the Sunday collection plate," for Solomon Peter Hale had by this point become "an evangelist of no mean order" who "wisecracked the scriptures to drive home his point." Local newspapers transcribed and published his talks, which were then picked up by other newspapers farther afield. But, noted Smith, "[a]s tape recorders were not invented every editor admitted that they could not take down SPH's lectures in shorthand as he utilized words not found in the average dictionary!"

According to Smith, Hale had a repertoire of oft-repeated "stock lectures"; Ingersoll resident Fred Ackert had told Smith that "as a boy he heard SPH address the public and Rev. Hale never varied so much as a syllable in any of his lectures on the same subject."

Smith most-repeated lectures took as their subjects "Women," "Eternal Punishment," and "The British Empire." The *Woodstock Times* summarized the sermon on women this way: "When de snake bit Eve de good Lawd put dem ahtside de garden ob Eben in de chilly atmosphere an' Adam said, 'Evie, we sho' had an early Fall!'"

Smith went on to provide a summary of Hale's life and career:

The Rev. Hale was an escaped slave from a Maryland plantation and crossed into Canada at Windsor in the mid-1850s and settled on a farm in Essex County. With a devout thirst for religious knowledge he soon learned to read and write and eventually was ordained in the ministry of the BME church. For a time he was a supply minister in Chatham, Dresden, Buxton, and Puce … the latter a small settlement fronting Lake St. Clair in Essex County. He became so popular he received a call to remain in Puce and he stayed there until the congregation dwindled almost to the vanishing point upon the termination of the Civil War in 1865.… For the next five years he served several churches as a supply and was eventually assigned to Ingersoll in the early [18]70s.… Some say that one picture is worth a thousand words. SPH reversed this old adage because he could spellbind his audience with words that were more descriptive than any picture produced. If the words were not in a dictionary he would create them on the spot!

Smith told of how he had discovered "thousands of old documents" while cleaning out the attic of a house in Ingersoll, among which were three letters that provided insight into how Hale was hired to give a lecture. Ingersoll resident William Hoagg, who had invented (and patented) a furnace for heating large buildings, travelled around Ontario and Quebec, and apparently also acted in the capacity of Hale's agent. "He journeyed to Galt and met the school trustees, which were headed by a Mr. Graham," wrote Smith. "When Hoagg returned to Ingersoll he received a letter from J. Y. Graham, a son of the trustee. The following letters speak for themselves."

GALT, JAN. 9, 1879 — Dear Mr. Hoaag — can you inform me whether or not a Coloured clergyman resides in Ingersoll by the name of the Rev. Solomon Peter Hale. This gent lately lectured in St. Marys on "The British Empire" and judging from one extract of his lecture it must have been as good as a circus. Another young chap and myself thought of asking S.P.H. to lecture here on the same subject. If he lives in Ingersoll please ask him how much he would charge, and when he could come. Omit names and put the affair at one of the Societies' doors as the old fellow frequently pokes fun at the ones employing him....

Hale asked for a fee of ten dollars for each evening's talk, a sum that Graham wanted reduced, as indicated in a follow-up letter:

GALT JAN. 16, 1879.
Dear Mr. Hoaag — we would like Rev. Hale to lecture on Tuesday evening, Feb. 4, subject "Eternal Punishment," and on Wednesday evening Feb. 5, subject "The British Empire." We will pay him $15 for the two lectures. He pays his own expenses. We pay for the hall and printing.

Try to get the old fellow to accept these terms, but if you can't we will have to take his $10 offer and make the most of it....

Hale accepted the offered terms, but, said Smith, he "apparently gave the citizens only a $7.50 lecture per evening instead of his usual spellbinder, but let Mr. Graham tell it in his own words":

GALT, FEB. 6th, 1879 — W. A. Hoagg, Esq.... Dear Sir (not the friendly "Dear Mr. Hoagg" as the salutation, as in the previous letter!) ... Possibly you may remember, our speculation came off 4th and 5th and I am sorry to say did not realize as much as we anticipated. Total amount received $38.10. Paid $15 to S. P. Hale and other expenses of $15.05 more, so $8.05 divided by two represents the profit. After the slim house we had the first night I was exceedingly thankful to have the matter end as satisfactorily as it did....

According to Smith, Hale ran into difficulties with his church around 1876:

[T]he yearly conference of the B.M.E. frowned on the activities of the Rev. gentleman, and he was admonished. It was reported that his clowning both in the pulpit but more so on the public platform, were placing the Coloured population in disrepute. It was mentioned that he was neglecting the spiritual needs of his flock during his absence on lecturing tours. Not only weddings had to be postponed, but funerals had to wait.

The next year, Hale was dismissed by the church conference, on the grounds that he had refused to share his earnings with other ministers "who preached at less lucrative locations." Hale, who had apparently also refused to accept an appointment in Puce, Ontario, which was located east of Windsor along Lake St. Clair, responded by saying that

he refused to go ... because the Conference absolutely refused to make provisions for himself or family [to keep] from starving to death. He cited instances occurring during his last sojourn at Puce whereby he subsisted on cornpone and fish, although he never put it as plain as that.... According to Harry Rowland of the Oxford Tribune, "Mr. Hale poetically referred to his previous existence in Puce depending upon 'the alimentary gastronomical demands for the Lake Saint Clair piscatorial delicacies subjoined with the farinaceous crop tickled from God's sunny soil'!"

Stanley J. Smith, "Hale's 'Discombobberation,' Delight to Many Audiences," *Ingersoll Tribune* (March 1956).

[Link to: James Sinclair on "the Coloured Church," Chapter 2; Stanley J. Smith on Solomon P. Hale and Black Speak, Chapter 3.]

The subject of this 1956 article by Smith was "Solomon Peter Hale, the fine old Coloured gentleman who could hold the attention of hundreds whenever and wherever he gave one of his 'Learned Expatiations.'" Smith wrote that Hale was not "an ordained minister"—not true—and mentioned Hale's association with "the B.M.E. church which used to be on Catherine Street." Smith went on:

> One gentleman who remembered Solomon Peter told us a bit about him. His home was near the "Nut Works," and the kindly gentleman was known to everyone. He was described as "almost a caricature of the Coloured preacher from the Deep South." His white whiskers were a striking contrast to his extremely dark skin. During the week he went from place to place whitewashing barns and fences, but on Sunday he donned his Prince Albert jacket and plug hat that always looked as if someone had sat on it. Solomon Peter Hale was an ex-slave and consequently received no formal education. Nevertheless his vocabulary was astounding and when he couldn't find the right word he simply made up one of his own. Whenever a church organization needed to raise some money they would invite Solomon Peter Hale to give a sermon and would be assured of a packed house. Solomon Peter died here about 1904, a very old man.

The balance of the article is a story about one of Hale's sermons that had been delivered in London. It first appeared in the Ingersoll Chronicle and had been "kindly loaned" to Smith by "a friend of the *Tribune*."

Brother Solomon's Learned Expatiation upon the Universal Recogriizande—The wherefore of the Discombobberation ob de Human Species. Solomon Peter Hale, the celebrated Coloured orator, of whom everyone has heard, made his inaugural appearance in London Thursday night. He delivered his oration on "Future Punishment" in one of the large rooms of Victoria Hall, and was greeted by an enthusiastic audience. Shortly before eight o'clock Solomon Peter strode majestically into the room, with the proverbial carpet-bag and gingham in hand. Having carefully deposited these in the corner, he took his seat upon the platform. A chairman was duly appointed, and the orator of the evening respectably introduced. He began by saying:—

"Mister Chairman, responsible and respectable hearers, in introducin' to you this momenshus question of eternal punishment I shall endeavour not to impersonate upon your important and meditative understandings. It may be probable that you are a people who will be actuated to laugh a little, or it may be comprehensible that you will be moved by feelings of de most insubordinate and serious complexions. In glancin' around upon your physiogenimes I see the existence of aptitude and competent energy. Then this momenshus question calls for your serious and magnanimous contemplation. The word 'Everlastin' Punishment' is an important interrogation. While elocution and rhetoric have been invested in the brains of the theological geniuses, we here from day to day dat der am no hell and if I tread on some of your finer feelin's you will have to give me scope. I know our political feelin's are fine, and ostracize more sanctemoneously than the nimble-fingered organist, as; she endeavours to touch up the minimums, crachatoes and stackets (Cheers). Your respectable capacity Mr. Chairman has no doubt been favored wid a great deal of augament on futuah punishment. Oh! When we look upon dat lovin' mother as she pressed that tender offspring to her gentle buzzum, and listen with all the universality of an obtuse ear to her caresses, can we trifle wid di awful and stupendous interrogation? (uproarious laughter)…

"In dis garden God placed among other curiosities a beautiful and conglomerate botancial specimen called de tree of good and evil. Now some of youeh whimperin' and unconsciable capacities will ask whether God didn't know that Adam would break dis law. Oh! I cry, why don't you prognosticate and impeach for mercy after askin' dat question! I shall not delay to reply. But, see, here comes de great enemy dat has depopulated de agrandizment of masculine humanity and waylaid the progress aposthumus advancement (Cheers). He don't come to Adam oh no? He knows dat dis masculine humanity would extenuate to him a peculiar conception, so he oscillated to dis femine woman. Dar you see de sub-tel serpent, friends, advancin' in expostulation like a masculine man in courtship and matrimony, (laughter). So she fell like a busted star and oh how dey anticipated when dey violated God's law…

"But what did Adam do, eh? What did Adam do I ask? Blamed it on his wife, as the associated masculine power and energy of to-day does. An den all those vegetables anatomies and umbrages lost their pronunciation, and de promulgated thunders of chaotic masses scared, him half to death. Wid perogative elucidation dey got some fig leaves and left de Garden of Eden and begotted Cain and A-Bill. Some of our theological geniuses apostrophize dis A-Bill and it will be to your moral obtuseness to know dat der are many Cains and A-Bills predicted in dis world, (laughter). But now we come to dis imponderable question of futuah punishment and I ask you to turn to St. Matthew, and read with me thusly: 'And these shall to out into everlasting punishment.' This is only a prefiguration, they say: and where it speaks to the rich man with his thousands of finances, high deposited in the sociality of agrandizment, and the poor man so revolutionized. They say it is only a metaphor. I believe every man can go to heaven. The capacity of our nobles are so arranged that they can have their plumpudding and Bristle carpet and fine houses, and will this prevent them from going to Heaven? Oh no! With all the socialities of sweet communion and abnormities of our air-tight stoves, with the vicissitudes of the organic and the tin-cup of the piano, we learn to go to heaven. (Cheers).

"The harm of riches is when under the concentration of contamination you squeeze the dollar too tight. The substantiated citizen may derogatize de poor boy, but (giggling) you can't expostulate the rich man's boy from playing with the poor man's boy. But not to monopolize dis discussion I will ask what cannon Farar and Mark Twain am going' to do in de face of dis Lazarous story? Dey can't do anything! I know it is getting popular to preach no hell, but (looking at a 13 year old boy in the front seat) when I see your patriarchiel phsiognomies I know dat you will not be schedulized by dis momenshus question. What do you go to chu'ch for (stroking his chin) tell me? What do you go to chu'ch for, if der ain't any hell."

The lecturer then closed with a brilliant peroration on "Majucians and southsayers, Nebuchnizzor and Socramothenes" under human auspices and the serious manner in which his modesty was shocked by the popular preaching of the day.

Charles Scoffin (1868–1954), White, Remembers Rev. Solomon Peter Hale (1948)[96]

We had some funny characters here. There was one outstanding one—Rev. Solomon Peter Hale. He was a great preacher and he could, at that time, read, and I know for I taught him his letters. He used to hold "Open Air" services in the Park and drew big crowds. Then, he got to preaching in the Coloured church over the river and would hold services at night. Us young whites would go there. There are things that stick in your memory and this is one. They would take up the collection and then start his oration. We would all drop a copper in and he would thank everyone for the donations. One old Coloured fellow would yell "Glory, Glory" and then S.P. Hale would ask some of the brothers to speak, so one night the "Glory" man started to pray and this was it—"Good Lord, send the angel Gabriel down on a chariot of fire and take Bro. Jones right up to Heaven." After the service was dismissed, someone suggested we pay Bro Jones a visit, so we went and I, being the kid of the bunch, I was elected to do the talking. I walked up to the door, rapped, rapped again, the I said, "Bro. Jones," then he asked me what I wanted, and I said, "This is the angel Gabriel come down to take Bro. Jones up to Heaven in a chariot of fire." "Now, look here you, go on away. Bro. Jones don't live here at all."

Charles Scoffin was born in Ingersoll on the southwest corner of Oxford and Dufferin Streets.

---

96. *Charles Scoffin Memoir* (1868–1954), Ingersoll Library.

Death Notice, Solomon Peter Hale (1816–1903)[97]

An Old Resident Dead

The death of Rev. Solomon Peter Hale occurred at his residence, Carnegie Street, yesterday, after an illness extending over several weeks. Deceased was in his 88th year and has been a resident of Ingersoll for many years. He was for several years pastor of the BME church [British Methodist Episcopal Church] here and was one of our best known citizens. The funeral takes place from his late residence tomorrow afternoon at 3 o'clock to the Ingersoll Rural Cemetery

Rev. Solomon Peter Hale

After a residence of so many years amongst us, not only as a minister but also as a lecturer of some note, and also as a most exemplary citizen in his everyday life, he passed away on Thursday last to the great beyond. It may not be amiss to note a few items of Mr. Hale's career. He was born a slave and after having attained to manhood became desirous of freedom and made a bold attempt in obtaining the same, and about fifty years ago arrived at the Fifty-Ninth Creek, County of Wentworth (near Winona), and was fortunate in getting employment with Hugh B. Wilson, Esq., brother of the Hon. John Wilson, for over eleven years, meantime buying his first wife out of slavery. Mr. Hale so lived that he merited the good will of that entire neighbourhood, and has had calls from several friends who knew him in those days. Of his ministry here, we all know of how diligently he laboured, until old age made it necessary to retire. His lectures, novel and in a style peculiarly his own, caused him to be sought after far and near. Perhaps no man in Ingersoll has or will leave this world with a better record of good will from all to all. His estimable widow has the sympathy of many friends.

---

97. *Ingersoll Chronicle*, 24 September 1903, p. 6; *Ingersoll Daily Chronicle*, 18 September 1903.

Ingersoll Newspapers Mock "Black Speak" (Negro Dialect)

Oxford Herald, 12 January 1860

A Negro's instructions for putting on a coat were: —Fust de right arm, den de lef, den gib one general convulshun.

Ingersoll Chronicle, 10 June 1869
BURSTING OF DAM AT SMITH'S MILLPOND

Owing to a defective plank which fastened the sluice gates of Mr. Jas. Smith's upper mill dam, one of them gave way on Monday morning about three o'clock, the consequences of which have proved very disastrous. The water from [his] Upper Pond rushed into [his] lower one with great force, soon overflowing the dam and banks. As all of the waste gates were shut down to save a good 'head,' the only escape for the water was over the embankment, which it soon swept away, and the vast volume of water from the two ponds rushed down the narrow channel, causing great consternation to the inhabitants along the banks of the 'classic stream.'

Several of Messrs. Noxon's saw logs which were floating in the pond and lying in the vicinity were washed away—some as far as the river. Numerous outbuildings, located in the backyards adjacent to the current, were also washed from their foundations and carried down with a mass of fence timber, cord wood, and almost every other conceivable thing usually to be found in the back premises of our citizens. The lower story of Mr. Hugh Clark's house was flooded to the depth of nearly four feet. The small bridge at the rear of Mr. Poole's property was entirely swept away.

Great alarm was experienced by the occupants of a large two-story house in the vicinity, owned by Mr. Poole, from whence expressions such as the following might have been heard to issue: *'dod drat it mudder, take dat ar chile out de cradle or he'll be drownded, sure!' 'Lor a*

Massa we'll all be drownded alive in our beds!' 'Get out ob dar right smart!' 'Dog on if all de furniture, if all de furniture won't be swept down de ribber!' and such like [my italics]. But the greatest harm they experienced was the fright, which soon subsided, as did the water, and soon left the ponds 'high and dry.' As soon as it was daylight the boys had great sport in catching the fish which were soon floundering about in all directions, astonished at the sudden subsidence of their natural element.

Emancipation Day Observances in Ingersoll
James Sinclair on Emancipation Day, *Ingersoll Chronicle*, 22 August 1907

As the first of August was always observed by those people as Emancipation Day to celebrate the liberation of the slaves of the West Indies by the British government [on 1 August 1834], unusual services were held, and the name of Wilberforce and his influence on behalf of their race was made the theme of their oration. On one occasion a large gathering of these people held a monster picnic in a grove behind Dufferin Street, then a suitable woods. A feature of the occasion was an elaborate barbeque, when an ox was roasted whole, together with other animals. In the evening a grand ball was held in the old Jarvis Hall (which stood where the Campbell Block now stands), for which elaborate preparations were made.

Coloured Pride on Emancipation Day, 1st of August, 1864.
Ingersoll Chronicle, 5 August 1864

EMANCIPATION DAY. On Monday last the Coloured population of this town turned out en masse to celebrate the anniversary of the abolition of slavery in the British West Indies [on 1 August 1834]. As the event commemorated was one that would naturally fill the hearts with gratitude and joy, the gallant "Othellos" and their *blushing* "Dinahs" as they sauntered along the street in their gayest attire, did not allow their eye to dwell on the *dark* side of life's picture, judging from that peculiar cachinnation that greeted the ear at every corner of the street. About noon the masculine portion formed into procession, presenting a very imposing front as they marched through the town to the inspiring strains of the Scottish bagpipe. In the evening—so we are informed—a *ball* on a grand scale took place at the "Anglo-American." Dancing was kept up to the "witching hour of the night when church yards yawn," and the next day our Coloured neighbors seemed rather jaded from overindulgence in "the light fantastic toe."

Caveat

Elaborate celebrations of Emancipation Day were unusual in Ingersoll, not an annual event. In the event, the *Ingersoll Chronicle* made just two other references to local observances of Emancipation Day:

> EMANCIPATION DAY. The coloured inhabitants of this neighbourhood held a demonstration in town on Tuesday in commemoration of the emancipation of their brethren in the West India islands, an event which occurred on the 1st August, 1834. (*Ingersoll Chronicle*, 3 August 1876)

> The annual celebration of the British Emancipation Act was observed at Clifton [*Niagara Falls*] Monday. Excursions of coloured people arrived from stations on the G.W.R. Loop Line from Detroit, Chatham, and intermediate points. It rained nearly the whole day.
> [Ingersoll]. Sunday was Emancipation Day. Some of our coloured population joined their brethren at *Niagara Falls* on Monday. (*Ingersoll Chronicle*, 5 August 1880)

CHAPTER SIX
Black-White Collisions in Ingersoll, 1860–80

Magistrate's Court before Reeve John Galliford, Esq.
Ingersoll Chronicle, 29 May 1857

Catherine Piper, a young Coloured girl, was charged with having stolen from Mr. James A. Fraser's store,[98] on the 20th inst., a cash box containing money notes of hand, etc.

Philip Box sworn—I am a clerk in Mr. Fraser's store. The cash box was in its place, on the 20th inst., at about 4 o'clock. Shortly after, Mr. Fraser had occasion to go to the box for some money, which he told me he was about sending to his brother, when it was discovered that the box was missing. I noticed the person called Griffin standing in Mr. Patterson's barn, in company with a suspicious looking character called Townsend, *alias* Dopp—saw accused about the door also. I was led to suspect she was concerned with the robbery from a conversation I had with Griffin, who told me she knew where the box was. I then procured a warrant for her arrest, and in company with Constable Swayze, proceeded to London, where I understood she had gone. Arrested the accused in the street, in London, and then proceeded to her aunt's, who said accused had given her $13. While waiting for the train at the London Railway station, at 11 p.m., accused said she knew nothing of the cash box, but that Griffin had told her the notes could be found beneath a log in rear of Watson's mill in this place. On arriving here I proceeded, in company with the constable and the accused,

---

98. James A. Fraser, dry goods store, near Patterson's Hotel, Thames Street (*Chronicle* advertisement).

at 1 o'clock a.m., to the spot, and found the cash box, which was buried under a log at Watson's Mill. The accused walked to the place without the slightest doubt as to the exact spot. The box produced is the one found, which is also the box Mr. Fraser lost.

Constable Swayze was sworn and corroborated the evidence of Mr. Box.

James A. Fraser sworn—the box produced (and its contents) belongs to me and is the one stolen from me on the 20th May.

An expensive silk cape worn by the accused was identified by Mr. G.A. Cameron as being his property, which had been stolen, it is supposed, by the accused.

The presiding magistrate committed the prisoner to jail, to take her trial at the July assizes.

The 1861 Census for Ingersoll enumerated Catherine A. Piper, age 17, one of seven Canadian-born Mulatto children of American-born parents, Thomas Piper, labourer, age 52, and his wife Elsa, 35. Thus, Catherine was 13 at the time of her alleged offence. The case was not heard in the July Assizes.

The White Magistrate, John Galliford (1811–75), Reeve of Ingersoll Village

Born England, served with the Royal Artillery in Montreal during the rebellion of 1837–38. Met Frances Hysop (1827–1901), a native of Ireland, who was visiting Montreal, and they married in Toronto. During the 1840s they removed to Ingersoll, where they raised ten children and lived out their lives. Boot & Shoe Maker, Freemason, and Church of England in religion. Municipal Honours: Reeve of Ingersoll Village 1852, 1856–58, 1863–64; Councillor 1853–55, 1859–60, 1862, 1870–72; mayor of Ingersoll (a town in 1865) in 1867–68.

1858. White Merchant Cheats Black Customer, Then Assaults Him

Ingersoll Chronicle, 11 June 1858

MAGISTRATE'S COURT

John McConaghan was summoned before His Worship [Reeve John Galliford, Esq.] on Saturday, charged with digging into a Negro named John Diggens. The last mentioned John, it appears, on Friday evening purchased from Mac what was supposed to be 50 lbs. of flour; but on returning home found the bag contained "only shorts" [coarse flour].[99] So on Saturday morning Diggens returned to the [merchant] and demanded flour or the dollar. Neither of which, it is alleged, Mac would do, but immediately pitched into Diggens, when a fight, of course, ensued. The upshot was—Diggens, it being supposed having been worsted in the fight—the summoning of McConaghan to appear to answer the charge of assault. Mac protested his innocence of being the aggressor, but His Worship thought otherwise and fined him $2 and $3.50 costs.

In 1858 John Diggens was a US-born labourer, age 25, Negro, married to Mary, age 20, Mulatto (1861 Census). He headed a family of five in 1861 and of six in 1871. John McConaghan: unidentified.

1858. Black Fined for Assaulting White Bigot

Ingersoll Chronicle, 25 June 1858

AN ASSAULT AND WHAT IT COST

On Monday, before John Galliford, Esq., a Negro named George Piner was charged with assaulting William Harris of West Oxford. The assault, it seems, was committed in consequence about some remarks made by Harris about "niggers" in general and Ingersoll "niggers" in particular, saying that the "white folks" would soon be obliged to emigrate, the "Coloured population" were becoming so numerous and so

99. Middlings and shorts: flour from coarser screens (50 and 30 mesh), which contains the germ, coarsely ground endosperm, and some finely ground bran.

disagreeable. Piner was standing on the opposite side of the street at the time the remarks of Harris were made, immediately after which he stepped across the road and deliberately struck Harris in the face. In order to forcibly impress upon Mr. Piner's mind the desirability of not making himself "too familiar" with strangers, His Worship fined him $4 and costs—in all $7.50.

The 1861 Census enumerated George Piner, age 28 [25 in 1858], a labourer, married to Sarah, age 21; they were Episcopal Methodist immigrants from the US and the parents of George, Jr., born in Canada West in 1858. William Harris, yeoman, age 27 [24 in 1858], was an Irish Anglican immigrant who had married in 1855 and was the father of four children under age 5.

1858. A Spat between Coloured Gamblers

Ingersoll Chronicle, 12 November 1858

A GAMBLING SCRAPE

A Coloured man, Calvin Jones, who keeps a barber shop in this place, was brought before John McDonald and David Canfield, Esqs. on Monday last, charged with "clandestinely obtaining from Lewis Barry (another Coloured man) two coats, a waistcoat, and $4.50 in money." The facts of the case appeared to be these— Jones and Barry had previously been in the habit of gambling together, and on one occasion in London, Barry won all the money Jones had, besides his coat, shoes, etc. On Saturday last, Barry entered Jones's shop and shortly after—first, however, warming the inner man with a few horns of spirits—they proceeded to the back room of a saloon on King Street and commenced playing at cards for money. Fortune, it appeared, favoured Jones on this occasion—he having won all of Barry's money, together with his coat and waistcoat. Barry having thus rid himself of his money and his "personal property," felt aggrieved and sought relief in the "halls of justice." The evidence adduced … was very contradictory; but one fact was clearly established, namely that both Jones and Barry are gamblers—*professional* gamblers we might say.

The decision of the presiding magistrates was deferred until Wednesday—Jones in the meantime being liberated on bail.

In justice to the young man, Murray, who keeps the saloon referred to, we would state, that on his discovering that the parties were gambling, he at once ordered them out of the house.

WEDNESDAY—the magistrates ordered Jones to return the coats to Barry, and the latter was ordered to pay the costs.

1861 Census: Calvin Jones 62, a US-born labourer, and Ellen Jones, age 59, US-born, lived on their own in a frame dwelling.

1864. Magistrate Galliford Fines a White Bully
Ingersoll Chronicle, 23 September 1864
DISGRACEFUL ROWDYISM

One of those disgusting exhibitions ... that exemplifies as perfection the inherent brutality of the rowdy "native and to the manor born," disgraced our town on Monday afternoon. It appears that a noted specimen of this stamp, familiarly termed Jake Harris and who in pugilistic matters ... is a perfect "I am Sir Oliver, and when I open my lips let the dog bark," took into his head on the occasion in question, when well primed with his favourite beverage, to kick everything before him that came within the reach of his pedal extremities. Having exhausted his [?] on some innocent whelps—of the canine race—he drew himself up in drunken [dignity?] before the door of one Jeffrey, who happens to be a Coloured man that keeps an eating house. At the time Levi Matthews—similar in complexion to the landlord—was standing peacefully outside when Mr. Harris, with his characteristic politeness (?), enquired of him, "how many d---n niggers are there here?" Of course such an interrogatory was well calculated to look as *Black* as thunder. He, however, in the blandest tone possible, replied,

"What do you mean by that? I don't consider myself a Black nigger, and I don't think you have a right to insult any person on the street." This conciliatory speech was received by his swarthy antagonist with the utmost scorn, who warned him "not to give any of his slack or he would lose his mouth in two minutes." The terrific threat, of course, did not intimidate Mr. M. who then coolly remarked, "Well then bust ahead." To make a long story short a regular combat in dog fashion style took place between the belligerents, in which the Coloured gentleman eventually succeeded in eating away a portion of Harris's hand, and would have probably devoured more of the raw material so bountifully provided for him were it not that they were separated in time to prevent a further evidence of his appetite for uncooked dainties. When the case was brought before His Worship, the Reeve, he very properly inflicted a fine of $10 and costs upon the prisoner Harris, who, from the testimony adduced, was the aggressor and richly deserved, we think, all that he received both personally and pecuniarily.

1861 Census. Jacob Jeffrey, 50 [in 1864], labourer, married to Matilda, age 52. We have no information about Levi Matthews (victim) and Jake Harris (the bully).

1864. A Black Man's Gunshot Answers White Stone Throwers

Ingersoll Chronicle, 23 September 1864

On Wednesday evening another Coloured gentleman of the name of Hall was introduced to His Worship for firing among three of the N. Oxford Rifles who were returning from practice at Ingersoll. The accused admitted the fact, but assigned as his motive for the civilized form of warfare—he it would appear was determined to shoot his game and not act the part of a *cannibal*—that stones were thrown at his shanty, and that he suspected one of the trio had bestowed on him that mode of attention, which merited a discharge of his gun in return.

Mr. Henderson, the Reeve of North Oxford and Captain of the Rifles, stated in his evidence that had such been the case, he would have heard the noise at the toll-gate. Shearer, the first witness being sworn stated that no insult was offered by any of the party, and believes the prisoner to be the man who fired the shot, which lodged in the calf of Olden's leg and prevented him from being present at the trial. The case was sent to the Assizes.

The Ingersoll Chronicle *covered the Assizes on 28 October. There was no mention of this incident.*

1864. Coloured Barber Battles White Bartender
Ingersoll Chronicle, 2 September 1864
A BARBER'S ONSLAUGHT WITH A RAZOR

On Tuesday last many of the inhabitants of our peaceful town were struck dumb … on hearing that a Coloured gentleman of the tonsorial profession had misapplied the [tool] that is usually employed for the [cheek?] on the throat of the [White] barkeeper who [officiates?] at Brady's Hotel. Numbers flocked to the establishment to ascertain for themselves if the wounds were really serious … a thousand tongues had circulated far and wide that the unfortunate man's jugular had been seriously severed by the well [?] razor. Happily their worst fears were not realized, for although the object of their solicitude had keenly felt the ugly cut that he had received—on his neck 2 inches in length—at the hands of his opponent, still by sticking plaster [?] the incision was successfully closed, and Kirk, we are happy to state, at the present moment is out of danger and is the enjoyment of his wonted health.

A warrant having been issued for the arrest of King, the culprit was brought before the magistrates at the Town Hall in the evening. Long before the time appointed for his trial, the building was besieged by an anxious and excited crowd [who] the moment the doors were opened rushed upstairs to listen to the proceedings. Order having been restored, the Justice of the Peace, John Galliford and D.M. Robertson, Esqrs., commenced the investigation. On the prisoner's being arraigned, he appeared perfectly calm and self-possessed and did not appear to exhibit the slightest concern to the critical position in which he was placed, while the ironical smile that played across his swarthy countenance would lead one to suppose that he regarded the surrounding with ineffable contempt. The testimony throughout the prosecution and defence did not present any marked shades of difference, and the cross examination on both sides, we are free to confess, intimately blended with the tragic, comic, sublime, and ridiculous. From the mass of evidence adduced, it is pretty clear that King and Kirk had no love for each other, although it is questionable whether the former was justified in using the deadly weapon in the manner that he did.

John Kirk [the White bartender], being sworn, testified as follows: I heard that King [the Coloured barber] said I had been abusing his [King's] employer, Mr. Wanzer. I went down to the bar to ascertain the fact and asked what this [meant?]. I did not know his name as I asked the question. King came. When he came in I said, here he is, let him answer the question. He went on to say that [he?], Wanzer and a few more niggers was the [cause?] of me and other skedaddlers being here, told him he was a liar, and with that he called me a d-----d liar. I then went right up towards him. As I went up he took the razor out of the strop that was on the shelf; he had it open with one hand; I could not say who struck first. Brice the constable broke it up. King laid over in Woodstock for trial at the Assizes of the 13th instance.

Ingersoll Chronicle, *28 October 1864. Fall Assizes at Woodstock. No mention. John Kirk, White bartender at Brady's Hotel. [?] King, the Black, was a barber.*

1865. White Man Sexually Assaults a Black Woman

Ingersoll Chronicle, 22 September 1865

POLICE COURT

Matthew Torrance of London appeared before His Worship, the Mayor, Adam Oliver, Esq., charged by one Mrs. Sarah Maria Howard (Coloured) with attempting to assault her. J. McCaughey, Esq., appeared for the prisoner and requested His Worship to have the witnesses removed from the court. Complainant said she had only one witness, a little girl, who was requested by His Worship to withdraw.

Mrs. Howard deposed as follows: Yesterday between twelve and one o'clock the prisoner came to my house and said that I kept a dissipated house; that Mr. Jones and Mrs. Alice Williams told him so. I told him to leave as no one lived with me save a girl 12 years old. He said he would not leave until he got what he came for. He then came forward and made an attempt to take hold of me and again said that he would not go away until he got what he came for. I ran and picked up the axe and said I would chop him if he came near me. I said I would complain to the Mayor. He said do not and I will leave. He then went away. Swear positively that the prisoner is the same man.

After being cross examined by Mr. McCaughey, the girl, who appeared to be a very intelligent Coloured girl, was brought into court. She identified the prisoner as being the man who assaulted her adopted mother, and selected him from half a dozen other persons who had been placed beside him. The difference between her statement and Mrs. Howard's was in regard to the time the assault took place, the witness stating that it took place a little before the 11:15 train went west.

G.T. Barnwell, Stationmaster, was called. Who testified that the prisoner was employed by the G.W.R. and was whitewashing the stationhouse yesterday, and it was utterly impossible for the prisoner to have been at the complainant's house between the hours of 12 and 1, the house is over half a mile from the station, and he had seen him in the waiting room at least half a dozen times between 12 and 1 o'clock.

After more evidence was produced to prove the prisoner was at the station at the time the assault was said to have taken place, His Worship decided to dismiss the case, saying that he had no doubt that an assault had been committed, but thought they made a mistake as to identity.

The 1861 Census enumerated Sarah M. Howard, age 21 [25 in 1865], born Canada West, married to William H. Howard, age 27, born United States, labourer. Living with them was Mary Anne Steele, age 22, born Canada West, and Steele's two children.

1878. Dominion Day.
A Tavern Brawl, a White Mob, and the K.K.K.

Ingersoll Chronicle, 4 July 1878
BAD WORK!
THREE MEN MURDEROUSLY ATTACKED BY NIGGERS.
CUT WITH RAZORS!
THE PEOPLE TURN OUT AND DEMOLISH A BARBER SHOP.
EXCITEMENT IN TOWN.
TWO OF THE VILLAINS ARRESTED!

Considerable excitement has prevailed in town the past few days over the outrage by niggers Monday night. A barber named Neil, a hard case from London, and who had served several years in the penitentiary, accompanied by three others, Duncan, Parker, and Williams, demanded liquor of the proprietor of the McMurray House,[100] who refused when the men became boisterous and Mr. McMurray found it necessary to eject them from the house. When doing so, and when as far as the door with Duncan, Neil struck Mr. McMurray in the face and followed up with several more, the rest of the gang assisting. A number

---
100. Formerly the Anglo-American Hotel, southwest corner of Carroll and Queen Streets, proprietor William McMurray.

of Mr. McMurray's friends who were present took his part and the row became general, the barbers using razors. In the melee Mr. McMurray received a cut on the arm below the elbow in the fleshy part and in the chest. Constable [J. B.] Capron received several cuts about the head, and the hostler at the house had his arms severely cut. The barbers did not confine themselves to razors, but used stones, breaking the windows in front of the house.

The constable called on the men present to keep the peace, when the White men desisted and the barbers fled. In a few moments a crowd of about two hundred men gathered, when it was suggested that the fire alarm be sounded, the fire torches be procured, and a general search made. The hint was not long in being carried into effect. But in the meantime the barber shop and dwelling of Duncan (which were in the same building) were searched, the fugitives not being found, some of the more impulsive in the party proceeded to demolish the barbershop, and not a pane of glass or a mirror was left unbroken in the place. The mob would have undoubtedly torn down the other barbershops in town but for a few timely remarks by Mr. James Brady,[101] when the mob attacked the houses occupied by Coloured people, which were searched, and in one of them occupied by a family named Mann, disreputable characters, one of the parties named Williams was found. He escaped, however, by jumping off the roof and disappeared. A shot was fired after him by someone in the party, but without effect. The search was kept up until about three o'clock in the morning, but was unsuccessful. Williams was captured Tuesday evening on Col. Skinner's farm near Woodstock, and Parker was found under John Crotty's barn last evening. On Tuesday evening a mob numbering about one hundred and fifty proceeded to the different Coloured houses in town, notifying all Coloured people to leave by Saturday night. Had the men, Neil and Duncan, been caught on Monday night, they would in all

101. James Brady, hotel keeper, Brady House (former Mansion House).

probability have been lynched. Now, however, that the excitement is subsiding, we do not look for any disturbance should they be captured. The law is strong, and they will no doubt receive their just punishment if caught. The action of the mob in ordering the Coloured people to leave town will not be endorsed by right-thinking people. There are about half a dozen disreputable houses in town which the authorities should put down, but mob law must never obtain a foothold in this fair Canada of ours.

Same Incident, Oxford Tribune, 3 July 1878
THE STABBING CASE

Between one and two o'clock on Tuesday morning a serious row took place in front of the McMurray House. Some Coloured men—barbers—called for liquor, and on being refused, smashed several panes of glass, etc. of the hotel. The proprietor, Mr. McMurray, in attempting to quiet them, was attacked in a savage manner by one of the Negroes, who stabbed him in the body slightly and made several horrible gashes in his arm. Chief Constable Capron, in trying to arrest the Negroes, was knocked senseless and cut severely about the head. The hostler of McMurray House was slightly cut on the arm. None of the wounds are dangerous. The Coloured men escaped arrest at the time but as the constables are on their track it is expected they will soon be taken. After the disturbance the barber shop in which the Coloured man who stabbed McMurray was thought to be hid, was completely wrecked by stones thrown by the excited crowd.

There was considerable excitement in the town on Tuesday and a number of citizens, together with constables Capron, Carroll, and Heeney, started for Beachville, where, it was said, the Negroes were hiding. After a great deal of searching constables Carroll and Heeney captured a man named Jack Williams, one of the men, about three miles east of here, as he was coming out of a woods. He is supposed to be one of the ring leaders. On his person was found a razor and dirk knife. The constables had to bring him around the back way, fearing that the mob would lynch him. They are still looking for the others. Mr. McMurray is very weak from loss of blood, and his medical advisors have advised him to keep his room.

A large mob, numbering about 150 men were on the streets this morning notifying the Coloured people to leave town by Saturday noon. They threaten to break into the Hook & Ladder Company's hall and take their apparatus to pull down a rookery on King Street, and one on Thames north, kept by a disreputable character named Joseph Mann, where Neil, the man who did the stabbing escaped the mob the night before. No further damage is reported except the smashing of windows. The feeling is intense. Constables Heeney and Capron are both on the track of Neil.

Threats of violence having been freely made, the Mayor has issued the following timely

PROCLAMATION

Whereas it has been credibly reported to me that certain parties not having the fear of the law, of the good order of the community before their eyes, have been making threats to do personal violence to the Coloured people of the town, and ordering them to leave within a given time, thereby inciting a disturbance from which serious consequences may ensure.

These are therefore to caution all persons against any breach of the law towards the Coloured or any other of our citizens as no distinction will be made in its application to the offenders.

Charles Chadwick, Mayor
Ingersoll, July 3, 1878

Up to the hour of going to press (Thursday morning) only two of the Negroes had been captured. Parker, the second one, a stranger, was taken last evening by Wm. O'Neil while hiding under a barn on the farm of Mr. John Crotty, North Oxford. Efforts are still being made to capture the balance of the gang.

Another "proclamation" has been issued in large sheet form and heavy painted letters, and posted opposite the Post Office, ordering the Coloured people occupying three specified houses in town to "slide out." It is signed "Keno, Captain, K.K.K."

Excerpt, Charles Scoffin Memoir, 1868–1954, Ingersoll Library
We had a lot of Coloured people here at that time and they decided to run them out of town. They did, but some returned. There was a house opposite Wellington St. on the north side of King—a one story, 3 apartments, and the whites tore that down. There was an old slave lived at the corner of Wellington and King named George Washington Bevins. They didn't interfere with him. He claimed he was 102 years old.

Charles Scoffin: White, born and raised in Ingersoll. He was 9 years old on Dominion Day, 1878, when his family lived on King Street E., near the centre of the riot.

CHAPTER SEVEN
"Aunt Hattie,"
A Hard Life in Ingersoll, 1862–1913

Harriett Ann ("Aunt Hattie") Wright (1833–1913), pictured above, was a Coloured resident of the Ingersoll area for 51 years. She had been born in the United States (12 January 1833) and came to Canada in 1862 at age 29. About 1864 she married Benjamin Wright, whom the 1861 Census enumerated as a 34-year-old, American-born Baptist labourer, living alone in a West Oxford shanty. The 1871 Census enumerated Benjamin and Harriett in West Oxford Township with four children: William (born 1865), Charles Fuller (adopted? born 1867), Isaiah (January, 1871) and Benjamin, Jr. (1873). The Wrights were "dirt poor" and illiterate.

By Census Day, 1881, Benjamin had left the marital home, which now was in Ingersoll (a shanty on Thamesford Road, Bell Street); under 1881 Census rules, if the marriage was intact, Benjamin should have been listed as "temporarily absent" on Census Day. One may surmise, therefore, that Benjamin was no longer domiciled with his wife and their three sons—William, age 16, a labourer; Isaiah, age 12; and Benjamin, Jr., age 8; Hattie worked as a general servant.[102]

In 1886 her son Benjamin, Jr., burned his mother's Bell Street shanty and was sentenced to five years in the provincial reformatory for arson (discussed below). In 1891 Harriett lived alone, a lodger at 195 Bell Street. Her absent husband Benjamin died about 1896: thus, the Town Directory for 1894–95 listed Harriett as "Mrs.," while that for 1897 recorded her as "widow Benjamin." By 1908 she had moved from Bell Street to Tunis Street. There she died, "frozen to death," in February 1913. Her death notice in the *Ingersoll Chronicle* gave the details:

> "AUNTIE" WRIGHT DEAD—Auntie Wright died at the Alexandra Hospital, between 1 and 2 o'clock this afternoon 20 minutes after being admitted. Today Mayor Coleridge and Chief Fish visited her home on Tunis St., and found her with her hands and feet frozen. They at once called the ambulance and had her removed to the hospital where she died as stated above. De-

---

102. The 1881 Census for West Nissouri Township enumerated one Benjamin Wright, American-born African labourer, a Baptist, aged 65, married to an Ontario-born African, Charlotte, aged 24.

ceased had been a resident of Ingersoll for many years and was a familiar figure on the streets. She had resided alone for years and during the past 2 or 3 years had been very feeble. Members of the council for many years have tried to persuade deceased to go to the House of Refuge at Woodstock, but she refused and it is said that members of the Indigent Committee have found the door locked against them when they went to visit her to see if she needed food or fuel. Apparently her reason for locking the door when members of the council visited her was that she feared they would take her to the Refuge. The council has kept her in fuel and food and when her home was visited today she had supply of both. (*Ingersoll Chronicle*, 6 February 1913)

We know something of her sons Isaiah and Benjamin. Her eldest son, William, possibly was the person enumerated as a foundry worker in Hamilton in 1891: his census age, 26, squares with the previous census, and his parents were American-born.

1886. "Aunt Hattie's" Son Benjamin, Age 13, Arsonist
A YOUNG FIRE BUG SENT DOWN
(*Ingersoll Chronicle*, 9 September 1886)

Our citizens will no doubt experience a sense of relief when they learn that one fire bug has been discovered, tried, and sentenced to five years in prison. At the fire which destroyed the shanty occupied by Mrs. Wright (Coloured), Chief Wilson's suspicions were aroused that some member of the family had set fire to the building, and he immediately set to work to discover the culprit. He succeeded so well that he suggested to Ben, a lad of [thirteen] years of age, that he knew something about the matter. Of course the boy stoutly denied knowing anything about the matter. Notwithstanding [the boy's denial], Constable Wilson caused a warrant to be issued for his arrest. The lad in the meantime had gone to Woodstock. The chief, however, by writing him and telling him his mother was going to London, easily induced him to come home, when he was promptly arrested. He still declared his innocence, until, while being examined before the magistrate, Constable Wilson confronted him with a pewter cup in which he had borrowed a quantity of coal oil from a neighbour, stating his mother had sent him for it. The young rascal then asked the chief if he would let him off if he told the truth. The imp then told the following story which we give in his own words: "My mother had thrashed me and I told her she would never whip me again in that house. I borrowed some coal oil from a neighbour and set the house on fire. I did not know [if] there was anybody in the house at the time."

Mr. Chadwick sentenced him to five years in the reformatory.[103] The boy afterwards confessed to Mr. Wilson that he had torched two other houses, one belonging to a man named Chambers; his reason for doing so [was] that Mr. Sudworth, who had charge of the property, threatened to lick him and hand him over to the constable for stealing cherries. He thought he would leave him with no house to watch, so he had set fire to it. The other [house], occupied by a man named Johnston, he set on fire because one night a man named Roberts came to their place drunk and would not go away till his mother threatened to strike him with an axe. Everybody living around there said the house where Roberts lived would be better burned down, so he had set fire to it and burned it down.[104]

---

103. The Reformatory (1859–1903) was located at Penetanguishene. See *Chronicle*, 11 May 1860.
104. Data from the 1881 Ingersoll Census: Harriett Wright (Coloured), US born, general servant, married (husband not enumerated). Her three children were William, 16, labourer; Isaiah, 10; and Ben, 8.

1905. "Aunt Hattie's" Son, Isaiah, Death by Drunken Misadventure

Excerpts from the *Ingersoll Chronicle*, 5 and 12 October 1905; 8 March 1906

On 6 May 1889 Isaiah married Matilda Collins, age 19, of Ingersoll, but the marriage was a brief one—possibly she died.[105] In the event, at age 25 Isaiah married Mary Preston, age 19, in 1895.[106] In 1900–01 he and his wife, age 30, were living with his mother-in-law, Mary Preston, on Carnegie Street (on the north side of the river).

But Isaiah was a drunk and petty thief. In 1896 Isaiah was "SENT DOWN … was on Monday before the Police Magistrate on a charge of drunkenness. He was found guilty and fined $5 and costs or twenty days in the County jail. The funds were not forthcoming and he was consequently escorted to the public boarding house."[107] In 1897 "Isaiah Wright, the Coloured cook at the [Woodstock] jail was not visibly affected by the news of the death of his three months' old child in Ingersoll, says the *Sentinel-Review*. He still sings 'There'll be a hot time in the old town,' and there is not a happier prisoner in the jail than he."[108] In 1898 "Isaiah Wright and John Henderson were arrested Saturday night on a charge of stealing chickens from Mr. William Ireland. Isaiah appeared before the police magistrate this morning and was remanded until Friday."[109]

In October, 1905 Isaiah's dead body was found in the Thames River, near the Wonham Street Bridge, after he had been missing for a few days.[110] His wife Mary testified that he was a habitual drunk:

---

105. *Ingersoll Chronicle*, 9 May 1889; Ingersoll vital statistics, Schedule B, marriage registrations, 1889.
106. London vital statistics, Schedule B, marriage registrations.
107. *Ingersoll Chronicle*, 16 July 1896.
108. *Ingersoll Chronicle*, 30 September 1897.
109. *Ingersoll Chronicle*, 31 March 1898.
110. *Ingersoll Chronicle*, 5–6 October 1905; 8 March 1906; Ingersoll Cemetery Rural Burial Register, 26 September 1905.

Mrs. Wright, widow of the late Isaiah Wright, was the first and only new witness called. She last saw her husband alive three weeks ago last Friday, at a quarter to five in the afternoon, at the McMurray House. She made enquiries on the following day as to his whereabouts, but found no trace of him. On the second day of his disappearance she became alarmed. Her husband had sometimes gone away and stayed without telling her.

Cross examined by J.C. Hegler, witness said she had been married over ten years. Her husband drank and sometimes created trouble at home. It was no unusual circumstance for him to stay away a week or so without telling her where he was. He very seldom took any meals at home. He did not tell her where he was going when she last saw him. He had not been drinking up to the time she saw him that day.

Four of his drinking companions on the Wonham Street bridge were charged with his murder, but in March 1906, the judge at the Spring Assizes in Woodstock acquitted them all. No murder had occurred; rather it was death by misadventure:

> THE TRIAL ONLY LASTED TWO HOURS
> Crown Prosecutor did not ask for a Conviction
> IN WRIGHT MURDER CASE
> The Four Ingersoll Men Acquitted at Woodstock Last Night
> Ewart Bell, Geo. Dennis, Geo. Bower, and Thomas Wilson, all of Ingersoll, were tonight found not guilty on the charge of the murder of the late Isaiah Wright of Ingersoll, last September. The trial lasted two hours and purely circumstantial evidence was offered, leaving a very reasonable doubt of the agency of the prisoners. It was shown that Wright was on the bridge with the prisoners on the night of his last appearance alive, that they were all having a

good time, and that Wright, who was a habitual drunkard, was intoxicated. At least two of the prisoners were there after it was uncertain that Wright was on the bridge. However, the medical testimony was that a blow discovered on the back of the head was not sufficient to cause death, and might have been caused by Wright having fallen off the railing of the bridge, and striking his head, and the condition of the body, as shown in the post-mortem, was compatible with the theory that intoxication had caused unconsciousness, and that in this state he had fallen into the water while he was either dead or unconscious before reaching the water. Upon the evidence Crown Prosecutor Arnoldi of Toronto did not ask for a conviction. T.C. Robinette of Toronto and J.C. Hegler, K.C. of Ingersoll defended.

THE DEAD MAN.

CHAPTER EIGHT
Black-race Entertainment for Ingersoll Whites: In the Town Hall and in the Street

Nineteenth-century Ingersoll hosted a range of popular entertainments (concerts, theatre, public lectures, society meetings, excursions, processions). Among them were performances by Blacks which flattered fashionable White belief in White-race supremacy. Although popular, Black-race entertainments were something less than a craze. As reported below, the *Ingersoll Chronicle* advertised one or two of these events per year.

The events included indoor stage-minstrel shows, outdoor street-minstrel performances (*Darktown Fire Brigade*), *Jubilee Singers* concerts, theatre (*Uncle Tom's Cabin*), and standalone concerts (*Blind Tom, Black Pianist*). Touring American troupes brought these events to Ingersoll, and local troupes hosted a few (*Ingersoll Minstrels, Woodstock Minstrels* and *London Minstrels*).

These forms of Black-race entertainment evolved, and the literature describing them is rich, complex, and beyond the scope of this study. What follows is a brief, general guide to their performances in Ingersoll.

Minstrelsy

Minstrelsy staged comic variety shows that mocked practically everyone (ethnic groups, social climbers, rural and urban folk, southerners and northerners), not just Blacks. But it was racist as far as Blacks were concerned. The principal comedians in a show—typically White actors—posed as lower class African Americans, using blackface and dialect.[111] Their comic routines featured stereotyped depictions of Black Americans. There were a few minstrel troupes with Black actors, which one could identify by their use of one of three designations: "Georgia," "Coloured," and "Slave" (e.g., *Dave Picket's Coloured King's Players of Dixie*, in Ingersoll, 1899). "Negro" indicated Whites in blackface.[112]

Street Minstrelsy: The *Darktown Fire Brigade*

The *Darktown Fire Brigade* was a street minstrel show that depicted Negro firemen as comically incompetent buffoons. Whereas stage minstrelsy variety shows had many comic targets, *Darktown* performances in the street, with White actors in blackface, focused exclusively on mocking Blacks. On four occasions Ingersoll hosted *Darktown* performances: Dominion Day, 1890; Queen Victoria's Diamond Jubilee celebration, 22 June 1897; and the 24th of May Queen's Birthday celebrations, 1899 and 1910.

Jubilee Singers

During the 1870s African American *Jubilee Singers* performed slave-plantation sketches and songs, initially to raise money for cash-strapped Negro universities in Nashville and New Orleans. By the 1880s when their performances reached Ingersoll, however, they operated as independent for-profit entities.

Whereas minstrel shows presented Black culture as parody, *Jubilee Singers* framed it as Black pride—"Spiritual songs of slavery were 'genuine jewels' that Blacks brought from their bondage." Black religious

---

111. Tim Brooks, *The Blackface Minstrel Show in Mass Media: 20th Century Performances on Radio, Records, Film and Television* (Jefferson, NC: McFarland & Co., 2020), p. 11. Blackface was black makeup, usually burnt cork.
112. Cheryl Thompson, "Black Minstrelsy on Canadian Stages: Nostalgia for Plantation Slavery in the Nineteenth and Twentieth Centuries," *Journal of the Canadian Historical Association* volume 31, no. (2021), pp. 67–94.

harmony singing was a precursor of Gospel music.[113]

Three troupes of jubilee singers performed in Ingersoll: the *Original Nashville Students* (1883); the *New Orleans University Jubilee Singers* (1886); and the *Fisk University Jubilee Singers* of Nashville, Tennessee (1888).[114] Their performances highlighted Old-South plantation songs, of course. In its review of the 1886 concert of the *New Orleans Jubilee Singers*, however, the *Ingersoll Chronicle* highlighted solos of "Swanee River" and "Coming through the Rye"; the former had been written in 1851 by a White northerner who had never visited the South, and the latter was a Scottish song.

Uncle Tom's Cabin, Theatre Plays

Uncle Tom's Cabin (1852) was the best-selling novel in 19th-century America. It did not come from Black slave culture. Its author was a Northern-State White Abolitionist, Harriet Beecher Stowe. The book and the plays it inspired were powerful indictments of slavery, but they also helped to popularize negative stereotypes about Black people: "Uncle Tom," too eager to please White people; the "happy darky"; the light-skinned "tragic mulatto," comfortable in neither the White world or the Black world; the dark-skinned female "mammy"; and the "pickaninny" stereotype of black children.[115]

Uncle Tom theatre troupes staged four performances in Ingersoll (1879, 1880, 1893, and 1899). In 1900 a non–*Uncle Tom* troupe narrowly missed performing in Ingersoll:

---

113. Lynn Abbott, "'Do Thyself a' no Harm': The Jubilee Singing Phenomenon and the 'Only Original New Orleans University Singers,'" https://www.google.com/search?client=firefox-b-d&q=new+orleans+university+jubilee+singers; Graham, *Spirituals and the Birth*.
114. The cash-strapped Black universities in Nashville and New Orleans had been founded by the biracial, abolitionist American Missionary Society, which also had supported the Rev. Lewis C. Chambers, the Coloured pastor of the British Episcopal Methodist Church in Ingersoll during the early 1860s. The *Original Nashville Students*, who were neither students nor from Nashville, were an ensemble of eight or nine African American singers formed in Chicago in 1882. This troupe worked under the auspices of the Redpath Lyceum Bureau, a Boston organization devoted to adult education. See Graham, *Spirituals and the Birth*, ch. 4.
115. https://en.wikipedia.org/wiki/Uncle_Tom%27s_Cabin.

Thirty Coloured people struck the town Thursday morning with the intention of giving the performance "A Trip to Coon Town" in the Town Hall in the evening. No arrangements had been made by their representative for hotel accommodation and when the "professional people" arrived the rates of the hotels given them were too high for them and they left on the afternoon for Woodstock. Consequently the people did not have the pleasure of seeing their performance.[116]

Black Entertainments (Dates from *Ingersoll Chronicle*)	
23 October 1873	Minstrel, McAllister & Polley
2 April 1874	Minstrel, Benedict & Clark
23 September 1875	Blind Tom, Black Pianist
29 June 1876	Minstrel, Centennial
10 May 1877	Blind Tom, Black Pianist
2 January 1879	Uncle Tom's Cabin, Lottie Combination
13 May 1880	Uncle Tom's Cabin, Wilkinsons
8 June 1882	Minstrel, Duprez & Benedict
3 May 1883	Jubilee Singers, Nashville Students
4 June 1885	Minstrel, Woodstock Amateur Minstrels.
11 June 1885	Minstrel, Georgia Minstrels
23 December 1886	Jubilee Singers, New Orleans University
5 July 1888	Minstrel, San Francisco Minstrels
1 November 1888	Jubilee Singers, Fisk University
8 November 1888	Minstrel, Clark's Female Minstrels
14 February 1889	Minstrel. Woodstock Minstrels
3 July 1890	Minstrel, Darktown Fire Brigade
16 April 1891	Minstrel, London Minstrels
17 November 1892	Minstrel, Guy Brothers
23 February 1893	Uncle Tom's Cabin, Stowes Co.
4 May 1893	*Kaffir Choir from Africa*
26 November 1896	Minstrel, Guy Brothers
22 June 1897	Minstrel, Darktown Fire Brigade
30 March 1899	Uncle Tom's Cabin, Stetsons
13 April 1899	Minstrel, Dave Picket's Coloured
11 May 1899	Minstrel, Darktown Fire Brigade

116. *Ingersoll Chronicle*, 25 January 1900.

Black Entertainments (Dates from *Ingersoll Chronicle*)	
26 October 1899	*Minstrel, Ingersoll Minstrels*
10 May 1900	*Minstrel, Ingersoll Minstrels*
6 December 1900	*Minstrel, Guy Brothers*
26 May 1910	*Minstrel, Darktown Fire Brigade*

MINSTREL SHOW
(*Ingersoll Chronicle*, 23 October 1873)

The Town Hall has been engaged for tomorrow (Friday) by the *McAllister & Polley Minstrels* [unidentified] a company which comprises some first rate performers. The *Adrian Press* says of them: Their jests, sayings and actions are free from low vulgarisms so characteristic of shows of this kind, and every performance was in good taste. The end men did not overdo and the specialties were all first class. McAllister probably has no superior in his Ethiopian representations, and we pronounce the acrobatic dance of Wayne and Lovely the finest performance ever introduced by a troupe of this kind.

MINSTREL SHOW
(*Ingersoll Chronicle*, April 2, 1874)

Minstrels tonight. *Benedict & Clark's Minstrels* [unidentified] appear at the Town Hall tonight and will no doubt draw a large audience. The Company performed the other evening in Hamilton, and the *Times* of that city says of them: "The programme consists of musical selections from first class orchestra, comic songs, dances, and well-arranged special minstrel business which is presented in the most laughable manner possible. There is nothing in the performance that would offend the most fastidious."

"BLIND TOM," BLACK PIANIST
(*Ingersoll Chronicle*, 23 September 1875; 10 May 1877)

Thomas "Blind Tom" Wiggins (1849–1908) was an American pianist and composer who had been born into slavery in Georgia. In 1865 the United States abolished slavery. In 1866, at age 16, he began a European concert tour. In 1875 he began touring the United States and Canada.

[23 September 1875] The greatest musical prodigy of the age, the most marvelous musical genius living, will be in the Town Hall, Ingersoll, on Thursday evening next, 30th September. The wonderful Negro boy pianist, Blind Tom, the son of ordinary field hands, untutored and sightless from birth—his very soul overflowing with musical genius, is presented to a critically discriminating public as surpassing everything hitherto known in the world as a musical phenomenon. There is no art about him. God has given him a guide, but it is a silent one—that of Nature herself—unlike the great masters of the day, whose manipulations result from deep and unwearied study; his instruction comes from a Higher Power, and this philosophers are pleased to term genius, which enables him, without a knowledge of either language, to sing in German, French, and English, and without understanding a single rudiment of written music to compose gems of rare artistic ability, and to perform the most difficult operatic pieces, not only Brilliantly and Beautifully, but with all the correctness, purity of expression, skill and excellence of the most distinguished artist. He can execute three airs at once, each in a different key, and perform music correctly with his back to the instrument… Doors open at 7 o'clock. Commence at 8 P.M. Admission 50 cents, Children 25 cents. Reserved Seats 75 cents, Children 50 cents.

[10 May 1877] BLIND TOM, the Negro boy pianist, will be here in the town hall on Saturday the 19th inst. Those who have seen this great musical wonder will go again, and those who have not yet witnessed his wonderful performances should not fail to go.

"Blind Tom"

MINSTREL SHOW
Ingersoll Chronicle, 29 June 1876

CENTENNIAL MINSTRELS [unidentified]. This organization gave an entertainment in the Music Hall[117] last night and were received by a full house. Their performances gave good satisfaction. Morgan in his "Negro specialties" was very laughable. The singing of Messrs. McGraw and Lenihan were repeatedly encored. They have four end men and the company will no doubt meet with success on their tour.

117. Above Royal Hotel, east side of Thames St., south of St. Andrews Street.

UNCLE TOM'S CABIN
Ingersoll Chronicle, 2 January 1879

UNCLE TOM'S CABIN. The *Lottie Combination and 5th Avenue Theatre Company* [unidentified] played "Uncle Tom's Cabin" in the Town Hall here Monday evening last two a fair audience. The play was rendered exceedingly well.

UNCLE TOM'S CABIN
Ingersoll Chronicle, 13 January 1880

UNCLE TOM'S CABIN. The famous Wilkinsons[118] will appear at Town Hall, Ingersoll, for one night only, on Friday, May 14th, presenting their great specialty, "Uncle Tom's Cabin." Their success has been great in every part of the States. The press and people all pronounce their representation of "Uncle Tom's Cabin" unequalled by any company. General admission 25 cents. All coupon tickets 35 cents. Seats may be secured at Woodcock's Book Store. Referring to their *third* appearance in Syracuse the *Courier* says:— Critics have puzzled their brains a good deal to account for the wonderful vitality, the astonishing

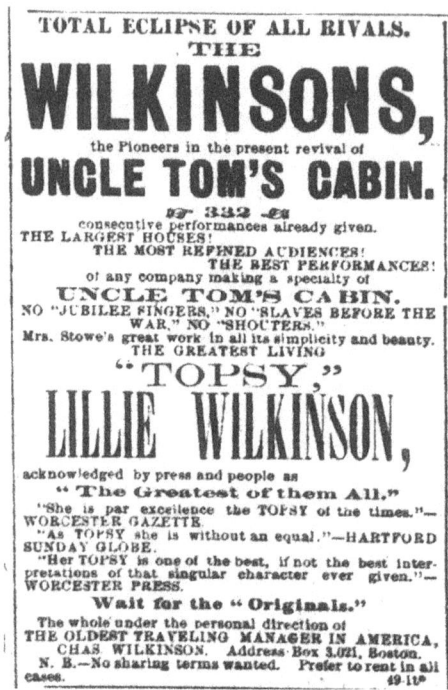

Charles Wilkinson (1830–1888) was a native of Connecticut. The Lillie in the poster was actually Leila Layton, born in England and Wilkinson's wife.

hold that the play of *Uncle Tom's Cabin* has upon the public. Year after

118. The Wilkinsons were New England Whites. https://nutfieldgenealogy.blogspot.com/2011/03/wilkinsons-in-theater-business.html.

year it is played, and always before crowded houses, when presented by good talent. But few women have made a reputation for themselves as actresses have gained any credit for themselves in the delineation of *Topsy*, the incorrigible wench of Mrs. Stowe's creation. Mrs. G.C. Howard and Lilly Wilkinson are about the only ones who have been able, year after year, to play this character to large and delighted audiences; and it is generally conceded that Miss Wilkinson stands at the head. Mr. Charles Wilkinson, the oldest travelling manager in America, will appear in his great specialty, Gumption Cute, as played by him in 1853. Georgia L. Fox, daughter of the late George L. Fox, will personate *Little Eva*, with Lillie Wilkinson as *Topsy*. The company embraces eighteen artists.

MINSTREL SHOW [American Blackface Troupe]
(*Ingersoll Chronicle*, 1 and 8 June 1882)

Town Hall, 6 June. *Duprez & Benedict's* Company of twenty-five minstrels gave first class entertainment in the Town Hall on Thursday evening to a large and appreciative audience, there being a large number of ladies present, a new feature in Ingersoll. The company is far ahead of the majority of smaller organizations travelling. Not one act or one word was said objectionable to any lady present.

JUBILEE SINGERS, THE NASHVILLE STUDENTS[119]
(*Ingersoll Chronicle*, 3 and 10 May 1883)

[3 May] This company of Negro plantation singers are advertised to appear in the Town Hall, Ingersoll, on Friday evening, May 11th. Its members, it is stated, were with one or two exceptions were all slaves. They appear in full plantation costumes in a new programme replete with jubilee singing, presenting plantation, social, river, and cabin

---

119. The Company were neither students nor from Nashville. The troupe was organized in Chicago in 1882 and operated under the auspices of the Redpath Lyceum Bureau of Boston, which promoted adult education.

songs. Following are three newspaper extracts from the large number before us:—

If you desire to see the darkey as he appears at home, upon the plantation, and his meetings, do not fail to attend one of the concerts given by the Original Nashville Students. —*Chicago Inter-Ocean.*

The Original Nashville Students, who are just closing a season of one month in this city, have been remarkably successful in giving a pleasing entertainment and in drawing crowded houses; and in the first place they give the most original and unique concert ever given by a jubilee party. —*Chicago Tribune.*

The Original Nashville Students who appear here this week are the sensation of the season. Their performance last night at the Opera House made such a hit that they were compelled to respond to eight encores before the audience was satisfied. We can only say that they are the most complete organization of this kind now on the road. —*Cincinnati Enquirer.*

[10 May 1883] THE NASHVILLE STUDENTS JUBILEE SINGERS. The entertainment given in the Town Hall by the Jubilee Singers on Tuesday evening was a musical treat. The concert was mostly a representation of the music of the coloured people of the south and is expressive of deep religious sentiment, while being odd and in quaint language. The rendition of the various songs and choruses were good, and the appearance of the singers in plantation costumes and the gestures of the different actors created great outbursts of laughter. There was only a fair sized audience, but everyone seemed pleased with the entertainment.

MINSTREL SHOW, WOODSTOCK AMATEUR MINSTRELS
(Ingersoll Chronicle, 4 and 18 June 1885)

[4 June] The *Woodstock Sentinel-Review* says that the amateur minstrels of that town are a 'treat to any audience as they are the most refined and talented minstrel company that ever appeared here.' *Woodstock Amateur Minstrels*. This company composed of 30 of Woodstock's young men will make their debut in Ingersoll at the Town Hall on Friday evening 12th inst. under the auspices of the Dufferin Lacrosse Club. They have played to crowded houses three different times in Woodstock and on the last occasion hundreds had to be turned away. Don't fail to see them.

[18 June] The *Woodstock Amateur Minstrels*, who appeared her under the auspices of the Dufferin Lacrosse Club in the Town Hall on Friday evening were greeted with a packed house, the ladies turning out in large numbers. The entertainment given was one of the best of the kind ever given here, and certainly far above the average professional minstrel troupes. They gave entire satisfaction and were heartily applauded.

MINSTREL SHOW
(Ingersoll Chronicle, 11 June 1885)

THE *GEORGIA MINSTRELS* [Black performers][120] were greeted with a packed twenty-five cent house, while the reserved seats were but sparsely occupied. The performers, with one or two exceptions, do not deserve to be ranked higher than third class, and the jokes and sets were do hoary-headed and bowed down with age that if our ancestor Noah had been present he would have recognized them as old acquaintances. The singing, too, was poor, but there were two sets that deserve praise, viz. the eccentric dancing of Tom Williams and the dancing of George Jackson.

Formed in Georgia in 1865, the original troupe comprised ex-slaves under a White owner/manager. Charles Callendar bought the troupe in 1872 and managed it into the 1880s. The words "Callender" and "Georgia" came to be synonymous with black minstrelsy, and the success of the Georgia Minstrels spawned numerous imitators.

JUBILEE SINGERS, NEW ORLEANS UNIVERSITY JUBILEE SINGERS
(Ingersoll Chronicle, 23 and 30 December, 1886; 6 and 13 January, 1887)

The Charles St. Methodist Church[121] here engaged the original university singers of New Orleans for next Wednesday evening, December 29th, on which occasion they will appear in the Town Hall in

---

120. https://www.jamesarsenault.com/pages/books/6350/a-schwabe-artist/the-original-georgia-minstrels?soldItem=true.
121. Formerly the Methodist Episcopal Church, 1841–84. Not to be confused with the Coloured British Methodist Episcopal Church, 1870–99.

one of their grand concerts. Prices of admission have been placed low to give everybody an opportunity of hearing this renowned company which is pronounced the first company of the character on the continent. Hear them and satisfy yourselves. They sing the plantation melodies in the original style. Seats now on sale at Richardson's jewelry store.

The *New Orleans Jubilee Singers* appeared in the Town Hall under the auspices of the Charles Street Methodist Church. On account of the [Ontario provincial] election excitement the audience was not as large as it would have been under ordinary circumstances. The current expression of opinion is that they are without exception the best company of Jubilee Singers that ever visited this town. The singing of Miss T[illie] Jones the leading Sopranoist was of the highest order. The rendition of "Swanee River," as was also "Coming through the Rye."[122]

All the members of the troupe distinguished themselves and every selection with the exception of two was encored. We are glad to announce that they are to return shortly.

6 January 1887. Coming Again

The *New Orleans Jubilee Singers*, that so delighted the audience in the Town Hall on the 29th Dec., are coming again next Monday evening. The programme will be entirely different from the last. This is the best company of Jubilee Singers on the continent, and strange to say their rates are the cheapest, tickets for reserved seats being only 35 cents. The solos given by Miss Jones, "Swanee River" and "Coming through the Rye," were worth the money alone the last time they were here. Their manager, Mr. Thomas, is to be congratulated upon securing a company of singers that are without exception star singers throughout. Be sure and hear the great bass soloist as well as Miss Jones. Reserved tickets at Harry Richardson's. Secure them at once as they are already in great demand.

122. Stephen Foster, a White northerner who had yet to visit the South, wrote "Swanee River" (a.k.a. "Old Folks at Home") in 1851. "Coming through the Rye" is a Scottish song.

[13 January 1887] The *New Orleans University Jubilee Singers* appeared in the Town Hall on Monday evening to a large audience. The singing was above the average.

JUBILEE SINGERS, FISK UNIVERSITY JUBILEE SINGERS[123]
(*Ingersoll Chronicle*, 1 and 15 November 1886)

[1 November] This well known company of sweet singers will give one of their concerts in the Town Hall on Thanksgiving evening, the 15th inst. They are at present in the east singing to crowded houses and are better than ever. Tickets for sale at H. Richardson's jewelry store at an early date.

[15 November] THE FISKS. Remember that the best concert of the season will be given tonight in the Town Hall by the Fisk University Singers. Admission to all parts of the hall, 50c.

JUBILEE SINGERS
(*Ingersoll Chronicle*, 12 August 1897)

Three Coloured vocalists delighted a number of our citizens on Tuesday

---

123. The above photograph of the original Fisk University Jubilee Singers (1872–78) is housed in the Fisk University Archives and in the collection of the Library of Congress.

night with their excellent rendering of several Negro melodies. They were splendid singers and possessed good voices which harmonized almost perfectly. They played their accompaniments on the guitar and mandolins.

MINSTREL SHOW, SAN FRANCISCO MINSTRELS
(*Ingersoll Chronicle*, 5 July 1888)

MINSTRELS [Blackface]. The *San Francisco Minstrels* performed at the Town Hall on Thursday night before a large audience. They have a fine band and excellent orchestra. The singing is good, that of the quartette particularly so, some very beautiful harmonies being produced. Caswell's xylophone solo, French's banjo specialties, Mather's clog dance, and Healey & Thompson's old Kentucky home character act, were all much applauded. Some of the dialogue was a little tame and tedious, but on the whole the show is quite as good as any need expect to see at this time of year. [Blackface]

MINSTREL SHOW, CLARK'S "FEMALE MINSTRELS"
A MISERABLE SHOW
(*Ingersoll Chronicle*, 8 November 1888)

Clark's "Female Minstrels and Arabian Nights Entertainment" [unidentified] appeared at the Town Hall Thursday night to a good house, and a more thoroughly disgusted crowd never left the hall at the conclusion of a performance. The company, which consists of three men, two fair variety stage singers and dancers—and six homely-looking females, the stickiest of sticks, gave a performance that would discredit to a Canal street concert saloon, when those institutions were in full blast. Whoever told those females in this company that they had talent for the stage should be prosecuted, and the females sent back to the scullery. With the exception of a song and dance and clog by the two female comedians, there was not a meritorious feature in the whole performance.

MINSTREL SHOW, WOODSTOCK AMATEUR MINSTRELS
(*Ingersoll Chronicle*, 31 January and 14 February, 1889)
FUN, WIT & MELODY

[31 January 1889] The *Dufferin Lacrosse Club* have arranged with the Woodstock Minstrel company to give a performance here on Thurs. evening Feb. 14th. A Woodstock *Sentinel-Review* reporter visited their rooms the other night and sat through a rehearsal. Speaking of the programme he says: "The choruses are taken by 35 well trained voices and are very effective. The orchestra consists of seven or eight pieces and there will be no defect in that department. There are six end men, three on each side, and they are all live men, not a stick among them. The customary 'gags' and repartees are indulged in; but in this case the gag business is not overdone, and the jokes are mostly original and local, without being insipid or offensive. Some of the choruses are exceedingly pretty; better than anything of the kind heard from professional minstrels. The first part concludes with a spectacular allegory, or stationary burlesque, or whatever you would like to call it, taken it is claimed from that marvelous spectacular affair, "The Fall of Rome," as produced by the Kiralfes of Staten Island, but certainly a unique and daring improvement on the original. The second part consists of vocal solos, quartettes and specialties. Of course it would never do to give the specialities away; but one of them may be hinted at. It is the funniest thing ever seen upon the stage. That is the mounted sword contest between two expert swordsmen, both of whose bodies, it may be remarked, afford ample scope for the operation of each other's weapon. With this is incorporated a Spanish bull fight by the same artists. If these don't bring down the house the fault will be with the house. Another feature is the female impersonation act of Mr. Hazelton, who dresses for the occasion with as much elegance as a lady for her first ball. But it is impossible to describe the many attractive features. They are all good. If you don't believe this go and see for yourself.

[14 February 1889] The hall was jammed full on Monday night with an audience desirous of hearing this company's performance. For amateurs it was good. Billy Farrell's club swinging and dancing and Lewis' specialty, "We'll have to mortgage this farm," being particularly worthy of mention. Miss Hazelton overdid things in his encore and spoilt the effect entirely. One pleasing feature of the entertainment which was not on the programme was the presentation of a very beautiful diamond ring to Mr. James F. McGachie by the Dufferin Lacrosse Club. After the curtain had dropped on the first part Mr. Hegler on behalf of the club came to the platform and called Mr. McGachie from among the company, and after a few complimentary remarks Mr. Vance presented him with the ring in recognition of the many services rendered by him to the lacrosse club. Mr. McGachie made as happy a reply as could be expected under the circumstances, thanking the boys for their handsome present... After the performance the Dufferins entertained the minstrels and guests to an oyster supper at the Atlantic House....

JUBILEE SINGERS, TENNESSEAN JUBILEE SINGERS
(*Ingersoll Chronicle*, 23 January 1890)

Will give one of their popular entertainments in the Town Hall on Thursday evening next.

MINSTRELS IN DOMINION DAY PROCESSION
(*Ingersoll Chronicle*, 26 June and 3 July 1890)
THE ORIENTAL PROCESSION[124]

[26 June] The Darktown Fire Brigade will give an exhibition of their skill in extinguishing a fire. Don't miss it.

[3 July] The first event of the day's programme was the procession of Orientals. It formed in the park and marched through the principal streets ... The procession was the best of its kind ever witnessed in this

---

124. *Ingersoll Chronicle*, 26 June 1890, p. 4, "And the Band Played Annie Rooney"; 3 July 1890, "A Grand Day's Sport ... the Orientals."

town. It was led by a band of Wild Western Cowboys ... followed by a dray containing the furniture to be given away in the evening to the person holding the lucky number, then followed the *Darktown Fire Brigade*...

The *Darktown Fire Brigade* was perhaps the best—at any rate they took first prize. They had a miniature house erected on a large dray, through the open doors of which could be seen the participants engaged in their household duties; a short distance in the rear followed the engine, hose reel, and firemen. As the procession approached the corner of King and Thames Streets, the house caught fire, the alarm sounded, and the alacrity with which the call was responded to would do credit even to the Ingersoll brigade themselves. The hooks and ladders were speedily on hand and the work of rescuing the inmates and extinguishing the flames was successfully accomplished. It was a thrilling exhibition and thoroughly enjoyed by the crowds that lines the streets...

Next in order of merit was the minstrel troupe [*The Original Comedy Company*] which captured the fifth prize. They were not the original Christies, but they no doubt acted their parts equally as well and created much amusement for the spectators by their comical antics and fantastic costumes.

MINSTREL SHOW, LONDON MINSTRELS
(*Ingersoll Chronicle*, 16 April 1891)

The I.A.A.A. [Ingersoll Amateur Athletic Association] have secured the *London Instrumental Minstrel Company* for a grand entertainment in the Town Hall tomorrow (Friday) evening. This is a first class company, and an enjoyable entertainment may be expected. Admission 25c and 50c. Seats can be reserved at Richardson's jewelry store.

MINSTREL SHOW, GUY BROTHERS [Blackface][125]
(*Ingersoll Chronicle*, 17 and 24 November 1892)

[17 November] GUY BROTHERS MINSTRELS. This excellent company will appear in the Town Hall on Tuesday evening next. This is said to be one of the best shows on the road and gives a refined entertainment.

Owen Sound Times Oct. 23 says:— "The Guy Bros. Minstrels performed in the Town Hall last night, and a larger crowd or better entertainment had not been in the hall for years. Standing room was at a premium before 8 o'clock. Hundreds were turned away, and to satisfy the crowd the company had to be persuaded to postpone and engagement and remain in Owen Sound another night. Every number on it was excellent. The songs were all splendid. The jokes were original and extremely funny. The stock drill and dancing was excellent. Venerson and McDonald in their horizontal bar performance were good, and their 'Chinese laundry' brought down the house. The Negro impersonation of Mr. W.H. Guy was excellent, and his dialect is perfect and his actions, taken all around were ludicrous. E.A. Pratin's violin selections and imitations were well received. Mr. H. McVey's club swinging was a fine feature of the program. Eddie McDonald, the contortionist, is superb. Some of his feats are simply wonderful. 'Save the pieces,' the concluding number in which the trick cottage is introduced is a perfect whirlwind of fun. The orchestra is one of the best ever heard here. Everything is refined, the course jokes in which some organizations delight being conspicuously absent." Town Hall, Ingersoll, Tuesday next. Seats on sale at Richardsons.

125. A story in the *New York Times* (13 June 1942, p. 15) reports the death of the last surviving member of the Guy Brothers troupe.

[24 November] GUY BROS. MINSTRELS. The above troupe appeared in the Town Hall in an old fashioned minstrel performance on Tuesday evening to a crowded house. The large audience expressed their appreciation of the entertainment by frequent and hearty bursts of applause.

KAFFIR CHOIR, AFRICA
(*Ingersoll Chronicle*, 4 May 1893)

A NOVEL ENTERTAINMENT. The most novel and interesting entertainment which has ever been given before an Ingersoll audience has been booked for Tuesday evening, May 16, at the Town Hall. The native African choir is the only Kaffir choir of its kind in the world and has appeared before Her Majesty Queen Victoria at Osborne.... They are now making for the first time a tour of Canada, and have been met with enthusiastic receptions in all of the large cities. They represent seven distinct African tribes, viz.: Amoxora, Fingo, Temba, Ropidi, Basanti, Zulu, and Cape. Their concert, in which they appear clad in the costumes of their ancestors, and go through the native dance and "warble their wood-notes wild," has proved very attractive, and all who are fond of beautiful harmony, sweet sounds, droll, rough musical periods, good humour and pathos, should not fail to hear them. They are appearing at only a few points in Ontario and are secured at large expense. In the City of Toronto they are to appear for three nights under a guarantee of twelve hundred dollars, and it is hoped that they will receive such a reception here as their merits should entitle them to.

[There was no mention of the show in the *Chronicle*'s 18 May issue.]

UNCLE TOM'S CABIN, STOWE'S UNCLE TOM'S CABIN CO.
(*Ingersoll Chronicle*, 23 February 1893)

Regarding the above company which will appear in the Town Hall tomorrow night, Mr. George T. Claris, manager of the St. Thomas Opera House says: *Stowe's Uncle Tom's Cabin Co.,* with a perfect cast, gave two performances at the Opera House here today. The receipts at the matinee were the largest—two to one—in the history of the house, and hundreds were turned away at night.

[There was no mention of the snow in the *Chronicle* for 2 March.]

MINSTREL SHOW, GUY BROTHERS [Blackface]
(*Ingersoll Chronicle*, 26 November 1896)

A large and appreciative audience greeted the appearance of *Guy Bros.* the old time favourites in the Town Hall Friday night. The entertainment was first class, the singing, dancing and specialties were up to date. The Guy Bros. have introduced a number of new specialties this year, which add materially to the show. The statuary work of the Guy Bros. is excellent and received much applause. The orchestra is second to none in the country and rendered sweet music.

MINSTREL SHOW, GUY BROTHERS [Blackface]
(*Ingersoll Chronicle*, 6 December 1900)

GUY BROTHERS MINSTRELS appeared in the Town Hall Monday night and gave their performance to a crowded house. The show is as good as in former years. The band music on the street at noon was much appreciated by a large crowd of citizens.

UNCLE TOM'S CABIN
(*Ingersoll Chronicle*, 30 March 1899)

STETSON'S BIG DOUBLE UNCLE TOM'S CABIN CO.[126] at the Town Hall on Tuesday evening of this week. Especial mention is deserved to the many pleasant specialties. The two Topsies are the best ever seen

---

126. White and Coloured musicians and drum majors, Coloured quartette, ca. 1895. https://www.jamesarsenault.com/pages/books/5493/stetson-s-big-double-uncle-tom-s-cabin-co-or-life-among-the-lowly-our-colored-corps-in-songs-and-dances?soldItem=true.

and are accomplished dancers. The *Lone Star Quartette* render some pleasant Negro melodies in a fine manner.

MINSTREL SHOW,
DAVE PICKETT'S COLOURED KING'S PLAYERS OF DIXIE[127]
(Ingersoll Chronicle, 6 and 20 April 1899)

[6 April] *Dave Pickett's Coloured King's Players of Dixie* were greeted with a full house in the Town Hall Monday night. The audience was made up of principally young men, and they thoroughly enjoyed the coon dancing and singing. Probably the best thing they put on is the trick and fancy banjo playing by D. Pickett.

[20 April] *Dave Pickett's Coloured King's Players of Dixie* and Cake Walkers were not so successful on their second appearance in Ingersoll at the Town Hall Thursday night. About a handful of people found

127. Ref. Dave Pickett's Negro Band Quartet & Comedy Company, "D" Index to African American Newspaper Articles, Grand Rapids Public Library, 1830–1935.

their way to the Town Hall and listened to their programme, which was a repetition of the one given here a few nights ago.

CAKE WALK[128]
(*Ingersoll Chronicle*, 9 and 23 January 1890)

There will be a grand concert and cake walk in the town hall on the 28th inst. All those who wish to spend an enjoyable evening should take it in. [also 23 January, 1890].

MINSTREL SHOW, INGERSOLL MINSTRELS
(*Ingersoll Chronicle*, 26 October 1899
and 25 January, 15 March, and 10 May 1900)

[26 October 1899] The *Ingersoll Minstrels* had an excellent practice Monday night, and are making good progress with the programme for their coming entertainment. The first part will be given in gorgeous military costumes and will consist of the very latest songs, jokes, and gags. Look for an evening of music, mirth and song when this great military aggregation make their appearance.

[25 January 1900] The *Ingersoll Minstrels* gave their performance in Salford Saturday night under the auspices of the Independent Order of Foresters Court in that place. The attendance was good considering the inclement weather, and those present showed their appreciation by frequent and enthusiastic applause.

[15 March 1900] The *Ingersoll Minstrels* intend giving another performance sometime next month. Everything will be completely new from the rise of the curtain on the first part until the last act in the olio. The music will be under the direction of A.L. McCarty, and he has received professional copies of all the very latest songs that are being used by

128. Cake walk: a dancing contest among African Americans in which a cake was awarded as a prize.

all the big minstrel shows. The jokes and gags will all be new, many of which will be local. Mr. McCarty corresponds with a number of professional friends and has all the gags etc., being used by Dumont's Minstrels of Philadelphia, which is a permanent organization in that city. The costumes will be all new and elegant, and the curtain will rise on the swellest First Part ever presented to an Ingersoll audience.

[10 May 1900]
THE INGERSOLL MINSTRELS SCORE ANOTHER SUCCESS AT THE TOWN HALL TUESDAY NIGHT. A BRIGHT AND PLEASING ENTERTAINMENT GIVEN BEFORE A LARGE AUDIENCE – MUSIC, MIRTH, AND JOLLITY REIGN SUPREME – THE SWELL COONS HAVE A HIGH OLD TIME, WHICH CONCLUDES WITH A GEORGIA CAKE WALK.

The third performance under the auspices of the Ingersoll Minstrels took place at the Town Hall Tuesday night [and] was the closing of the season. While the attendance was not quite as large as on previous occasions, the hall was well filled, and the entertainment was, if anything, better, and the large audience was exceedingly well amused throughout the evening.

For nearly half an hour prior to commencing the programme proper the Ideal Orchestra rendered choice music which was thoroughly enjoyed. This is an organization possessing the merit of excellence, and the music discoursed was harmonious and pleasing.

The first part consisted of the typical minstrel performance, consisting of songs, ballads, and choruses, and upon the rising of the curtain a very pretty scene presented itself. The burnt cork artists wore white costumes and were arranged in semi-circular and straight rows, with the interlocutor on a dais in the centre. The stage decorations were pure white, giving a most pleasing effect. The four end men, Messrs. Scoffin, Kay, McCarty, and McDonald, carried their parts like professionals, while their jokes were new and for the most part good. The soloists were Messrs. Joe McCarty, P.G. Kilborn, J.H. Murray, Alex McDonald, Chas. Phillips, N.E. McCarty, Chas. Scoffin, W.H. Price, Chas. Crooker, and Cliff Kay.

The olio consisted of selections by the male quartette, Messrs. Murray, Price, McCarty, and Crooker; cornet solo by J.H. Murray; an amusing exhibition by the shadowscope; trombone solo by Dell Mayberry' comicalties by McDonald and Scoffin, comedians, during which some excellent step dances were given by members of the company. Billy McLeod also gave a splendid exhibition of buck dancing. A.L. McCarty gave a clarinet solo in his well known style, after which came the grand cake walk. Three couples competed for the prize, which, so far as the audience could judge, was an elaborate affair. The grotesque actions of the dancers caused lots of merriment and made a fitting finale to a most meritorious entertainment. The cake was awarded to the couple receiving the most generous applause from the audience, and the honours appeared to be about qually divided between No. 2 and No. 3, the latter however winning. Master Lou Edwards made a very efficient drum major.

The entertainment was a most gratifying success, and we trust that this will not be the last time that the Ingersoll Minstrels will cater to the amusement of the public. The entire performance was given without a hitch, everything moving as clock work, and without any tedious delays between acts, as is too often the case with amateur entertainments.

Mr. F.P. Leake was the efficient stage manager and interlocutor, while Mr. A.L. McCarty was the capable music director. The committee of management was Messrs. C. Crooker, R.A. Hayden, N.E. McCarty, C. Scoffin, and C.L. Henderson.

THEATRE, A TRIP TO COON TOWN
(*Ingersoll Chronicle*, 25 January, 1900)

Thirty Coloured people struck the town Thursday morning with the intention of giving the performance "A Trip to Coon Town" in the Town Hall in the evening. No arrangements had been made by their representative for hotel accommodation and when the "professional people" arrived the rates of the hotels given them were too high for them and they left on the afternoon for Woodstock. Consequently the people did not have the pleasure of seeing their performance.

Street Minstrelsy: The *Darktown Fire Brigade*

The *Darktown Fire Brigade* was a street minstrel show that depicted Negro firemen as comically-incompetent buffoons. On four occasions, Ingersoll hosted *Darktown* performances: Dominion Day, 1890; Queen Victoria's Diamond Jubilee celebration, 22 June 1897; and the 24th of May Queen's Birthday celebrations, 1899 and 1910.

Brigade performances were popular with Ingersoll Whites when the Coloured population in town was becoming an historical memory. The Black Census population had shrunk from 150 in 1861 (6% of population) to 29 in 1911 (0.6% of population).

The *Darktown* theme was popularized in lithograph cartoons. As a 21st-century authority writes,

> The American printing firm Currier & Ives (1834–1907) produced *Darktown*, a lithographic series chronicling a fictional African American community. From the mid-1870s into the 1890s, Currier & Ives commissioned various illustrators to produce more than one hundred scenes of this fictional, segregated community that reinforced pervasive negative stereotypes about Black Americans—namely newly emancipated slaves—through caricature and inscriptions written in a highly exaggerated vernacular. The *Darktown* series captured nativist and racist attitudes that persisted after Reconstruction (1865–77), the period following the Civil War in which former Confederate states were

Blacks in a White Place: Ingersoll, Canada West and Ontario, 1850–1921

reintegrated into the United States. As states and localities in the American South began to implement Jim Crow laws, a White, middle-class audience collected these prints. Though Currier & Ives is most often associated with idyllic winter scenes and depictions of horseracing featuring White participants, the dehumanizing imagery of *Darktown* was among the firm's most popular—thousands of re-strikes from the original lithographic stones were issued by other publishers after the company liquidated in 1907.[129]

Following are two pages of a *Darktown* screenplay for street and indoor performances and two representative lithographic cartoons.

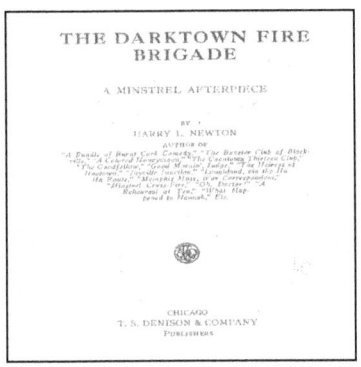

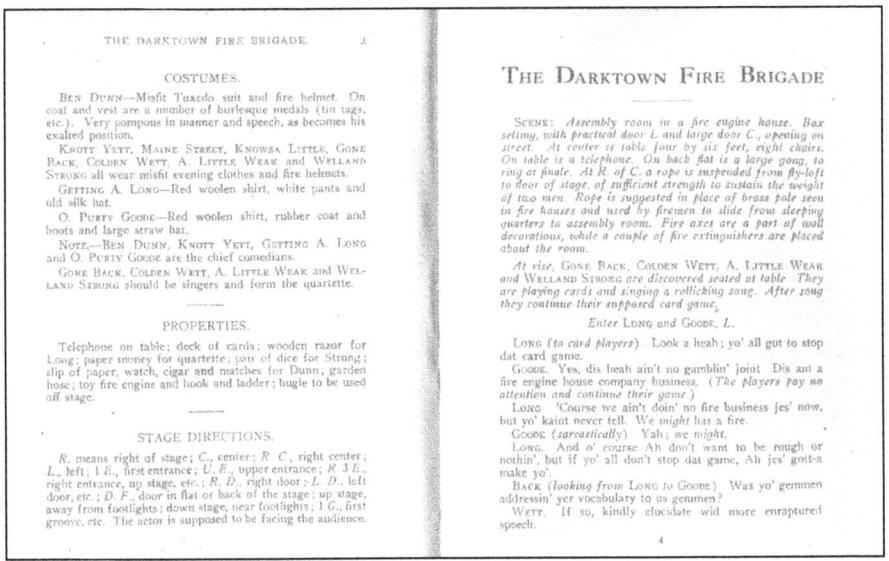

129. Clark Art Institute, Williamstown, Mass.

Two Currier & Ives prints from the *Darktown Comics* series, from 1887 (top) and 1888 (bottom). By 1884, the *Darktown Comics* series accounted for roughly one-third of the company's output.

Racist Advertising

Advertisement for Karn Pianos and Pipe Organs, D.W. Karn Co., Woodstock, 1903

D.W. Karn Co., located at 532 Dundas St., Woodstock. Founded in 1867 as the Woodstock Organ Factory. Renamed the D.W. Karn Piano & Organ Co., 1873. Dennis Karn was mayor of Woodstock in 1889. In 1896, S.R. Warren and Son Organ Company of Toronto bought out Karn. In 1901 Dennis Karn retired.[130]

---

130. https://woodstocknewsgroup.weebly.com/karn-organ-and-piano.html.

Depicting Negroes as Buffoons apparently was acceptable advertising in Ingersoll during the 1880s. John Russell was proprietor of the Ingersoll Foundry and Agricultural Works, near the northeast corner of Charles and Thames Streets, during the years 1881–86.[131] *(Image courtesy of the Ingersoll Cheese and Agricultural Museum)*

Late Nineteenth and Early Twentieth Century Appearances of the *Darktown Fire Brigade*

1897. The *Darktown Fire Brigade* at the Queen's Diamond Jubilee Celebration in Ingersoll, 22 June

(*Ingersoll Chronicle*, 24 June 1897)

Great interest centred in the exhibition of the *Darktown Fire Brigade*, and certainly it was the funniest thing that occurred during the day. An old house on the town square inhabited by a family of darkies in some mysterious manner caught fire (probably from the chimney). The fire alarm was rung immediately, but before the gallant brigade responded the unfortunate family had succeeded in recuperating most of the fur-

---

131. John Russell of Hamilton and William Russell of Dundas purchased the business from Thomas Brown & Co. "30 to 50 hands to be employed," *Ingersoll Chronicle*, 17 November 1881, "The Ingersoll Foundry"; *John Russell & Co. Catalogue*, Ingersoll, 1883; *Ingersoll Directories*, 1881, 1883–84, 1885–86.

niture. Just then the company came up and after "due delay" had two splendid streams of water about a foot in length playing on the fire and the darkies generally, from their engine, which looked like a water barrel and a couple of pumps to the uninitiated spectators. In spite of the bravest efforts of the firemen, spurred on as they were by the Chief and his speaking-trumpet, the palatial residence was totally destroyed by fire. One of the unfortunate family [members] was compelled to leap from an up stair window to escape the flames, and when he dropped into the net, ready for him in the street below, one of the company let his corner fall, and the rescued man came heavily to the ground. Was uninjured. By regrettable oversight the insurance policy was allowed to run out the day before and so the building was a total loss.

> 1899. The *Darktown Fire Brigade*, Ingersoll, Queen's Birthday
> (sponsor: Ancient Order of Foresters)
> DARK TOWN FIRE BRIGADE. WILL BE A FEATURE OF OUR QUEEN'S
> BIRTHDAY CELEBRATION
> (*Ingersoll Chronicle*, 11 and May and 1 June 1899)

The committee have made arrangements with the DARK TOWN FIRE BRIGADE to give an exhibition at 11 a.m. ...

Those who witnessed the comical antics of the brigade when in parade here a few years ago will be delighted at the opportunity to see the gentlemen of colour once more.

[18 May 1899] The Dark Town Fire Company erected their house on Wednesday evening.

The Dark Town Fire Brigade will give their exhibition on the vacant lot in front of the Noxon works where everyone can have a good view...

Don't miss the Dark Town Fire Brigade exhibition at 11 o'clock. Their exhibition is alone worth coming to see. Synopsis of their programme: House to Let—The application of a tenant—The arrival of a family and household furniture—The putting of the house to rights—The young people engage in plantation songs and dances—The explosion of a lamp causing a fire—The Dark Town Brigade to the rescue—Narrow escape of occupants—The rescue—The Brigade on parade.

[1 June 1899] The *Darktown Fire Brigade* was the main attraction of the morning, and for upwards of two hours they held the attention of an immense audience. Shortly after nine o'clock the 'happy family' moved to their new place of abode, a dwelling for their convenience having been erected on the vacant lot just north of the C.P.R. depot. The 'moving act' created a great deal of amusement, as did also the antics of the 'coons' during the time that elapsed prior to the 'fire scene.'

Shortly after eleven o'clock the shanty caught on fire, the alarm sounded, and in an incredibly short space of time the 'Darktown Fire Brigade' arrived on the scene with their engine and hook and ladder apparatus, and with great bravery rescued the inmates from their perilous position, many of whom had hair-breadth escapes. Some of the onlookers in their eagerness to see all that was going on got too close to the burning building and got pretty well drenched by the hosemen of the brigade who apparently had great difficulty in controlling the nozzle, owing no doubt to the powerful stream that was thrown. The act was very funny and was greatly enjoyed by the hundreds of spectators present.

1910. "Aunt Hattie" and the *Darktown Fire Brigade*, Ingersoll, Victoria Day (Caledonian Society)
VICTORIA DAY IN INGERSOLL, DARK TOWN FIRE BRIGADE
(*Ingersoll Chronicle*, 26 May 1910)

The next attraction was the exhibition by the Dark Town Fire Brigade. The scene of the conflagration was a small cabin, of Virginia style, on

King Street east near the tannery. Shortly after the crowd had congregated flames broke out in the roof of the cabin and above their crackling could be heard the cries of the frantic inmates. The alarm was sounded at the fire hall, and the "Dark Town Fire Brigade" responded. Their run was neither spectacular [n]or thrilling, while their fire fighting appliances would have been considered ancient many years ago. The life-saving net consisted of a large roll of fine wire. They arrived on the scene just as the occupants of the cabin were in great danger of 'perishing.' For a few minutes some 'heroic' work was witnessed, and eventually all of the occupants of the house were rescued. The exhibition was of the true burlesque nature and afforded a great deal of amusement for old and young.

Darktown Fire Brigade, Ingersoll, 24 May 1910

A postcard describing the Victoria Day proceedings includes a reference to "Aunt Hattie," the subject of an earlier chapter in this book. "Aunt Hattie" was still alive and living in Ingersoll in 1910; she did not

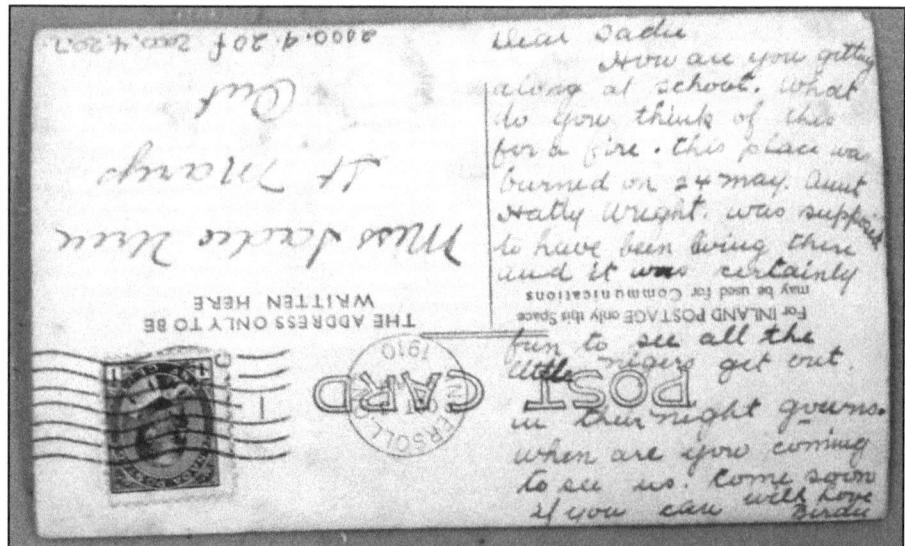

die until three years later, in 1913, though her house had burnt down in 1886. The message on the back of the postcard reads: "What do you think of this [i.e., the image on the previous page] for a fire. This place was burned on 24 May. Aunt Hatty [sic] Wright was supposed to have been living there and it was certainly fun to see all the little nigers [sic] get out in their night gowns."

Conclusion

- Blacks first came to the Ingersoll area about 1857. Their population peaked during the early 1860s at some 200, but fell into decline during and after the 1880s. The peak census population (1861) was 6% of the Town population and 3% of population in the Ingersoll area (the Village and its contiguous townships).
- A quest for jobs underlay the influx of Blacks to Ingersoll before and during the American Civil War years. Beginning in the 1880s, the rise of job markets in great cities caused job-seeking Blacks to bypass small places such as Ingersoll.
- Conversely, the history of Ingersoll Blacks was not primarily about runaway slaves, White abolitionist heroes, and the Underground Railway. By Wayne's estimates, four Blacks in five entering Canada from the United States were Free Blacks, not runaways. On entering Canada, even fugitives (under American law) became immigrants (under Canadian law)—runaways no longer unless they returned to the United States before the abolition of American slavery in 1865.
- Pre–Civil War Blacks in Ingersoll differed from local Whites; Blacks were more heavily male; more of them were illiterate; more of them had been born in the United States.
- Blacks differed culturally from Whites, as evidenced in their preference for Coloured institutions, religious practices, and their Negro dialect. White racism reinforced racial separateness in Ingersoll.
- Ingersoll Whites found local Blacks to be peculiar, amusing, primitive, and in some cases unhygienic and bad smelling. They patronized entertainments that featured unflattering Black stereotypes.

- Relations between Blacks and Whites in Ingersoll were sometimes abrasive, with street fights and in one instance a White race riot.
- Yet the documentary record does evidence instances of Black-White cordiality, notably prominent White support of Black cake walk concerts put on by the financially distressed BMEC congregation during the 1880s and 1890s.
- Local histories of Ingersoll Blacks have been false narratives, expressing the racial bias of White supremacy and small-town local boosterism. For that very reason, they are rich source materials for understanding Ingersoll's historical memory of 19th-century Blacks—which has become problematic in our 21st-century times.

APPENDIX A
Counting Blacks in Censuses, 1852–1921

Seven of the eight censuses undertaken during the period of study collected information about "Race." However, the questions put to the people changed from Census to Census, and published statistics tallied from the manuscript Census are problematic.

Appendix A navigates shortcomings in manuscript censuses to obtain a statistical profile of Blacks in Ingersoll for the Censuses of 1852, 1861, 1871, 1881, 1901, 1911, and 1921. The 1891 Census did not ask a question about Race. Some enumerations asked questions about literacy (over 20, *can't read, can't write*); and some did not (1852, 1881). The 1842 manuscript Census (for heads of households) is not extant for Oxford County. The 1852 manuscript Census is not extant for North Oxford Township.

Documentary Sources of Information in Census Enumerations

Schedules of Questions and Printed Forms Issued to Enumerators

The Government Census Office designed the Census *schedules* which contained the questions put to individuals in the population. As the office acknowledged in 1871, "the questions put cannot embrace everything of interest, but must, on the contrary, be limited to matters of leading importance to the whole Dominion. There are even many matters of general interest, which must be omitted, as well because of the intricacies they present, as of the necessity there is to limit the number of the questions asked."

The enumerators, one for each Census sub-district, received printed forms with the scheduled questions on which to record the responses of individuals. The printed forms, when completed by the enumerator, constitute the *manuscript Census. Published statistics* are the tallies by Census officials in Ottawa of information in the manuscript Census.

Each first page of printed forms for the 1861 manuscript Census records the responses of 50 individuals. Below are listed the first 11 questions on page one of the printed forms:

Column 1.   Name of inmates
Column 2.   Profession, trade or occupation
Column 3.   Place of birth
Column 4.   Religion
Column 5.   Residence if out of limits
Column 6.   Age next birthday
Column 7.   Sex: male
Column 8.   Sex: female
Column 9.   Married or single
Column 10. Coloured persons—Negroes
Column 11. Indians, if any
[… etc.]

The Government Census Office issued "Instructions to the Enumerators" to detail how responses to the scheduled questions were to be recorded. The instruction for the 1901 variable, "racial or tribal origin," for example, directed that *"only pure whites will be classed as whites."*

The instructions stated when the enumeration was to commence (e.g., 14 January in 1861; 2 April in 1871). The information collected was for *Census Day*, the day preceding the start of the enumeration.

Census Districts, Census Sub-Districts, and Divisions

- *Counties* were Census *Districts* before Confederation. Thus, *Oxford County* was a Census district.
- *Electoral Districts* of the House of Commons were Census *Districts* after Confederation. Thus, Oxford County held two Census Districts, *Oxford North* and *Oxford South*.[132]
- *Municipalities* (Ingersoll Town, West Oxford Township, etc.) were Census *Sub-Districts*.
- A *Sub-District* was divided into *Divisions*, one for each enumerator. Between 1881 and 1921 the County population declined from 50,154 to 46,172, but the number of Divisions soared, from 31 to 92; ergo the mean population per enumerator dropped from 1,618 in 1881 to 509 in 1921.

Persons to be Enumerated (the Enumerator's Instructions)

- **In 1861 it read:** "In the first column you will enter the name of every person who sojourned in each house, on the night of Sunday, the 13th of January, as well as members of the family who are temporarily absent, but whose usual residence it is."
- **In 1871 and 1881 it read:** "The principle adopted for the registration of the population is that which is called by statists the ... *population de jure*; that is the population legally *domiciled* within the territory of the Dominion, and including all persons who may be temporarily absent from their place of abode, whether at the fisheries, at sea, or in the forest wilderness. All persons are to be registered in the province and particular locality in which their home, family dwelling, or place of abode is situated, although they may happen to be in other parts of the Dominion. ..."

---

132. After John A. Macdonald's drastic redistribution of ridings in 1882, municipalities in the Oxford ridings no longer corresponded with county boundaries. See George Emery, *Principles and Gerrymanders: Parliamentary Redistribution of Ridings in Ontario, 1840–1954* (Montreal and Kingston: McGill-Queen's University Press, 2016).

Census by Census Appraisal of the Data for Blacks, 1852–1921

1852 Census, Canada West

Census Day was Sunday, 11 January 1852—exactly one year later than was normal for an 1851 Census, which is how Library and Archives Canada treats it.

Relevant Question on the Census Schedule: Column 10. "Coloured persons—Negroes."

Column 1. Names of inmates
Column 2. Profession, trade or occupation
Column 3. Place of birth.
Column 4. Religion
Column 5. Residence if out of limits
Column 6. Age next birthday
Column 7. Sex: male
Column 8. Sex: female
Column 9. Married or single
Column 10. Coloured persons—Negroes

Enumerator's Instruction: "Cols. 10 & 11—You will at once apprehend by the term 'Coloured persons,' is meant 'Negroes.' Column 11 asks: Indians if any.

- The manuscript Census for North Oxford Township is not extant.
- The manuscript Census page with Column 10 (*Coloured persons—Negroes*) is not on microfilm.
- Thomas S. Shenston, county clerk and census commissioner for Oxford County, published the number of Blacks that were enumerated in the County. The count was zero for Ingersoll Village and its contiguous townships.

1861 Census, Canada West

Census Day was Sunday, 13 January 1861. The American Civil War began in April 1861.

Relevant Question on the Census Schedule: Column 13: "Coloured, Mulatto, Indian."

Enumerator's Instruction: "In this column mark a figure (1) [for] every Coloured person's name, i.e. Negro or negress. If Mulatto, mark M after his or her name—thus, (1) M; and if Indian, mark Ind."

The Manuscript Census is reasonably complete and reliable for the Race question.

The Published Statistics are low and unreliable. The published total for Oxford County is 281; the count from the manuscript Census is 551. The problem arises from sloppy tallies by clerks and supervisors in the government Census Office.[133]

1871 Census, Ontario

Census Day: 2 April 1871.

Relevant Question on the Census Schedule: Column 13: "Origin" (replaces the 1861 Census Column 13: "Coloured, Mulatto, Indian")

Enumerator's Instruction: "Column 13. Origin is to be scrupulously entered, as given by the person questioned; in the manner shown in the specimen schedule, by the words English, Irish, Scotch, *African*, Indian, German, French, and so forth."

Published statistics for African origin in Oxford County are equal to 99% of the persons reported as African in the Manuscript Census. Thus, in contrast to the 1861 Census experience, the clerks in the Census Office gave reliable tallies for "African" in the manuscript Census.

1881 Census, Ontario

Census Day: 4 April 1881.

---

133. Michael Wayne, "The Black Population of Canada West," pp. 465–85.

Relevant Question on the Census Schedule: Column 13: "Origin" (unchanged from 1871)

Enumerator's Instruction (unchanged from 1871):

Column 13. Origin: "Indicated by a country name which might be different from the country of birth."

"Column 13. Origin is to be scrupulously entered, as given by the person questioned; in the manner shown in the specimen schedule, by the words English, Irish, Scotch, *African*, Indian, German, French, and so forth."

No question for "Read and Write."

Manuscript Census. "Origin" proved to be an ambiguous question in 1881. Inmates in the hundreds gave "Canadian" or "American" as their "Origin." Nothing in the enumerators' instructions proscribed such entries (presumably covered by "and so forth"). Oxford County's "Africans" were among those who used the new terms.

Thus, published statistics for "African" origin captured just 58% (158 of 273) of "Africans" who were enumerated in Oxford County. The published tallies missed Blacks who gave their "Origin" as "Canadian" or "American," but who

- had been enumerated as "African" in the 1871 Census, and/or
- in the 1881 Census, were flagged as "Coloured" in the column for the enumerator's comments.
- Or in the 1881 Census were listed as B.M.E.C. in Religion.

Examples:
- Ingersoll, 103 Blacks, of which 30 gave their origin as "American."
- Oxford North Township: all 5 Blacks (by my count) gave their origin as "American."
- Dereham Township, 30 Blacks (my count). Of these, 20 gave their origin as "Canadian" (8 cases) or "American" (12 cases).
- Norwich South Township, 68 Blacks (my count). Of these, 47 re-

ported their origin as "American" (34 cases), "Ontario" (8 cases); one "West Indies" (1 case) and "don't know" (3 cases). Ten heads of households were reported as "Coloured" in the column for the enumerator's "comments."

1891 Census, Ontario: No Information about "Race"

Census Day: 6 April 1891.

Relevant Questions on the Census Schedule: None.

The 1891 Census schedule does not ask about "colour" (as in 1852, 1861, and 1901) or "Origin" (as in 1871, 1881, 1901, 1911, and 1921).

Microfilm copy of the enumerators' returns for 1891 is incomplete. The published Census reports Ingersoll's population at 4,573; the count from microfilm copies is 1,553 (33% complete).

Census Statistics for Blacks in 1891: None exist.

There are questions for "Read and Write."

1901 Census, Ontario

Census Day: 31 March 1901.

Three Relevant Questions on the Census Schedule:

- Column 5: "Colour"
- Column 14: "Racial or Tribal Origin"
- Column 15. Nationality

Enumerator's Instruction for Column 5: "Colour": "The races of men will be designated by the use of 'w' for white, 'r' for red, 'b' for Black and 'y' for yellow. The whites are, of course, the Caucasian race, the reds are the American Indian, the Blacks are the African or Negro, and the yellows are the Mongolian (Japanese and Chinese). *But only pure whites will be classed as whites;* the Children begotten of marriages between whites and any one of the other races will be classed as red, Black or yellow, as the case may be, irrespective of the degree of colour.

Enumerator's Instruction for Column 14: "Racial or Tribal Origin": "*Among whites* the racial or tribal origin is traced through the father, as in English, Scotch, Irish, Welsh, French, German, Italian, Scandinavian, etc. ...A person whose father is English, but whose mother is 'American' or 'Canadian' in a racial sense, as there are no races of men so called [American, Canadian]. 'Japanese,' 'Chinese' *and* '*Negro*' are proper racial terms [for non-whites]; but in the case of Indians the names of their *tribes* should be given, as 'Chippewa,' 'Cree,' etc. Persons of mixed white and red blood—commonly known as 'breeds'—will be described by addition of the initial letters 'f.b.' for French breed, 'e.b.' for English breed, 's.b.' for Scotch breed and 'i.b.' for Irish breed.

The published statistics were tallied for Column 14, "Racial or Tribal Origin," only. The manuscript statistics for Column 5, "Colour," were not used.

Published Statistics. For Oxford County, the published tally for "Racial Origin" missed 8% of the unpublished tally for "Coloured" in Column 5. The undercounts were for

- Ingersoll (8 cases). The incorrect entries were "English," 5 cases; "French," one case; and "not known," 2 cases.
- South Norwich (13 cases). The incorrect entries were "German," 10 cases; "English," 4 cases; no data, 1 case.

1911 Census, Ontario

Census Day: 1 June 1911.

Relevant Question on the Census Schedule: Column 14 (Racial or Tribal Origin).

The variable "Colour" is discontinued. The variable "Nationality" (Column 15) is continued as a home for entries such as "Canadian" and "American," but the enumerators' instruction did not explicitly proscribe them for "Racial Origin."

Enumerator's Instruction for Column 14: "Racial or Tribal Origin": The racial or tribal origin, column 14, is usually traced through the father, as in English, Scotch, Irish, Welsh, French, German, Italian, Danish, Swedish, Norwegian, Bohemian, Ruthenian, Bukovinian, Galician, Bulgarian, Chinese, Japanese, Polish, Jewish, etc. A person whose father is English but whose mother is Scotch, Irish, French or other race will be ranked as English, and so with any of the others. In the case of Indians the origin is traced "through the mother, and names of their tribes should be given, as 'Chippewa,' 'Cree,'" etc. *The children be-gotten of marriages between white and Black or yellow races will be classed as Negro or Mongolian, (Chinese or Japanese) as the case may be.*

(Oxford County "Africans" were generally recorded as such. An exception was four Ingersoll Africans who gave their Racial Origin as "Canadian.")

1921 Census, Ontario

Census Day: 1 June 1921.

Relevant Question on the Census Schedule: Column 21 (Racial or Tribal Origin).

Enumerator's Instruction for Column 21: The racial or tribal origin is usually traced through the father, as in English, Scotch, Irish, Welsh, French, German, Italian, Danish, Swedish, Norwegian, Bohemian, Ruthenian, Bukovinian, Galician, Bulgarian, Chinese, Japanese, Polish, Jewish, etc. A person whose father is English but "whose mother is Scotch, Irish, French or other race will be ranked as English, and so with any of the others. In the case of Indians the origin is traced through the mother, and names of their tribes should be given, as 'Chippewa,' 'Cree,' etc. *The children begotten of marriages between white and Black or yellow races will be classed as Negro or Mongolian (Chinese or Japanese), as the case may be. The words Canadian" or "American" must not be used for this purpose, as they express "Nationality" or "Citizenship" but not a "Race or people."*

For the first time the enumerator's instructions for "origin" (1871–1921) specified that "Canadian" and "American" were terms for nationality, not Race.

The published tallies for Oxford County Negroes generally accord with tallies calculated from the manuscript Census, but with one curious exception. The published count for Woodstock was 45; despite four sweeps of the manuscript Census, the writer found only 33.

APPENDIX B
Michael Wayne's Interpretation

Source: Michael Wayne, "The Black Population of Canada West on the Eve of the American Civil War," *Histoire Sociale/Social History*, vol. 28, no. 56 (1995, November).

- Of 17,053 Blacks, 9,806 (57%) stated "US" as their place of birth, and 6,906 (40%) stated "Canada West."
- 744 US-born Blacks reported a particular US state for place of birth; of these 521 (70%) came from Slave States.
- Some Slave-State Blacks were *free*, not slaves. In Wayne's sample, 83% of the 521 Slave-State Blacks came from Maryland, where 49.5% of Blacks were free; Virginia, 10.6% were free; and Kentucky, 4.5% free. In Slave States, moreover, free Blacks could exit to Canada more easily than slaves.
- Historians estimate that 75–80% of runaway slaves were men. "Men were more likely than women to have opportunities to travel beyond the plantation and to learn to read and write; women were less likely to be sold away from their children and as a result had arguably stronger emotional ties to their family."
- Thus, if all 521 Slave-State Blacks were fugitives, then from 390.8 to 416.8 (75–80%) would have been men.
- Of the 521, however, just 324 (62%) were men. Thus, "simple algebra establishes that only 49 per cent of Blacks from the Southern States were runaway slaves while 51 per cent were free."[134]

---

134. Wayne, "Black Population of Canbada West," p. 474 and n. 26. "Let x equal the number of females from the South who were fugitive slaves and y the number of females who were free. Then $x + y = 197$ (the total number of women indicating they had been born in the slave states). Similarly, $3x + y = 324$ (the total number of men indicating they had been born in the

- By extension to 17,053 Blacks in Canada West, 6,864 of (70%) 9,806 US-born Blacks were from Southern States, and of these 3,363 (49%) were fugitives. This represented 19.7% of all 17,053 Blacks in Canada West.

Wayne discusses considers what might qualify his estimates, such as the probable under-enumeration of Blacks in the Census.[135] However, his estimates are sufficiently robust to uproot conventional wisdom. Fugitives and their children were not 75% of Canada West's Black population; 30 to 40%, he judges, is more reasonable.

---

slave states), since it is assumed that males represented three out of every four runaways and that free men and women came to Canada West in more or less equal numbers. Solving for x and y allows us to determine the percentage of Blacks who were fugitives." For the "simple algebra," see below.

135. Wayne judges that undercounts miss up to 20% of Blacks in some United States communities; see Wayne, "The Black Population of Canada West," pp. 469–70.

Elaboration of Wayne's "Simple Algebra" (courtesy Jamie Emery).

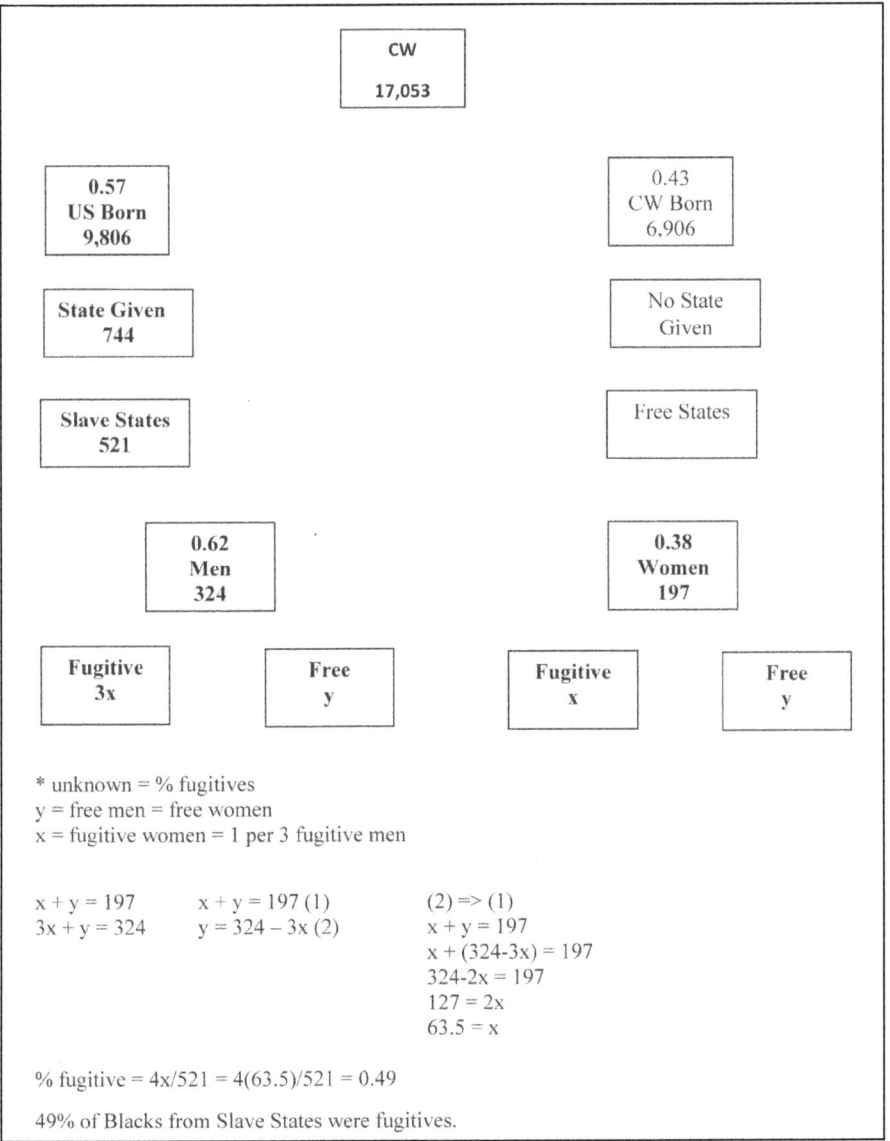

APPENDIX C
Ingersoll and Township Blacks Enumerated in Censuses, 1861–1921

Ingersoll 1861

Number of Blacks: 150. Number of Whites in Black Households: 5.

Family Name	First Name	Age	Birth-place	Religion	Married	Profession	Race
Arnhous	Bluher	22	USA	E Meth		labourer	Black
Beuford	John	41	USA	E. Meth		gunsmith	Black
Bedford	Alexander	12	CW	E. Meth			Black
Bevens	Washington	50	USA	E. Meth	M	labourer	Black
Bevens	Maria	45	USA	E. Meth	M		Black
Bevens	Irene	6	CW	E. Meth			Black
Brice	Anna M.	50	USA	E. Meth	M		Black
Brice	Charles	49	USA	E. Meth	M	labourer	Black
Brice	Joshua	23	USA	E. Meth		labourer	Black
Brice	Caleb	22	USA	E. Meth		labourer	Black
Brice	Washington	19	USA	E. Meth			Black
Brice	Mathew	14	USA	E. Meth			Black
Brice	Charles	12	USA	E. Meth			Black
Brice	Mordicai	10	USA	E. Meth			Black
Brice	Mary C.	8	CW	E. Meth			Black
Bryce	Joshua	23	USA	W. Meth		porter	Black
Bryce	Washington	21	CW	Baptist		waiter	Black
Buck	Jacob	24	CW	E. Meth			Black
Butler	Peter	37	USA	Baptist	M	plasterer	Mulatto
Butler	Ellen	34	USA	Baptist	M		Mulatto
Carter	Jane	39	USA	Baptist	M		Mulatto
Carter	John	37	USA	Baptist	M	labourer	Black
Carter	Charles	13	USA	Baptist			Black
Darnell	James	36	USA	E Meth	M	barber	Black
Darnell	Rachel	21	USA	E Meth	M		Mulatto

Family Name	First Name	Age	Birth-place	Religion	Married	Profession	Race
Davis	Daniel	24	USA	Meth	M	labourer	Black
Davis	Rebecca	23	USA	Meth	M		Black
Davis	Martha J.	2	CW	Meth			Black
Diggens	John	29	USA	E Meth	M	labourer	Black
Diggens	Mary	24	USA	E Meth	M		Mulatto
Diggens	Julia	5	CW	E Meth			Mulatto
Diggens	Benjamin	3	CW	E Meth			Mulatto
Diggens	Mary T.	1	CW	E Meth			Mulatto
Duke	Henry	33	USA	E Meth	M		Black
Duke	Grace	32	USA	E Meth	M		Mulatto
Duke	John Wesley	19	USA	E Meth			Mulatto
Graham	Wm Henry	35	USA	Baptist	M	labourer	Mulatto
Graham	Adeline	29	USA	Baptist	M		Mulatto
Graham	Eliza	5	CW	Baptist			Mulatto
Graham	Mary	3	CW	Baptist			Mulatto
Graham	Martha	1	CW	Baptist			Mulatto
Grayham	Emeline	26	USA	Baptist	M		Black
Grayham	Caledonia B.	7	USA	Baptist			Black
Green	Preston	30	USA	Meth	M	labourer	Black
Green	Mary	29	USA	Meth	M		Black
Hubbard	Henson	25	USA	Baptist	M		Black
Hubbard	Hannah A.	22	USA	Baptist	M		Black
Hubbard	Lewis G.	4	CW	Baptist			Black
Harden	Charles	40	USA	E. Meth	M		Black
Harden	Mary	22	USA	E. Meth	M		Black
Harper	Charity	44	USA	E. Meth			Black
Henderson	Susannah	24	USA	E. Meth	M		Black
Henderson	Charles	6	CW	E. Meth			Black
Henderson	Rheuben A.	4	CW	E. Meth			Black
Henderson	Caleb A.	2	CW	E. Meth			Black
Holmes	John	34	USA	E. Meth	M	labourer	Black
Howard	Wm H.	25	USA	E Meth	M		Mulatto
Howard	Sarah M.	22	CW	E Meth	M		Mulatto
Huffman	Nancy	39	USA	E. Meth			Black
Jackson	Rebecca	46	USA	E. Meth	M		Black
Jackson	Peter	45	USA	E. Meth	M		Black

Blacks in a White Place: Ingersoll, Canada West and Ontario, 1850–1921

Family Name	First Name	Age	Birthplace	Religion	Married	Profession	Race
Jeffrey	Matilda	50	CW	E Meth	M		Black
Jeffrey	Jacob	48	CW	E Meth	M	labourer	Black
John	Lucas	37	USA	E. Meth			Black
Johnstone	Burch	26	USA	E. Meth	M		Black
Johnstone	Lovina	23	USA	E. Meth	M		Black
Johnstone	Adison N.	17	USA	E. Meth			Black
Jones	Calvin	63	USA	Baptist	M	labourer	Mulatto
Jones	Ellen	60	USA	Baptist	M		Black
Lawrence	Eliza Ann	58	USA	E Meth			Black
Martin	Catherine	19	CW	Baptist			**WHITE**
Meradith	George	30	USA	E. Meth	M	labourer	Black
Meradith	Ann	21	CW	E. Meth	M		Black
Meradith	John	3	CW	E. Meth			Black
Meradith	George	2	CW	E. Meth			Black
Miner	John	46	USA	E Meth	M	barber	Black
Miner	Eliza Ann	27	CW	Baptist	M		**WHITE**
Miner	Jane	12	CW	E Meth			Black
Moore	William H.	25	USA	Baptist			Black
Wallace	John	30	USA	E. Meth	M	labourer	Black
Orm	John	34	USA	Baptist		labourer	Black
Owens	Ostin	46	USA	E Meth	M	barber	Mulatto
Owens	Francis	27	USA	E Meth	M		Mulatto
Peterson	Samuel	52	USA	E. Meth	M	labourer	Black
Peterson	Elizabeth	40	USA	E. Meth	M		Black
Peterson	Louisa	19	CW	E. Meth			Black
Peterson	John	12	CW	E. Meth			Black
Peterson	Francis	8	CW	E. Meth			Black
Piner	George	29	USA	E. Meth	M	labourer	Black
Piner	Sarah E.	22	USA	E. Meth	M		Black
Piner	George	2	CW	E. Meth			Black
Piper	Thomas	52	USA	FC Pres	M	labourer	Mulatto
Piper	Elsa Ann	35	USA	FC Pres	M		Mulatto
Piper	Sarah	31	Ireland	Episcopal	M		**WHITE**
Piper	Catherine A.	18	CW	FC Pres			Mulatto
Piper	Elizabeth	16	CW	FC Pres			Mulatto
Piper	George	12	CW	FC Pres			Mulatto

Family Name	First Name	Age	Birth-place	Religion	Married	Profession	Race
Piper	Amanda	8	CW	FC Pres			Mulatto
Piper	Ann E.	7	CW	Episcopal			Mulatto
Piper	Thomas	6	CW	FC Pres			Mulatto
Piper	William	6	CW	Episcopal			Mulatto
Piper	Thomas	5	CW	Episcopal			Mulatto
Piper	William	4	CW	FC Pres			Mulatto
Piper	John	3	CW	Episcopal			Mulatto
Piper	Amelia J.	2	CW	FC Pres			Mulatto
Piper	Jacob	1	CW	Episcopal			Mulatto
Price	John	14	USA	E. Meth			Black
Roff	Jacob	45	USA	E. Meth			Black
Roff	Frances A.	12	USA	E. Meth			Black
Sandey	Thomas	22	USA	E Meth		barber	Black
Scott	Wesley	4	CW	E. Meth			Black
Smith	Curtis	47	USA	C of E	M	labourer	Black
Smith	Susannah	42	CW	C of E	M		Black
Smith	James	40	USA	E. Meth	M		Black
Smith	Charles	24	USA	Meth		labourer	Black
Smith	Mary	24	USA	E. Meth	M		Black
Smith	George	18	CW	C of E			Black
Smith	John	16	CW	C of E			Black
Smith	Hannah A.	15	CW	C of E			Black
Smith	Hariett	14	CW	C of E			Black
Smith	Robert	11	CW	C of E			Black
Smith	Susannah	9	CW	C of E			Black
Smith	Curtis	6	CW	C of E			Black
Smith	Irena	4	CW	E. Meth			Black
Smith	Wm.	4	CW	C of E			Black
Smith	William	3	CW	E. Meth			Black
Smith	James	2	CW	E. Meth			Black
Smith	Henry	2	CW	C of E			Black
Sommers	Noah	38	USA	Meth	M	labourer	Black
Sommers	Emma	18	USA	Meth	M		**WHITE**
Sommers	Lucretia	3	CW	Meth			Black
Sommers	Isaac	1	CW	Meth			Black
Steele	Mary Ann	23	CW	E Meth			Mulatto

Family Name	First Name	Age	Birthplace	Religion	Married	Profession	Race
Steele	Sarah J.	6	CW	E Meth			Mulatto
Steele	Daniel H.	4	CW	E Meth			Mulatto
Thomas	Washington	20	USA	Baptist		waiter	Black
Thompson	Lydia	48	USA	Meth			Black
Thompson	Moses	21	CW	Episcopal			Black
Thompson	Catherine	15	CW	RC			Black
Walton	John	45	USA	Baptist	M	labourer	Black
Walton	Ellen	23	CW	RC	M		Black
Walton	William	7	CW	RC			Black
Walton	Louis	4	CW	RC			Black
Walton	Albert	3	CW	RC			Black
Walton	Franklin	1	CW	RC			Black
Washington	Eliza	17	CW	E Meth		servant	Mulatto
Williams	Thomas	56	USA	E. Meth	M	labourer	Black
Williams	Martha J.	53	USA	E. Meth	M		Black
Williams	Isaac	32	CW	Episcopal	M	labourer	Black
Williams	Asenath A.	30	CW	W Meth	M		**WHITE**
Williams	Emma	2	CW	W Meth			Mulatto
Willis	Mary	26	USA	E Meth	S		Mulatto
Willis	Rosena	5	CW	E Meth			Mulatto
Willis	Rebecca	5	CW	E Meth			Mulatto
Willis	Melia A.	1	CW	E Meth			Mulatto

Oxford North 1861

Number of Blacks: 18. Number of Whites in Black Households: 0.

Family Name	First Name	Age	Birthplace	Religion	Married	Profession	Race
Anderson	Robert	25	USA	EM		labourer	Black
Brown	John	17	USA	Baptist			Black
Fram	Richard	41	USA-NJ	RC			Black
Jones	Wilson	30	USA	EM			Black
McKinney	Richard	27	USA-VA	EM	M		Black
McKinney	Anne	34	USA-NY	EM	M		Black
Nelson	Sandford	30	USA	FC Pres			Black
Oakley	Charles	33	USA-NY	EM	M		Black
Oakley	Jane	34	USA-NY	EM	M		Black

Family Name	First Name	Age	Birth-place	Religion	Married	Profession	Race
Oakley	Julianne	8	USA-NY	EM			Black
Oakley	Charles S	6	USA-NY	EM			Black
Oakley	Sarah	4	CW	EM			Black
Sanders	Rheuben	47	USA-Ga	Baptist			Black
Sanders	William L	12	USA-LA	Baptist			Black
Washington	George	35	USA	EM	M	labourer	Black
Washington	Mary J	20	CW	EM	M		Black
Washington	Mary C	3	CW	EM			Black
Washington	George Mott	1	CW	EM			Black

Oxford West 1861

Number of Blacks: 30. Number of Whites in Black Households: 0.

Family Name	First Name	Age	Birth-place	Religion	Married	Profession	Race
Burnet	John H	67	USA-NY	Baptist	W	potter	Black
Clark	John H	20	USA	none		labourer	Black
Galloway	Charles	65	USA	Advent	M	brickmaker	Black
Galloway	Barbara	39	USA	Advent	M		Black
Galloway	Anne E	18	USA	Baptist			Black
Galloway	Susannah	17	USA	Advent			Black
Galloway	Joseph	12	USA	Advent			Black
Galloway	Benjamin	10	CW	Advent			Black
Galloway	Mary A.	7	CW	Advent			Black
Galloway	Arch	4	CW	Advent			Black
Galloway	John	1	CW	Advent			Black
Johnston	Jeremiah	27	USA	Baptist			Black
Galloway	Elizabeth	18	USA	WM			Black
Fry	George	28	USA	Baptist	M	labourer	Black
Fry	Harriett	23	USA	Baptist	M		Black
Hall	David	49	USA	EM	M	labourer	Black
Hall	Hariett	39	USA	EM	M		Black
Hall	Lenora	17	CW	EM			Black
Hall	Elizabeth	15	CW	EM			Black
Hall	Francis	13	CW	EM			Black
Hall	John	11	CW	EM			Black
Hall	Sinderella	9	CW	EM			Black

Family Name	First Name	Age	Birthplace	Religion	Married	Profession	Race
Livers	Harkless	78	USA-VA	WM	M		Black
Livers	Harriet	34	USA-VA	C OF E	M		Black
Livers	Benjamin	5	USA-VA	C OF E			Black
Nichlas	Christopher	52	USA-NY	Baptist		labourer	Black
Nichlas	Lydia	35	USA-NY	Baptist			Black
Harris	John H	25	USA	WM		labourer	Black
Shanklin	Isiah	14	CW	none			Black
Write	Benjamin	35	USA	Baptist			Black

Ingersoll 1871

Number of Blacks: 106. Number of Whites in Black Households: 3.

Family Name	First Name	Age	Where Born	Religion	Married	Profession	Racial Origin
Bass	William	16	Ont	C. Presby.			African
Bedford	Francis	26	Ont	RC	M	labourer	African
Bedford	Anne	17	Ont	RC	M		African
Bevins	Washington	65	USA	W. Meth	M	white washer	African
Bevins	Maria	55	USA	W. Meth	M		African
Bevins	Reva	16	Ont	W. Meth			African
Bird	Charles	43	USA	W. Meth	M	labourer	African
Bird	Mary	29	USA	W. Meth			African
Bird	James	9	Ont	W. Meth			African
Bird	Harriet	4	Ont	W. Meth			African
Brown	Enoch	51	USA	BA	M	lumberman	African
Brown	Emaline	40	USA	FW Bapt	W		African
Brown	Maria	39	USA	BA	M		African
Brown	Isabella	17	USA	FW Bapt			African
Brown	Louisa	15	Ont	BA			African
Brown	Ida	13	Ont	BA			African
Brown	Elita	10	Ont	BA			African
Brown	Mary	8	Ont	BA			African
Brown	Ernest	2	Ont	BA			African
Carey	Charles	57	France	RC	M	barber	**IRISH**
Carey	Mary	32	USA	W. Meth	M		African

Family Name	First Name	Age	Where Born	Religion	Married	Profession	Racial Origin
Carey	Fred W.	9	Ont	RC			African
Carey	Charles H.	7	Ont	RC			African
Collins	Matilda	2	Ont	ME			African
Davis	John	14	Ont	W. Meth		barber	African
Degroat	Martha	48	USA	W. Meth	W		African
Degroat	Catherine	16	Ont	W. Meth			African
Degroat	Miranda	10	Ont	W. Meth			African
Digens	Mary	infant	Ont	WM			African
Digens	John	40	USA	WM	M	labourer	African
Digens	Mary	30	USA	WM	M		African
Digens	Benjamin	12	Ont	WM			African
Digens	Freeman	9	Ont	WM			African
Digens	Josiah	6	Ont	WM			African
Douglass	Minnie	2	Ont	C of E			African
Gaines	Robert	39	Ont	C. Presby.	M	barber	African
Gaines	Hattie	35	USA	C. Presby.	M		African
Gaines	Artridge	8	Ont	C. Presby.			African
Graham	Adeline	38	USA	FW Bapt	W		African
Graham	Eliza	16	USA	FW Bapt			African
Graham	May	11	Ont	FW Bapt			African
Graham	Martha	9	Ont	FW Bapt			African
Graham	Ellen	7	Ont	FW Bapt			African
Graham	Emma	5	Ont	FW Bapt			African
Graham	Harry	3	Ont	FW Bapt			African
Graham	Joseph	2	Ont	FW Bapt			African
Hall	David	60	USA	W. Meth	M		African
Hall	Harriet	47	USA	W. Meth	M		African
Hall	John	21	Ont	W. Meth			African
Hall	Cinderella	19	Ont	W. Meth			African
Hall	Walter	11	Ont	W. Meth			African
Hall	Charles	6	Ont	W. Meth			African
Holmes	Elizabeth	45	Scot	WM	M		**SCOTCH**
Holmes	Henry	41	USA	W. Meth	M	plasterer	African
Howard	William	50	USA	WM	M	labourer	African
Howard	Sarah	34	Quebec	WM	M		African

Blacks in a White Place: Ingersoll, Canada West and Ontario, 1850–1921

Family Name	First Name	Age	Where Born	Religion	Married	Profession	Racial Origin
James	Joseph	48	USA	RC	W	labourer	African
Johnston	Mary	14	Ont	WM		labourer	African
Jones	Ellen	80	USA	Baptist	M		African
Lee	William H.	30	USA	C of E	M	barber	African
Lee	Alice C.	25	no data	C of E	M		African
Lee	Anne	5	no data	C of E			African
Lee	M. E. (FEM)	3	no data	C of E			African
Lee	Eliza	2	no data	C of E			African
Lives	Hariett	46	USA	C of E	W		African
Lives	Benjamin	13	Ont	C of E			African
Mann	Archibald	50	USA	CC Bapt	W	carpenter	African
Mann	Josephine	9	Ont	W. Meth			African
Mann	Emma	3	Ont	W. Meth			African
Meredith	George	56	USA	Baptist	M	labourer	African
Mitchell	Elizabeth	9	Ont	WM			African
Mitchell	Charles	7	Ont	WM			African
Pierson	Eva	infant	Ont	WM			African
Pierson	Matilda	25	USA	WM	M		African
Pierson	James	22	USA	WM	M	labourer	African
Piper	William	16	Ont	RC			African
Piper	Thomas	14	Ont	RC			African
Piper	John	13	Ont	RC			African
Piper	Ida	10	Ont	RC			African
Piper	Samuel	7	Ont	RC			African
Piper	Israel	4	Ont	RC			African
Preston	Thomas	50	USA	W. Meth	M	labourer	African
Preston	Mary Ann	38	USA	W. Meth	M		African
Preston	Susannah	8	USA	W. Meth			African
Rue	John	51	USA	Bapt	M	labourer	African
Rue	Sarah	46	IRELAND	RC	M		**IRISH**
Saunders	Rheuben	60	USA	FW Bapt	W	labourer	African
Shanklin	Margaretta	44	Ont	W. Meth	W		African
Shanklin	Jane	15	Ont	W. Meth			African
Shanklin	Banjamin	10	Ont	W. Meth			African
Shanklin	Hillary	8	Ont	W. Meth			African
Shanklin	John	3	Ont	W. Meth			African

Family Name	First Name	Age	Where Born	Religion	Married	Profession	Racial Origin
Smothers	John	30	USA	W. Meth	M	labourer	African
Smothers	Anne	27	USA	C of E	M		African
Sullivan	John	50	USA	EM		labourer	African
Tolbert	Catherine	68	USA	W. Meth	W		African
Truhon	R.V.	23	Ont	W. Meth			African
Truhon	Phoebe	3	Ont	W. Meth			African
Vanpatter	Henry	27	Ont	W. Meth	M	labourer	African
Vanpatter	Margaret	26	Ont	W. Meth	M		African
Vanpatter	John	22	Ont	WM		plasterer	African
Vanpatter	John	3	Ont	W. Meth			African
Vanpatter	Henry	2	Ont	W. Meth			African
Vanpatter	Minnie	0.58	Ont	W. Meth			African
Washington	Thomas	58	USA	Baptist		labourer	African
Washington	Maria	30	USA	Baptist	M		African
Washington	Annie	4	Ont	Baptist			African
Washington	George	3	Ont	Baptist			African
Willis	Rosa	14	Ont	CC Baptist			African

North Oxford 1871

Number of Blacks: 3. Number of Whites in Black Households: 0.

Family Name	First Name	Age	Where Born	Religion	Married	Profession	Racial Origin
Harris	Hannah	48	Ont	WM	M		African
Harris	Calvin	14	Ont	WM			African
Harris	Catherine	6	Ont	WM			African

West Oxford 1871

Number of Blacks: 48. Number of Whites in Black Households: 0.

Family Name	First Name	Age	Where Born	Religion	Married	Profession	Racial Origin
Bell	Charlotte	20	USA	Baptist	M		African
Bell	Henrietta	3	Ont	Baptist			African
Burnett	John	79	USA	FW Baptist			African
Butler	William	46	USA	WM	M	labourer	African

Blacks in a White Place: Ingersoll, Canada West and Ontario, 1850–1921

Family Name	First Name	Age	Where Born	Religion	Married	Profession	Racial Origin
Butler	Anna	43	USA	WM	M		African
Butler	Margaret	21	USA	WM			African
Butler	James	19	USA	WM		labourer	African
Butler	Anna	16	USA	WM			African
Butler	Lorenzo	15	Ont	WM			African
Butler	Anna	14	Ont	WM			African
Butler	Theophilus	11	Ont	WM			African
Butler	Albert	9	Ont	WM			African
Butler	Geneva	7	Ont	WM			African
Butler	Isaac	5	Ont	WM			African
Butler	Frederick	4	Ont	WM			African
Cooper	John	52	USA	Baptist	M	labourer	African
Cooper	Caroline	40	USA	Baptist	M		African
Cooper	Martha	17	Ont	Baptist			African
Cooper	Edward	16	Ont	Baptist			African
Cooper	William	12	Ont	Baptist			African
Cooper	Henry	9	Ont	Baptist			African
Fuller	Charles	4	Ont	Baptist			African
Henry	Peter	40	USA	Baptist		labourer	African
Minor	John	50	USA	EM	M	labourer	African
Minor	Eliza A	36	Ont	EM	M		African
Minor	May j	22	Ont	EM			African
Minor	Eliza a	6	Ont	EM			African
Minor	Margaret	4	Ont	EM			African
Minor	William H	1	Ont	EM			African
Washington	Mariah	22	USA	EM	W		African
Washington	Emile	5	USA	EM			African
Washington	James H	2	USA	EM			African
Munson	Cornelius	63	USA	Baptist	M	labourer	African
Munson	Letitia	65	USA	Baptist	M		African
Munson	Frederick	4	USA	Baptist			African
Owens	William	30	Ont	EM	M		African
Owens	Mary	29	Ont	EM	M		African
Owens	Elijah	7	Ont	EM			African
Owens	Joseph	5	Ont	EM			African
Owens	John	4	Ont	EM			African

Family Name	First Name	Age	Where Born	Religion	Married	Profession	Racial Origin
Owens	Robert	infant	Ont	EM			African
Truman	Phoebe	19	Ont	Baptist			African
Truman	Mary	18	Ont	Baptist			African
Truman	Daniel	14	Ont	Baptist			African
Wright	Benjamin	47	USA	Baptist	M		African
Wright	Hannah	45	USA	Baptist	M		African
Wright	William	6	Ont	Baptist			African
Wright	Isaac	4	Ont	Baptist			African

Ingersoll 1881

Number of Blacks: 97. Number of Whites in Black Households: 2.

Family Name	First Name	Age	Birthplace	Religion	Married	Profession	Racial Origin
Anderson	Joseph	26	USA	Br Meth			American
Anderson	Mary	24	USA	Br Meth			American
Bedford	William	8	CW	Br Meth			USA
Bedford	May	5	CW	Br Meth			USA
Bedford	Anna	4	CW	Br Meth			USA
Bevins	Washington	75	USA	EM	M	labourer	African
Bevins	Marie	45	USA	EM	M		African
Bird	Charles	54	USA	EM	M		African
Bird	Mary	40	USA	EM	M		African
Bird	Calista	37	CW	Br Meth	M		African
Bird	James	30	CW	Br Meth	M		African
Bird	John	15	CW	Br Meth			African
Bird	Harriet	13	CW	EM			African
Bird	Isaac	7	CW	EM			African
Bird	William	7	CW	Br Meth			African
Bird	Thornton	5	CW	Br Meth			African
Bird	Prudence	3	CW	EM			African
Bird	Sydney	3	CW	Br Meth			African
Brown	John	50	USA	Meth	M		African
Brown	Mathilda	37	USA	Meth	M		African
Brown	William	16	USA	Meth			African
Brown	Emma	14	USA	Meth			African
Brown	Mary	10	USA	Meth			African

Blacks in a White Place: Ingersoll, Canada West and Ontario, 1850–1921

Family Name	First Name	Age	Birth-place	Religion	Married	Profession	Racial Origin
Brown	Elizabeth	4	USA	Meth			African
DeGrout	Lucinda	42	CW	Meth	W	washer-woman	Canadian
DeGrout	Charles	16	CW	Meth		labourer	American
Diggins	Carey	53	USA	Br Meth	M	labourer	American
Diggins	Mary Jane	31	USA	Br Meth	M		American
Diggins	Julia	24	CW	Br Meth			American
Diggins	Benjamin	22	CW	Br Meth		labourer	American
Diggins	Elizabeth	11	CW	Br Meth			American
Diggins	William	6	CW	Br Meth			American
Diggins	Hazy	4	CW	Br Meth			American
Diggins	Carey	2	CW	Br Meth			American
Fant	CREA (F)	infant	CW	Baptist	M		American
Fant	Willis	74	USA	Baptist	W	butcher	American
Fant	Alexander	29	USA	Baptist		labourer	American
Fant	Lelia Ann	19	USA	Baptist			American
Fuller	Hannah	24	CW	Baptist			African
Fuller	Charles	21	CW	Baptist	M		African
Fuller	Freddie	8	CW	Baptist			African
Hale	Peter S.	62	USA	Meth	M	minister	African
Hale	Juliana	44	USA	Br Meth	M		USA
Hall	David	69	USA	Meth	M	labourer	African
Hall	Harriet	54	USA	Meth	M		African
Hall	Walter	20	CW	Meth			African
Hall	Charles	18	CW	Meth			African
Holmes	Elizabeth	53	Scotland	Meth	M		SCOTCH
Holmes	Henry	50	USA	Meth	M	plasterer	African
Holmes	John V	29	CW	Br Meth			African
Holmes	Charles	16	CW	Meth			African
Hughes	Benjamin	50	USA	Br Meth	M	labourer	USA
Hughes	Mary Jane	35	CW	Br Meth	M		USA
Hughes	Henry Geo.	19	CW	Br Meth			USA
Hughes	James	16	CW	Br Meth			USA
Joiner	Mark	34	CW	Br Meth	M	barber	American
joiner	Ida	20	CW	Br Meth	M		American
joiner	John	3	CW	Br Meth			Canadian
joiner	William	2	CW	Br Meth			Canadian

Family Name	First Name	Age	Birth-place	Religion	Married	Profession	Racial Origin
joiner	Martin	0.5	CW	Br Meth			Canadian
Lillywhite	Sophie	70	CW	Br Meth			African
Lillywhite	Sophie	8	CW	Br Meth			African
Lillywhite	Martha	5	CW	Br Meth			African
Lillywhite	Clara	0.66	CW	Br Meth			African
Miner	George	26	CW	Br Meth		barber	American
Minor	Maggey	12	CW	EM			African
Moore	Robert L	64	USA	Br Meth	M	labourer	Mulatto
Moore	Maria	40	CW	Br Meth	M		Mulatto
Moore	Walse (F)	17	CW	Br Meth			Mulatto
Moore	Bertha	12	CW	Br Meth			Mulatto
Moore	Frederick	9	CW	Br Meth			Mulatto
Philips	Betsey	13	USA	no data			African
Piper	Sarah	51	Ireland	Br Meth	W		Irish
Piper	W.H.	24	CW	Br Meth		labourer	USA
Piper	John	22	CW	Br Meth			USA
Piper	Samuel	17	CW	Br Meth			USA
Piper	Ezra	14	CW	Br Meth			USA
Saunders	Rheuben	60	USA	FW Bapt	W	labourer	African
Sullivan	George W	50	USA	Br Meth		labourer	African
Sullivan	Elizabeth	40	USA	Meth			African
Sullivan	Elizabeth	35	USA	P Meth			African
Sullivan	Virginia	30	USA	Meth			African
Thomas	William	53	USA	Br Meth	W	labourer	African
Thomas	Alice	21	CW	Br Meth			African
Valentine	W.J.	33	CW	Br Meth		barber	American
Van Pater	Sarah	6	CW	Br Meth			African
Van Pater	George	4	CW	Br Meth			African
Van Pater	Arthur	3	CW	Br Meth			African
Van Pater	Amy	1	CW	Br Meth			African
Vanpatter	Henry	35	CW	Br Meth	M	labourer	African
Vanpatter	Margaret	34	CW	Br Meth	M		African
Vanpatter	John	13	CW	Br Meth			African
Vanpatter	Henry	12	CW	Br Meth			African
Vanpatter	Minnie	10	CW	Br Meth			African
Vanpatter	Charlie	8	CW	Br Meth			African

Family Name	First Name	Age	Birth-place	Religion	Married	Profession	Racial Origin
Wright	Harriet	50	USA	Br Meth		servant	Col'd
Wright	William	16	CW	Br Meth			Col'd
Wright	Isaiah	10	CW	Br Meth			Col'd
Wright	Benjamin	8	CW	Br Meth			Col'd

West Oxford 1881
No. of Blacks: 5.

Family Name	First Name	Age	Birth-place	Religion	Married	Profession	Racial Origin
Harris	Henry	65	USA	Meth	M	shoemaker	Indian71
Harris	Hannah	56	CW	Meth	M		Black71
Harris	Calvin	26	CW	Meth			Black71
Harris	Kate	18	CW	Meth			Black71
Smothers	Ann	34	USA	Meth			Black71
Hisson	Frederick	4	CW	Meth			Black

North Oxford 1881
No. of Blacks: 9.

Family Name	First Name	Age	Birth-place	Religion	Married	Profession	Racial Origin
Charles	Daniel	70	USA	Baptist	M		African
Charles	Mary	20	CW	Baptist	M		African
Munson	Commandis	64	USA	Presby	M		African
Munson	Letitia	63	USA	Presby	M		African
Munson	Sarah	18	USA	Presby			African
Munson	Frederick	14	USA	Presby			African
Munson	Ida	13	USA	Presby			African
Munson	Robert	3	CW	Presby			African
Munson	Charles	1	CW	Presby			African

Unidentified Table
No. of Blacks: 8.

Family Name	First Name	Age	Birth-place	Religion	Married	Profession	Racial Origin
Preston	Mary	61	Ont		W		African

Family Name	First Name	Age	Birth-place	Religion	Married	Profession	Racial Origin
Wright	Isaac	35	Ont		M		African
Wright	Mary	30	Ont		M		African
Wright	Harriett	68	USA	S. Army	W		African
Fant	Alexander	47	USA	Baptist	M	labourer	African
Fant	Margaret J.	31	Ont	Baptist	M		African
Fant	Edith	17	Ont	Baptist			African
Fant	Della M.	11	Ont	Baptist			African

Ingersoll 1901
No. of Blacks: 28.

Family Name	First Name	Age	Birth-place	Religion	Married	Profession	Racial Origin
Preston	Mary	61	Ont		W		African
Wright	Isaac	35	Ont		M		African
Wright	Mary	30	Ont		M		African
Wright	Harriett	68	USA	S. Arm	W		African
Fant	Alexander	47	USA	Baptist	M	labourer	African
Fant	Margaret J.	31	Ont	Baptist	M		African
Fant	Edith	17	Ont	Baptist			African
Fant	Della M.	11	Ont	Baptist			African
Fant	Minnie	9	Ont	Baptist			African
Fant	John H.	7	Ont	Baptist			African
Fant	Beatrice E.	4	Ont	Baptist			African
Fant	A. Marg.	2	Ont	Baptist			African
Anderson	Joseph	42	USA	Meth	W	labourer	African
Hale	Solomon	80	USA-Md	Meth	M	Preacher	African
Hale	Julia Ann	60	USA-Md	Meth	M		African
Degrost	Martha	69	USA	Meth	W		A[illeg]?
Degrost	Kate	45	Ont	Meth		Servant	A[illeg]?
Degrost	James	17	Ont	Meth			A[illeg]?
Degrost	Emma	11	Ont	Meth			A[illeg]?
Degrost	Ebner	7	Ont	Meth			A[illeg]?
Degrost	Martha A.	5	Ont	Meth			A[illeg]?
Moore	Maria	65	Ont	S. Arm	W		Eng
Moore	Fred	30	Ont	S. Arm	M	labourer	Eng
Vanpater	John H.	47	Ont	Meth	M	horse trad.	African

Blacks in a White Place: Ingersoll, Canada West and Ontario, 1850–1921

Family Name	First Name	Age	Birth-place	Religion	Married	Profession	Racial Origin
Vanpater	Edna	41	Ont	Meth	M		African
Vanpater	Gormon A.	14	Ont	Meth			African
Vanpater	Charles M.	9	Ont	Meth			African
Vanpater	Otto	4	Ont	Meth			African
Vanpater	Edgar C.	1	Ont	Meth			African
Vanpater	Edna	8	Ont	Meth			African
Vanpater	Beatrice M.	6	Ont	Meth			African
Smithser	John	65	Ont	Baptist	M	engineer	African
White	Joseph B.	70	USA	Meth	W		African
Henderson	Joseph	50	USA	Baptist	M	town labourer	African
Henderson	Phoebe	48	Ont	Baptist	M		African
Henderson	Anabel	31	Ont	Baptist		hotel clerk	African
Henderson	John	28	Ont	Baptist		hotel porter	African
Henderson	James	25	Ont	Baptist		labourer	African
Henderson	Levi	23	Ont	Baptist		labourer	African
Henderson	Moses	21	Ont	Baptist		scrubber	African
Henderson	William	20	Ont	Baptist			African
Henderson	Clara	18	Ont	Baptist			African
Henderson	George	16	Ont	Baptist			African
Henderson	Edith	11	Ont	Baptist			African
Henderson	Arthur	4	Ont	Baptist			African
Kelley	Fred	13	Ont	Baptist			African
Kelley	Charles	8	Ont	Baptist			African
Owens	Dan	30	Ont	Meth		labourer	Spanish
Carey	Charles E.	86	France	RC		barber	French
Chambers	George	70	France	C of E		r. farmer	Eng
Chambers	Mary Alice	52	France	C of E			Eng
Chambers	Zara	60	Ont	C of E			Eng
Moore	Effie	18	Ont	Meth	M		Eng
Smithser	Laura	17	Ont	C of E	M		Eng
White	Joseph	70	USA	Meth	W		African

207

West Oxford 1901
No. of Blacks: 7

Family Name	First Name	Age	Birth-place	Religion	Married	Profession	Racial Origin
Armour	Jane	65	Ireland	Pres	W		Irish
Armour	Sarah	30	Ont	Pres			Irish
Armour	Katie	25	Ont	Pres			Irish
Armour	Maggie	22	Ont	Pres			African
Armour	Winnie	3	Ont	Pres			Irish
Thompson	James	16	Ont	Meth		f. labourer	African
Henderson	John	28	Ont	Pres			African
Henderson	Frances	28	Ont	Pres			African
Henderson	Marnie	9	Ont	Pres			African
Henderson	Gertie	2	Ont	Pres			African
Henderson	Phoebe	1	Ont	Pres			African

North Oxford 1901
No. of Blacks: 0.

Ingersoll 1911
No. of Blacks: 29.

Family Name	First Name	Age	Birth-place	Religion	Married	Profession	Racial Origin
Henderson	Joshua	71	USA	Meth	M	labourer	Negro
Henderson	Phoebe	58	Ont	Meth	M		Negro
Martin	Arvilla	41	Ont	Meth		domestic	Negro
Henderson	Levi	35	Ont	Meth		labourer	Negro
Henderson	Moses	33	Ont	Meth		labourer	Negro
Henderson	William	31	Ont	Meth		labourer	Negro
Henderson	Clara	26	Ont	Meth		domestic	Negro
Henderson	George	28	Ont	Meth		labourer	Negro
Henderson	Edith	22	Ont	Meth		domestic	Negro
Henderson	Arthur	15	Ont	Meth		labourer	Negro
Fant	Alexander	55	USA	Meth	M		Negro
Fant	Maggie	38	Ont	Meth	M	domestic	Negro
Fant	Edith	23	Ont	Meth		domestic	Negro
Fant	Della May	21	Ont	Meth		domestic	Negro

Family Name	First Name	Age	Birth-place	Religion	Married	Profession	Racial Origin
Fant	Minnie	19	Ont	Meth			Negro
Fant	Beatrice	14	Ont	Meth			Negro
Fant	Daisy	12	Ont	Meth			Negro
Fant	John	16	Ont	Meth			Negro
Fant	Alexander	9	Ont	Meth			Negro
Fant	Ralph N	5	Ont	Meth			Negro
Fant	Douglas R.	5	Ont	Meth			Negro
Mann	Katherine	53	Ont	Meth		washer w.	Negro
Mann	James	27	Ont	Meth		labourer	Negro
Mann	Mattie	15	Ont	Meth			Negro
Wright	Hattie	75	USA	S .Arm	W		African
Henderson	James	38	Ont	Br. ME	M	labourer	Canadian
Henderson	Nora	32	Ont	Br. ME	M	domestic	Canadian
Henderson	William	15	Ont	Br. ME		labourer	Canadian
Johnston	Mary	50	Ont	Br. ME			Canadian

West Oxford 1911

No. of Blacks: 7.

Family Name	First Name	Age	Birth-place	Religion	Married	Profession	Racial Origin
Henderson	John	45	Ont	no church	M	labourer	Negro
Henderson	Francis	40	Ont	no church	M		Negro
Henderson	Mary	20	Ont	no church			Negro
Henderson	Gertie	16	Ont	no church			Negro
Henderson	Phoebe	14	Ont	no church			Negro
Henderson	Bertha	10	Ont	no church			Negro
Henderson	Jane	0.5	Ont	no church			Negro

North Oxford 1911

No. of Blacks: 0.

Ingersoll 1921
No. of Blacks: 28.

Family Name	First Name	Age	Birthplace	Religion	Married	Profession	Racial Origin
Mann	Catherine	64	Ont	Meth	W	char-woman	Negro
Mann	James	38	Ont	Meth		tinsmith	Negro
Mann	Mattie	24	Ont	Meth			Negro
Fant	Alexander	70	USA	Meth	M	labourer	Negro
Fant	Maggie	46	USA	Meth	M	none	Negro
Fant	Beatrice	23	USA	Meth		none	Negro
Fant	Daisy	20	USA	Meth		domestic	Negro
Fant	Alexander Jr	19	USA	Meth		labourer	Negro
Fant	Ralph	15	USA	Meth		student	Negro
Marshall	Ralph	15	Ont	Meth			Negro
Marshall	Edith	32	USA	Meth			Negro
Johnston	George	42	USA	Meth	M	labourer	Negro
Johnston	Edith	30	Ont	Meth	M		Negro
Johnston	Georgie	3	Ont	Meth			Negro
Johnston	Robert	2	Ont	Meth			Negro
Johnston	James	7 m	Ont	Meth			Negro
Anderson	Ralph	65	USA	Meth		labourer	African
Anderson	Clementine	65	Ont	Meth			African
Fant	John	26	Ont	Meth	M	labourer	Negro
Fant	Annie	25	Ont	Meth	M		Negro
Henderson	James	49	Ont	Meth	M	labourer	African
Henderson	Albert	47	Ont	Meth	M	labourer	African
Johnston	Mary	72	Ont	Meth			African
Henderson	John	49	Ont	Presby		farm helper	African
Henderson	Francis	48	Ont	Presby			African
Henderson	Phoebe	20	Ont	Presby			African
Henderson	Ruth	12	Ont	Presby		student	African
Henderson	Jean	10	Ont	Presby		student	African

West Oxford 1921; North Oxford 1921
No. of Blacks in Each Township: 0.

ACKNOWLEDGEMENTS

My thanks to Vicki Brenner, Local History Technician, Ingersoll Public Library, and Scott Gillies, Curator of the Ingersoll Cheese and Agricultural Museum, for supplying research materials and their unfailing interest and support. We three co-authored a recent book, *Public Celebrations in Ingersoll, 1855–1930*.

Hilary Neary generously shared her letters of the Coloured pastor in Ingersoll during the 1860s, Lewis Chambers, the subject of her just-published book (Hilary Bates Neary, *A Black American Missionary in Canada: The Life and Letters of Lewis Champion Chambers* (McGill-Queen's University Press, 2022).

Elaine Balpataky, my sister, gave expert scrutiny to drafts of the manuscript and contributed greatly to its quality.

THE AUTHOR

George Emery is Professor Emeritus of History, Western University (1968–2007). He is a graduate of VMS and IDCI in Ingersoll (1945–60), Queen's University (B.A., 1964), and the University of British Columbia (Ph.D., 1970). Now retired in London, he contributes to the local history of Oxford County (see below).

2023. With Debbie L. Kasman. *The Bodwells of Elgin Hall: Mount Elgin Hamlet, Dereham Township, Oxford County, 1848–2023* (Dereham Centre: DC Heritage Press).

2021. With Scott Gillies and Vicki Brenner. *Public Festivals in Ingersoll, 1855–1930* (Ingersoll: Ingersoll Historical Society).

2019. *Municipal Bonuses for Manufactures: How These Worked in Ingersoll, 1873–1927* (264 Oxford Street Press).

2019. *Millponds, Millstreams and People in Ingersoll, Ontario, 1819–2015* (264 Oxford Street Press).

2018. *Thomas Ingersoll, His Family, and the Founding of Ingersoll Village, Canada West, 1749–1852* (Ingersoll: Ingersoll Historical Society).

2016. *Principles and Gerrymanders: Parliamentary Redistribution of Ridings in Ontario, 1840–1954* (Montreal and Kingston: McGill-Queen's University Press).

2012. *Elections in Oxford County, 1837–1875: A Case Study of Democracy in Canada West and Early Ontario* (Toronto: University of Toronto Press).

2002. With Glenna Oliver Jamieson. *Adam Oliver of Ingersoll, 1823–1882: Lumberman, Millowner, Contractor, and Politician* (Ingersoll: Ingersoll Historical Society).

2001. *Noxons of Ingersoll: The Family and the Firm in Canada's Agricultural Implements Industry, 1856–1918* (Ingersoll: Ingersoll Historical Society).

2001. *The Methodist Church on the Prairies 1896–1914* (McGill-Queen's Studies in the History of Religion series. Montreal and Kingston: McGill-Queen's University Press).

1999. With J. C. Herbert Emery. *A Young Man's Benefit: The Independent Order of Odd Fellows and Sickness Insurance in the United States and Canada, 1860–1929* (Montreal and Kingston: McGill-Queen's University Press).

1993. *Facts of Life, the Social Construction of Vital Statistics, Ontario, 1869–1952* (Montreal and Kingston: McGill-Queen's University Press, 1999); see "Death in Ingersoll, 1880–1972," pp. 5–71.

www.ingramcontent.com/pod-product-compliance
Lightning Source LLC
Chambersburg PA
CBHW061734070526
44585CB00024B/2668